From statism to p

Modern societies currently lack positive alternative visions of the future. Many commentators have claimed that the only option is a return to free-market capitalism, in which success and survival depend on being as competitive as possible whether as a nation, firm or individual. Yet nations such as Germany and Japan, that might have provided a model of how to do this, are now seen to be failing, and the future for firms seems to be one of ceaseless adaptation to rapid change.

Paul Hirst argues that there are viable alternative futures. In *From statism to pluralism* he advances a model – associative democracy – that, he suggests, addresses the major obstacles to democracy today. Associative democracy is a way of revitalizing democratic accountability and economic governance, through devolving social affairs to voluntary self-governing associations. In a post-liberal society dominated by large, hierarchically-controlled organizations in both the private and public sectors, associative democracy provides a means to re-establish democratic ideals and liberal values.

These provocative and compelling essays from one of today's most lively and inventive thinkers, represent an attempt to re-state a practical third way between the discredited ideals of state socialism and *laissez-faire* capitalism. *From statism to pluralism* will be essential reading for all those interested in the ideological renewal of the left.

Paul Hirst is Professor of Social Theory, at Birkbeck College, University of London. He is the author of fourteen books including *Pre-capitalist modes of production* (1975, with Barry Hindess), *Marxism and historical writing* (1985), *After Thatcher?* (1989), *Associative democracy* (1993), and *Globalization in question* (1996, with Grahame Thompson). His work has been translated into German, Japanese, Portuguese and Spanish.

From statism to pluralism

Democracy, civil society and global politics

Paul Hirst

Birkbeck College, London

UCL
PRESS

First published in 1997 by UCL Press

UCL Press Limited
1 Gunpowder Square
London EC4A 3DE

and

1900 Frost Road, Suite 101
Bristol
Pennsylvania 19007-1598
USA

The name of University College London (UCL) is a registered
trade mark used by UCL Press with the consent of the owner.

British Library Cataloguing-in-Publication Data
A CIP catalogue record for this book is available from the British Library.

Library of Congress Cataloging-in-Publication Data are available

ISBNs: 1–85728–749–5 HB
         1–85728–750–9 PB

Typeset in Garamond by Solidus Ltd, Bristol, UK
Printed and bound by
T. J. International Ltd, Padstow, UK

Contents

Acknowledgements

I am specially grateful to Lars Bo Kaspersen and Jonathan Zeitlin for help and advice in preparing this collection, and to Caroline Wintersgill of UCL Press for her help and patience in the process of deciding what should be included. I owe a great debt to Jane Tinkler for preparing the manuscript.

The original places of publication of the following chapters were:

Chapter 2 in *Dissent* (New York) Spring 1994

Chapter 3 in David Held (ed.) *Prospects for Democracy*, Cambridge: Polity Press, 1993.

Chapter 4 in B. Pimlott, A. Wright and T. Flower (eds) *The Alternative*, London: W.H. Allen, 1990.

Chapter 5 in B. Hindess (ed.) *Reactions to the Right*, London: Routledge, 1990.

Chapter 6 in *Parliamentary Affairs* **48(2)**, 1995.

Chapter 7 in P. Hirst and S. Khilnani (eds) *Reinventing Democracy* Oxford: The Political Quarterly/Basil Blackwell, 1996.

Chapter 8 in *Renewal* **4(2)**, 1994.

Chapter 9 in *Australian Left Review* (Sydney) September 1992.

Chapter 10 in *Economy and Society* **20(2)**, 1991.

Chapter 11 in L. Freedman (ed.) *Military Intervention in European Politics*, The Political Quarterly/Basil Blackwell, 1994.

Chapter 12 in *London Review of Books*, **11(22)** 1989.

Chapter 13 in *Prospect* February 1996.

Chapter 14 in K. Dean (ed.) *Politics and the Ends of Identity*, Andover: Avebury, 1997.

Chapter 15 in *Renewal* **4(4)**, 1994.

1

Introduction

Modern societies appear to be trapped: between the increasingly oppressive actuality of a capitalist system drifting toward a restoration of *laissez faire*, and the absence of any viable alternative to it. Socialism – in the sense of a comprehensive alternative to the market system – is dead. The brutalities of actually existing socialism have fatally crippled the power of socialist ideas of any kind to motivate and inspire. Social democracy too seems muted and ineffective. The collapse of revolutionary socialism and the decline of wars between the major industrial states have removed the major justifications of social democracy for established elites – that it could prevent the worse evil of communism and that it could harness organized labour in the national war effort. Those elites have not merely turned against social democracy, but they also seem to have convinced significant sections of the population that a regulated economy and comprehensive social welfare are either unattainable or undesirable.

Modern politicians in the advanced states operate within a narrow political spectrum in which they all claim to be democrats and they all embrace the market system as the only possible form of economic organization. Yet the democracy they espouse is of a narrowly plebiscitarian variety, in which the people periodically choose who are to be their elected masters. The economic policies they advocate are those of the financial and business elites – "sound money" and the pursuit of microeconomic "efficiency". In these circumstances the electorate have a choice between variants of the same, and increasingly they are indifferent to the political process and cynical about what it can accomplish.

In these circumstances the people have been robbed of any kind of political hope, of an imagined collective future that would be attainable and better than the present. Given this then there is little that is worth striving for in the company of others. Hope is reduced to individual success in the competitive race and aspirations reduced to a desire for material things – to a second car or a swimming pool. This political climate has also robbed social theory of much of its purpose. It now has little to say about the general character and evolution of modern societies. The result is, on the one hand, an ironic postmodernism that denies the possibility of imagined futures founded upon a rigorous analysis of the present, and, on the other hand, a reduction of social action to economics, to the calculation of the rational self-interested agent. The critical forms of social theorizing retreat from social generality into a concern with specific issues, chiefly into an obsession with personal and group identities and with the particular discontents that arise from them.

The essays collected here are an attempt to respond to this situation: on the one hand, to argue that there are alternative imagined futures that can be defended and that are capable of motivating large numbers of citizens; and on the other hand, to claim that modern societies are not condemned to evolve into variants of a brutalized consumer capitalism that excludes increasing numbers of people from full social and economic citizenship. The approach to contemporary problems offered here is distinctive in two senses. First, in terms of political theory: the approach is to reason from existing political institutions and contemporary political problems toward possible alternatives. This is in contrast to the retreat of most of modern political theory from institutions and problems of governance, either into the elaboration of abstract normative concepts divorced from political actualities and possibilities, or, into the elaboration of methodological tools for an objective "political science". Secondly, these essays expound a definite political doctrine – associative democracy – that is, a practical third way between collectivist state socialism and *laissez-faire* capitalism. It is a restatement and renewal of ideas that have resurfaced after many decades of neglect. In a changed conjuncture these ideas are attracting increasing support as people from diverse political positions recognize the need for and the possibility of a reform and reshaping of existing institutions that goes beyond the decayed orthodoxies of the left and the right. The objective of such reform is to deepen and to extend democratic control, thus enabling more informed decisions and thereby more effective economic and social governance. The public mood is changing toward greater dissatisfaction and a willingness to contemplate change.

But change has to be clearly outlined and the alternatives not merely enticing but also practical and attainable. The modern public is tired of utopias – the twentieth century has been dominated by attempts to turn the utopias of the left and right into practical politics with disastrous consequences. Marxism is the chief of these and it foundered above all because at its core is the anti-political ideal of a stateless society without a complex division of labour. Marxism set its ultimate social goals outside of any institutional frame and made all forms of government mere makeshifts on the way to utopia. This was a fatal mixture in which the unattainable legitimated the most ruthless pragmatism in its futile pursuit.

Modern *laissez faire* is also utopian. This may seem paradoxical since in modern societies markets appear to be the dominant form of economic organization. But free-market doctrines are not satisfied with the messy actuality of modern commercial societies, they aim to turn them into pure free-market systems. In doing so they ignore wider issues of governance and institutions because they wish to make markets unfettered by all extraneous constraints. Markets will be the primary form of social governance. *Laissez-faire* ideologues imagine a social order sustained almost exclusively by means of the exchange of goods and services between its members. Thus co-ordination of the activities of social actors is primarily by sales and purchases – the market is an exchange of goods that integrates the society. In this view non-market institutions have a distinctly secondary role in social governance, they are confined at best to underpinning the market. Thus a system of soundly defended private property rights and a modicum of commercial probity on the part of traders are the main preconditions for a market society as conceived by its most ardent economic liberal advocates. In its own way this is as anti-political and anti-institutional a view as Marx's dreaming of the abolition of the division of labour in the *1844 Manuscripts*.

The notion of governance has been introduced here in a very general sense, one that goes beyond specifically governmental institutions and which can include markets as one of the principal means of governance. Governance in this broad meaning can be defined as the means by which an activity or ensemble of activities is controlled or directed, such that it delivers an acceptable range of outcomes according to some established social standard. Governance has become more problematic in recent decades as its prevailing forms have become more difficult to apply to changing conditions and activities and less certain in their outcomes. This failure of the prevailing methods of governance has meant that increasingly we have been stumbling in an organizational twilight in which there are no readily applicable and generalizable methods of how to control and direct social activities. Rapid social change has undermined both the means of governance – making it difficult to offer tested and reliable models of how to govern that are relatively easy to learn and to apply – and it has made it difficult to define what are acceptable outcomes by which to judge the efficacy of such means, since hitherto given distributions of resources or patterns of activity have been subject to rapid and unpredictable change.

Associative democracy is relevant once again because it addresses this crisis of governance. It offers means of control and co-ordination that can work in more complex and changing conditions, and it also points to new social standards by which to assess outcomes. Before considering it we need to look at how and why the prevailing forms of governance came to fail. There are three basic governance mechanisms and widespread models of social organization that have been dominant in modern industrial societies: hierarchy and imperative control; exchange – co-ordination through contracts and market transactions; and negotiated control – bargaining between the affected interests in an activity to co-ordinate their actions to attain agreed outcomes. These models are highly generalized – they could be applied to states, to industrial and social sectors, to companies and other enterprises. They were not inconsequential, however, since they provided a frame in which various specific methods and techniques of control could be placed – for example, surveillance is a distinct style of control, but it can operate best within a hierarchical structure in which superordinates survey subordinates. We will now consider each of those three mechanisms-models in turn.

1.1 Imperative control

In this model governance operates through a dominant agency with exclusive control over all aspects of the activity in question and which co-ordinates and directs through the hierarchical transmission of orders to subordinate agencies and personnel. As in the classic model of bureaucracy the subordinates receive orders and transmit evidence of compliance up the chain of command, thus ensuring that superordinates know whether the outcomes have been attained and providing the informational conditions for continued governance. Hierarchy is a bounded information system, in which the conditions of control are internalized in a structure of command. As such it is far wider than the notion of bureaucracy; bureaucratic organiz-ations being a subclass of imperative control. This mode of governance can operate in very different social and ideological circumstances.

State socialist centrally planned economies are instances of imperative control on the scale of a whole society – administrative structures replace markets as the main mechanism for the transmission of information and the allocation of resources. The planning apparatus requires all sectors and enterprises to comply with plan directives and targets and to provide indi-cators of compliance whereby their performance is monitored. Central planning is a distinct governmental model – one that could be copied and transmitted. It is the specific governmental apparatus of socialism, distinct from the general ideological postulates of writers like Engels who imagined that socialist societies would be simple to organize. However, apparently entirely opposed types of institutions could utilize what is the same basic model of governance. Thus company-level planning and the related practices of Fordist or Taylorist workplace organization control, in which the tasks of conception and execution are rigidly separated, are also instances of governance through imperative control. Both the capitalist and socialist variants are feasible governance strategies (at the price of authoritarianism in differing degrees), if the circumstances to be thus controlled are relatively stable and the outcomes can be set in terms of easily measured and monitored quanta.

These conditions apply less and less. Central planning failed partly because its existing control technologies were inadequate to the scale and scope of the activities to be co-ordinated and because consumers were no longer satisfied with being fitfully provisioned with a given range of goods. However, top-down company planning is also undermined once output shifts from stable runs of standardized goods and services, and a relatively undifferentiated output. Rapidly changing product mixes and an emphasis on customization and the quality of products weaken the capacity of imperative control from top to bottom at company level. This leads to three major changes: first, forcing the decentralization of decision-making to levels where appropriate information is available; secondly, the granting of greater autonomy to the producers of goods and deliverers of services; and thirdly, the development of more complex and multicentred methods of monitoring product quality and productive performance.[1]

Similar considerations apply to public services organized along traditional bureaucratic lines. Bureaucracy spread from the army, postal services and railways to such services as health, education and welfare – centralization improved both the quality of such services and their consistency. This form of provision was viable well into the twentieth century because the social services demanded were simple in character and the requirements for their delivery fairly uniform – elementary education, basic workers' housing, standard unemployment insurance, etc. They could be hierarchically admin-istered because they were easily replicable locally and uniform in character – leading to more or less standardized provision. New public services are more diverse in their mix and far more complex in their character. Publics are more demanding and less deferential. The professionals responsible for service delivery need to have more knowledge, and hence more discretion, and are consequently more difficult to control from above. Thus, for example, universities are more difficult to monitor than elementary schools as mass higher education comes close to being a commonly available public service. It is very difficult to decide centrally what should be taught in universities and to determine if the outcomes are satisfactory.

The collapse of state socialism is thus a spectacular special case of a more widespread failure of the most commonly adopted non-market mechanism for co-ordinating services and activities. It is a failure that stems from the increasing complexity and localization of activities, and from the information required to govern these dispersed services proving to be beyond the capacity of hierarchical monitoring. It is a failure that managers, both public and private, continue in the main to find threatening and in response to which they seek substitute means of supervisory control over necessarily diverse and dispersed activities. The "audit explosion" is thus as much a consequence of the failure of top-down control as it is an attempt to find ways of continuing it.[2] Accountability upwards and transparency of activities for supervisory agencies are sought through ever more detailed accounting procedures made possible by computerization, standardized reporting mechanisms also facilitated by information technology, formula-funding schemes, and centralized quality-control systems. In the main those mechanisms can only succeed in asserting central control at the price of losing the advantages gained by localism and flexibility. This is what has happened in much of the public sector in the UK – the result is a mess in which the benefits of localism are often lost and effective hierarchical control is not restored.

Consumers generally find the moves towards customized production and tailored commercial services more satisfactory than standardized mass products. However, there are some real virtues in standardization and uniformity, and this has been particularly the case in the non-market public service sector. Consumers here, particularly those who have been conditioned into social democratic expectations, find diversity disquieting – they expect services to be uniform and equally available between different localities and social situations. Uniformity of administration and bureaucratic service delivery ensured a degree of equality and universalism in provision of services to citizens – this was desired by socialists, social democrats, and administrative rationalists alike. Indeed, such common uniform services provided foci for national continuity and identity – thus nationalists and civic republicans could welcome such homogeneity as promoting national character and political culture. Citizenship and the techniques of bureaucratic governance were closely connected. An example of the political effects of such uniform public services is the old monopoly public broadcasting systems like the BBC; critics fear that a multiplicity of channels will undermine a common national media culture and, therefore, part of national identity.

1.2 Exchange

It may seem curious to say that markets as a form of governance share in a crisis of modern techniques of control and regulation of activities, for market institutions and ideas seem to be dominant. Yet markets are only effective means of co-ordinating a wide range of activities and governing the action of numerous social actors either if they are combined with a strong mix of non-market institutions and activities, or if a very wide range of substantive outcomes is deemed acceptable. The notion that "free" markets are a method of co-ordination in and of themselves, without the need for other complimentary institutions, is only true in special circumstances.

Free markets cannot be a generalized mechanism of mediating between socially distinct and divided labours unless the conditions of perfect competition and perfect information are close to being met. A society of freely interacting small producers and traders, where the means of livelihood are fairly equally distributed, might permit markets to be the dominant form of social governance. A minimalist state and voluntary association for non-market activities would supplement a society organized around exchange. In a society with large corporations, a complex division of labour, and very large numbers of wage workers, these conditions cannot be met.

Moreover, modern expectations are strongly substantive – people may be told that "you cannot buck the market", but still they expect modern corporate capitalism to deliver broad-based prosperity and growth. Modern populations will not just accept whatever market exchange happens to deliver, and the notion that weakly regulated markets will tend to provide broadly egalitarian outcomes – full employment, growth and acceptable living standards for the mass of people – is too improbable to be credible. The problem is that modern free-market rhetoric tends to work towards undermining the forms of social embeddedness in non-market institutions that have helped both to enhance the performance of capitalist economies and to mitigate their worst features.[3] Welfare provision, for example, has helped both to ameliorate the effects of markets, cushioning the effects of sickness and unemployment, thus contributing to the political stability of capitalism, and to sustain mass demand, sharing the benefits of prosperity and creating more consumers. A purely competitive society in which individuals rise and fall on their luck or efforts, in which they themselves make provision for contingencies and risks through private saving and insurance, is likely to be a highly unequal society and one in which consumption will tend to be rigidly divided between rich and poor. By contrast modern mass consumption capitalism requires broad-based prosperity, a solid middle class who consume the bulk of its products. That middle class, the social basis of high and rising effective demand, is not a creation of the market alone but of an ensemble of social institutions that prevent radical social differentiation: free education, public financial support for private housing, collective consumption through infrastructure and public investment, social insurance and public health provision. Free-market rhetoric is thus undermining the foundations of modern capitalism in its advocacy of policies that destroy or hollow out the social institutions that allow markets to work effectively and relatively fairly.

1.3 Negotiated control

The classic form of such governance through negotiation and bargaining between the agents in an activity is corporatism – the macroeconomic and microeconomic regulation of capitalism through co-ordination by bargains struck between the major organized interests at national and at plant level. Industry, organized labour and the state co-operate in order to secure sustainable commitments by each of the parties and thus to provide relatively certain expectations. This method of governance through negotiation has been one of the most effective institutional supports of the large-firm market economy in the post-1945 advanced world. But it has increasingly been threatened by economic and industrial changes that have made it more difficult to bargain through centralized organized interests. Divisions of labour and forms of manufacturing organization have changed radically since the early 1970s. The manufacturing workforce has differentiated as a consequence of the decline of standardized mass production. This has led in the advanced countries to both a smaller and more diverse industrial workforce, to a blurring of the blue-/white-collar boundary in changing structures of skill, and to a lower level of unionization. Unions are thus less representative of the whole labour force. Thus it is less possible to centralize bargaining through common representative forms and structures in which the union federations claim to represent "labour". At the same time, the structures of the firm have been changing rapidly. Increasingly, highly centralized top-down control has been abandoned in favour of more responsive forms of organization able to cope with changing demand, rapid innovation, and the flexible production of a wide range of goods. Decentralization, de-merger, the growth of interfirm partnerships, sustained relationships with subcontractors, the formation of *ad hoc* project groups – all these developments weaken the classic managerial line of command and also mean that the interests of industry (between firms and within firms) are more and more difficult to represent through trade associations and national business federations.[4]

Companies thus face a very real threat of the loss of imperative control; this makes them less readily identifiable as bargaining agents. New forms of negotiated governance – networks, partnerships, trust relationships – are more specific and more evanescent, and less capable of being synthesized into a "model" on a national scale. If industry and labour have suffered a degree of decomposition as social interests, then the state too is less of an effective corporatist partner than it was in the era of the post-1945 great boom. States have fewer capacities autonomously to set macroeconomic conditions and targets, and are subject to greater international constraints – although the fashionable concept of "globalization" is far from an accurate description of the international economy and the prospects for governmental action by national states are not as reduced as is often claimed.

However, the result of these changes is greatly to weaken negotiated governance in the form of corporatism – a simple model of governance through tripartite bargaining between the major interests. The decline of corporatism and the weakening of Keynesian demand management strategies has limited the scope for distinct national responses to changing economic circumstances. Not only have these general models of governance ceased to be effective guides to political actors, but their embodiment in distinctive "national" models in which specific historical legacies and specific institutional ensembles combine to provide distinctive patterns of governance is now increasingly under threat. Until recently specific national capitalisms could be held up as models to the laggards in industrial performance and economic governance – West Germany, Japan and Sweden being the most often cited examples.[5] The Swedish combination of comprehensive welfare, active full-employment policies, centralized corporatist bargaining, and highly concentrated, internationally competitive industrial companies has clearly unravelled, even though popular support for welfare institutions remains strong. Germany and Japan are both increasingly seen as problematic models suffering from weaknesses and constraints that are systemic rather than conjunctural. In Germany the training system, the system of negotiated governance within firms, and the governing functions of institutions like trade associations are increasingly seen to be failing and no longer delivering microeconomic efficiencies and sustained high productivity growth.[6] In Japan growth has slowed dramatically and full employment is under threat. If these difficulties persist they will call into question the key features of the post-1945 settlement – such as the system of lifetime employment for core workers in major corporations and the highly labour-intensive and inefficient public and private service sectors.[7]

Even the "Third Italy", seen as a model of effective subnational economic governance based on the institutions of an industrial district, has lost some of its appeal. Italian local economic regulation relies on intimate knowledge on the part of key actors and intense networks that serve to balance co-operation and competition between firms and other economic actors. The problem is how to sustain such relationships *and* to promote changes in products and working methods necessary to meet intensifying international competitive pressures. Many Italian districts seem too tied to given products and divisions of labour, because stability in routines and settled expectations are the price one tends to pay for trust and for effective local knowledge.[8]

National models were never easily or directly applicable from one country to another.[9] It was difficult to disentangle the specific institutional legacies and the attitudes and experiences that go to make up a national capitalist system, to separate key features that could be replicated elsewhere and exported. The USA could never deliberately "copy" Japan and Germany. What it could do is borrow firm-level practices and graft them on to existing companies. That might change company performance, but it was more difficult to alter wider institutions and patterns of governance. If national "models" had a role, it was to highlight weaknesses in other systems, like the UK or USA, and prompt a response that was possible within their political system and social relations. Models defined benchmarks of effective governance against which one could judge one's own system.

The problem now is that models at every level seem less applicable. This is not to say that there are no new forms of governance and no specific experiences from which others can learn. There are a great many examples of institutional and organizational innovation. Firms are engaged in many evolving experiences of partnership, of building networks, of creating new working practices, and of seeking new relationships with customers, suppliers and employees. Governance through negotiation continues to develop in many forms at local level: new relationships between companies, local authorities and public agencies, worker groups, and local associations and activists. Some of this experience is valuable beyond the locality and can be disseminated to others. Charles Sabel has perceptively examined these relationships which emphasize change in response to new conditions and learning, where the distinct participating actors monitor each other's performance, and create open and "experimental" democratic forms.[10] However, creating "learning by monitoring" relationships is difficult. The generalization of practices of "bootstrapping reform" may be possible, but it still requires local knowledge and partners who are capable of sustaining ongoing evolutionary relationships. Moreover, these practices need to be located in wider political and economic structures that are sympathetic to them and sustain them.

Thus the issue is not that nothing is happening in the creation of new forms of governance. It is that such changes are specific to definite localities, evanescent, and subject to constant revision. They are thus difficult to generalize or to learn from – in part because they are processes rather than a settled architecture of institutions. Learning has significant costs, not the least of which is that such experiences are manifold – which is one to copy? It is also that they are difficult to formularize and to replicate. Models of the old kind offered firms, societies and states that were seeking to catch up "second-best practice", that is, ways to do things by numbers, to copy other people's institutional designs and practices. Keynesian demand management was in theory at least available to any medium-sized industrial state with a large enough public sector and a competent civil service. "Fordism" was an ideal-typical model of industrial efficiency that could be copied and adapted to local circumstances by mediocre firms.

Models also meant that, for good or ill, much of society was following the same script; that fact ensured a degree of uniformity and an ability to grasp the prevailing institutional architecture. Such simplicity has significant advantages – societies where institutions are highly localized, very different and rapidly changing are hard places for all but the most talented and adaptable to live in and difficult for outsiders to break into. They make accountability above the level of the very local difficult and common standards all but impossible.

Those who hanker after the uniform governance of the nation state, replicated in the same way across the country, those who yearn for equal treatment and common rules, for social democratic fairness and common standards of life, and those who want settled and common industrial routines, all find this new and evanescent world threatening. We cannot easily go back to such forms of uniformity in governance, but we need to go beyond a situation where the only certainties are perpetual learning and institutions that only exist in evolution. We need models because otherwise success depends entirely on constant learning and most people are bad at that, and because otherwise valuable possibilities are lost in a welter of experiments. A world of examples cannot create an economic and political system. If the second best constantly fall behind the successful, missing every trick in forms of governance and economic performance, then in a world of localized experiments, some firms and areas will pull away from others and set quite different socio-economic standards. However, a patchwork world of this kind is unlikely to be a successful or sustainable one. Modern societies need to sustain broad-based prosperity. If it cannot be had by the old social-democratic nation state-based strategies then we must find new ones, adapted to less stable and standardized production regimes – that will have similar effects.

The danger at the moment is that the many successful local experiments in governance are difficult to generalize and too evanescent to standardize. The result is that failed models will continue to reassert themselves – staking claims on the future because of the uncertainty of the present. We have seen the tenaciousness of the free market model despite ample evidence of the damage it does to the social fabric of modern capitalism. One also finds that many companies are trying to reassert imperative control. Partnerships and project groups are fine for innovation but they create uncertain relationships of ownership and control when problems arise, and, more-over, employees in interfirm teams often escape line-management super-vision altogether. Many firms are breaking down into more "manageable" units, not merely decentralizing to get better local knowledge and control but to be focused enough that top management can re-establish supervisory control.

The other danger is the persistence of wholly inappropriate models because they have become untouchable shibboleths in the absence of alternatives. One such model is the liberal notion of a democratic state in a market society, with a clear division of public and private spheres, and of "civil society" as a realm of voluntary action and private freedom. Our politicians all subscribe to some variant of this idea because anything else is seen as heresy, a threat to democracy and the free market. Yet this liberal architecture is a gross misdescription of the structure of modern societies. There is now no clear divide between the public and the private spheres, between democracy and markets, public and private choice. In fact modern societies are dominated by very similar large organizations on both sides of the formal public–private divide: business corporations, big public bureaucracies, quangos, and many intermediate kinds of organizations. These are in the main weakly accountable to those to whom they provide services. Public institutions are seldom directly accountable to those they serve – only indirectly accountable through elected officials who are also responsible for many other activities. These officials function less and less as representatives and more as the elected senior managers of a corporate enterprise. Companies too are weakly governed: shareholder *political* rights mean little since most managements are self-appointing oligarchies sustained by proxy votes. Stock markets assert a very direct power over companies, but few would argue it is in the best interests of consumers, employees or long-term investment and performance. Customers may or may not have market power, but many dimensions of the organization and behaviour of companies cannot be altered by buying or not buying their products.

The space between public and private is crossed by a wide variety of large governments, neither answerable fully through democratic elections nor through the market choices of consumers. Much of public life is organized on the model of a business corporation. Much of private life is dominated by large corporate businesses. Thus we are faced with a postliberal organizational society in which the fundamental relationship on either side of the public–private divide is that between a service provider and its clients, and in which the old liberal relationships of citizens and representative government, sovereign consumer and neutral market mean less and less. For most purposes people are confronted by organizations, and even though those organizations directly affect their interests they have very little say in how they are run. The institutional architecture of a postliberal society is so different that conventional economic liberal measures to boost accountability are no longer effective: downsizing government simply shifts the governance functions of large organizations from one formal constitutional site to another, from public to private, or public to quasi-public – and attempting to restore the role of "markets" is not to remove individuals from the scope of governance, but to shift the agencies that perform the functions from state to corporate bureaucracies.

Responding to the new institutional architecture of a postliberal society requires that any schemes for democratization and reform cross the boundary between civil society and the state, that they explicitly tackle the broader issues of the governance powers of all organizations and not just confine their remedies to government and to the state. Civil society needs to be made "public", its organizations being accepted as governing powers over which citizens with significant affected interests should have a say proportionate to their involvement and the risk to their interests. Thus organizations – state and non-state – need to be treated as political not merely administrative or private and the relevant publics given a greater direct role as organizational "citizens". If supposedly private organizations are governmental, then many public bodies and government agencies are now structured as if they were private corporations – the senior managers of such organizations need to be brought under the democratic control of the affected interests with a stake in their decisions.

This may seem naive, but it is to do no more than to apply the classic liberal principles of government by consent and of the right to be represented in decisions that affect one's interests to the organizational governments of a postliberal society.[11] The point of the criticism of liberalism as a *description* of modern society is not to reject but rather to further liberal goals – to promote the freedom of the individual and the accountability of governing powers to her or him. Thus recognizing that the public–private divide is undermined and that civil society is organizational rather than private, individual and voluntary is a prelude to new measures of democratization, not to the totalitarian extension of state power over private life. The cause of democratic reform will continue to stall until it is recognized that the old liberal architecture is obsolete and that we need to develop democratic practices across the whole of society, considering it as an ensemble of forms of governance.

If this recognition does not occur, then we are faced with the consequences of the changes that are possible underneath the stasis and drift which follows from sticking to the old liberal model and the prevailing forms of governance associated with it. Until this change of outlook happens new freedoms cannot be developed or old ones defended. We are faced with the threat of a political and social system beyond control, the key failings of which cannot even be identified through the fog of liberal rhetoric. Postliberalism may currently be a descriptive term, but it could also develop into a more sinister reality, in which liberal freedoms are irretrievably lost.

This is not inevitable, but there is the potential for major incursions into democratic rights and personal liberty. Nation states are still important, but they are losing certain capacities for governance as many economic and environmental issues develop to a scale where only effective international governance is possible. The danger of clinging to the model of the sovereign nation state is that it will lose more of its powers in the process, as national-level government is weakened by the absence of an effective division of labour with international agencies. It is conceivable, although unlikely, that internationalized markets and transnational companies could evolve beyond all political control, subjecting populations to ungovernable market forces.[12] In the absence of some effective measures for restructuring corporate governance, companies (whether national or transnational) will exploit their "private" status to bring ever larger areas of social life under their control. Companies could evolve into truly private governments with wide powers over citizens. The public sphere will thus be eroded by private power, companies beginning to exercise influence and to administer activities beyond all democratic control – whether of shareholders, employees, consumers or local communities.

At the same time the scope for unmolested enjoyment of the "private sphere" by the individual will shrink. The demands on the part of the members of modern society for protection from a wider and wider range of contingencies and risks will diminish the scope of private freedom. Measures designed to protect and enhance individuals' lives will have the effect of imposing a wider and wider series of controls and constraints. The pressures to check child abuse, violence against women, to promote racial and sexual equality, to eliminate health hazards and environmental risks may be justified and the objectives worthy, but the effect of all these pleas for help and protection is to give vast powers to public officials to police the private lives of citizens and to intrude ever deeper into what was once the sphere of governance through the family. This may be inevitable, indeed necessary, but it further undermines the relevance of the liberal archi-tecture based on the separation of a private sphere of individual conduct from the intervention of the state. *All* family and private life is increasingly closely policed, now subjected to scrutiny against evolving norms rather than to intervention only when a definite law is broken. Thus, for example, the Child Support Agency in Britain – created with cross-party support for the worthy objective of making delinquent fathers contribute to the costs of raising their children – began systematically to examine and to suspend legally agreed private divorce settlements. Administrative discretion could thus overturn legally sanctioned private contracts – a threat to the classic liberal view of the rule of law.

The prospect would thus be of a range of public agencies with extensive and increasingly arbitrary "police" powers in the private domain, of private corporations beyond public control and yet able to govern by their decisions increasing areas of social life and impose their will on state agencies, and of states that are no longer the exclusive hierarchically controlling power for all activities within their territories, being forced to submit to the intervention of international market forces and governmental agencies and also to share power with private bodies. This combination of a publicly scrutinized private life, the power of unelected organizations and private governments and the overlapping of powers of governance within the same territory has not been seen since the Middle Ages. It would, however, have none of the governmental checks and balances of medieval constitutionalism. In such a world the liberal governmental model would cease to have meaning, and yet such a world is more than conceivable if present trends continue unchecked. Private and unaccountable government is currently able to grow unchecked – in the major financial markets, in media empires, in major corporations – because its actions are presented as non-governmental, as the private actions of free citizens in civil society.

Traditionalists respond to this by seeking to reassert the power of the nation state. They claim that such a state, democratically accountable and imposing common standards, can check the slide away from national uniformity and common citizenship. Yet they fail to realize that the state is simultaneously weaker in certain dimensions than it was, and yet is ever more overextended in providing a diverse range of services and seeking to regulate an ever-widening range of contingencies. As such it is too overloaded to act as an effective democratic overseer, and too enmeshed in trying to rationalize its own activities to offer a check to the growth of private and quasi-public managerial power. Indeed, elected politicians and career officials are eager to assert corporate models of management in the public service; the paradox is that they are often the ones that business has been abandoning in practice as it tries to become flexible and responsive.

Privatization and marketization are failing to confront the problems of modern public management, whilst reducing equality and fairness in the provision of public services. Yet social democracy has not enjoyed a real renaissance in response. It depended on an economic-governmental conjuncture that cannot readily be put back together again. The ideal of uniformity in the delivery of services and universalism in entitlements, of common national standards for all localities and citizens, leading to a substantial measure of equality in living conditions, was a worthy one. Even at the height of social democratic influence it was seldom attained. The problem is that modern societies are less occupationally homogeneous, the mass manual male working class has been superseded by a more differentiated and diversified workforce, they are also less "national" and more pluralistic in goals, cultures and social standards, and the range of modern public services is too wide and too diverse to be delivered to everybody and in the same way. Social democratic and Christian democratic welfare measures and social provision reinforced national political identity, civic consciousness and a spirit of public service – they thus provided some of the social foundations for an effective mass democracy. A measure of cultural and social homogeneity is essential to democracy as a decision procedure, especially in a centralized sovereign state. One has to be sufficiently like one's fellow citizens to trust them with legislative power over one.

The welfare state and democracy are intimately linked. One cannot build new forms of democracy without ensuring a measure of social security. Thus the decentralization of sovereign power has to be coupled with a welfare system and set of public services that is itself decentralized, but which ensures common minimum standards of provision. This can only be achieved by maintaining public funding and common minimum entitlements. Just as the division of state and civil society has become blurred, to which the most effective reform response is a new postliberal governmental architecture which "publicizes" civil society, giving it the forms and attributes of democratic public governance, so the present division between public and private provision in welfare needs to be overcome. An associationalist welfare system will combine public funding related to individual membership of voluntary bodies providing services with citizen choice over providers. Public funding and common basic minima are essential in order to sustain an adequate level of welfare and a suitable range of services for all. Public entitlements and choice need to be combined, not driven apart as economic liberals who seek to privatize welfare provision wish to do. The provision of services through publicly funded voluntary associations in which individuals can choose and can craft the specific services they want is compatible with the common basic entitlements that were central to classical social democracy.

Indeed, it is probably the only way social democratic aims can survive. Unless individuals in a more differentiated society have choice and will consume the public services that they pay for in the way that they want to, then public welfare will degenerate into poor relief. The advocacy of "targeting" welfare services, concentrating them on the poor, has begun to capture socialist and labour parties in the postsocial democratic era. It is a political disaster, that will promote the worst kind of social differentiation – creating services that only the desperate will consume through want of other choices but which all have to pay for. A decentralized society can be a diverse one, but it cannot be a polarized one. A new democratic welfare system based on provision through self-governing associations requires an adequate minimum of common security. A society divided between the poor and the excluded and the rest, will promote centralization and repression, not localism and choice. Thus diversity in provision, where all can choose the services they want and well-to-do can top up a common sufficient minimum, may actually be the only route left to a relatively fair and not grossly unequal society, in which all have access to services and taxpayers accept the necessity to spend on forms of collective consumption to a high standard.

Associative democracy provides new and clear models of governance that are applicable in the political system, in economic life and in welfare services. However, associationalism does not do this by proposing the replacement of the existing social order with an entirely new alternative. Rather it is a supplement to existing institutions that has the capacity to transform their workings rather than to supplant them. Associationalist governmental means can be added piecemeal and iteratively to existing institutions in an ongoing reform process. Thus it has the gradualist and reformist potential of classical and social democracy, but adapted to new conditions.

Associative democracy aims neither to abolish representative government nor to replace market exchange with some other allocative mechanism, rather to free the former from the encumbrance of an overextended and centralized public-service state and to anchor the latter in a complex of social institutions that enables it to attain socially desirable outcomes. Associationalism responds directly to the problems of how to democratize a postliberal organizational society, since it aims to promote governance through democratically legitimated voluntary associations. The conversion of public and private corporate hierarchies into self-governing bodies answerable to those they serve and who participate in them would thus answer to the greatest democratic deficits of our time – organizational government without consent and corporate control without representation.

The great advantage of associative democracy is that it offers a coherent model to guide reform initiatives across specific organizations and localities. It provides a means to linkup and to systematize local experiments. Suitably applied, associative democratic concepts are at once a coherent and a sufficiently loose-textured model that can help to convert many local experiments in decentralization, democratization, and negotiated govern-ance from one-offs into contributions to a move toward a new style of social governance.

This book consists of essays that are attempts to define and specify a model of such governance. Some of these essays (notably chapters 6 and 7) go beyond my earlier *Associative Democracy* (1994) in this respect, and some of those in Part III (notably chapters 13 to 15) utilize ideas developed in *Globalization in Question* (1996: with Grahame Thompson) to place the associative model in a context of international issues and forms of governance. The book is thus a synthesis of themes held somewhat apart in the other two distinct contributions. The essays collected here form a whole and are gathered into three related groups, each of which tackles a major theme and each of which follows on from the preceding one.

The first part consists of four essays that perform two distinct tasks: to outline the core principles of associative democratic governance, and to develop a radical criticism of the weaknesses and limits of modern repre-sentative democracy that explains why the supplement provided by the devolution of government to voluntary democratically controlled associ-ations is necessary. Unlike most critiques of the current state of repre-sentative democracy, which typically advocate its complete replacement by some other form of democracy, such as direct democracy, the reforms proposed here supplement existing representative institutions with new or reconfigured forms of governance and accountability.

The effect of such reforms would be to strengthen representative institutions and to enable them effectively to carry out their traditional three main functions: to provide society with a framework of basic laws to guide social actors; to oversee forms of public service provision to hold public officials accountable; and to protect the rights and interests of citizens. Currently the core democratic institutions do these basic jobs badly because government throughout the advanced world is too centralized and omnicompetent, democratic bodies are thus enmeshed in the direct responsibility for the provision and delivery of services in an extended public-service state. Democratic institutions are thus forced to two expedients which undermine them in the attempt to assert control: the substitution of managerial methods of accountability for political ones, and the proliferation of rules to cover every contingency, thus weakening the rule of law by its very complexity. Not only is representative government caught in the contradictory tasks of being at once service provider and overseer of the adequacy of provision, but the scale and scope of the activities for which the state is responsible are too great for detailed supervision by institutions like representative assemblies that were created to provide political control in an era of small government.

The aim is not to convert big government into small government, to govern less and to provide less through the commonweal, but to change the methods of government. Public funding combined with decentralized provision is the essence of associative democracy. Representative institutions continue to provide the basic rules and to set the fiscal framework, but associations are responsible for the provision of services to their members. Decentralization of governance through voluntary self-governing associations would place individuals under the subsidiary governments they have chosen for the specific purposes in question and in which they have some voice. Associations would compete to provide definite services and to obtain public funds proportionate to membership for public purposes. The affairs of such governments in civil society could thus be specific to them for most matters concerned with providing services to their members and need not directly concern the public power. Associations make their own rules and have their own forms of accountability. Only serious harms to other associations or to individual rights need concern the public power. Associations, because they are voluntary, could be lightly regulated, individuals having the option to leave if they found the services or style of delivery unsatisfactory.

The very features of an organizational society that currently push it towards rule proliferation and top-down managerial control would thus be reversed in an associatively governed civil society. Associationalism is the one doctrine of governance that can make a virtue of the dominance of civil society by organizations – converting them into particular governments or political societies that their members have chosen and given consent to. Associationalism is thus not mere localism, it can cope with large-scale organizations, nor does it rely primarily on direct democracy and its extensive requirements for participation. Of course, it does not exclude intense participative voluntary organizations for those who want them, but even the most active will choose a small range of organizations to be active in. What associative democracy offers is governance through choice and voice – the possibility of exit from unsatisfactory service providers and the chance to vote and to get involved in the associations one values. Thus it turns the unaccountable and often compulsory organizations that now dominate "civil society" into voluntarily membership representative governments.

Associative democracy extends the principles of the democratic revolution of the eighteenth century to the "private sphere" created by that revolution. The separation between public representative government and individual freedoms created the space for the growth of corporate power, corporations being perceived as voluntary associations of citizens. It also extends the principles of representative democracy into state administration – governance should as far as possible involve choice and voice in its methods of administration and service delivery. A democratically legitimated structure of top-down authority only allows periodic active input by the citizens, a plebiscite, not continuous involvement. Associative democracy allows for such involvement without dissolving administration into amateurism or forcing everyone to attend committees. It has the benefits of representative and direct democracy, whilst minimizing the costs of both.

These are large claims, but having worked on modernizing the associative democratic tradition for a decade I am ever more convinced that they are sustainable. The essays in Part I stretch over five years. Chapters 2 and 3 are the most recent and most developed statement of associative democratic principles. Chapter 4 still conceives associative democracy primarily as a form of socialism. This is not so much wrong, since associationalism is the best option for the continuation of the values of democratic socialism, but partial, since other political traditions can also appropriate and adopt the political institutions involved as means to pursue their political goals. Associationalism has the advantage that it can speak to different parts of the political spectrum. Thus genuine free-market libertarians who want to maximize individual choice and freedom may find associative democracy their best option, if they are concerned about the destructive consequences of unregulated markets and the growth of corporate power and yet fear the growth of an over-mighty centralized regulatory state. Associationalism can also provide a political model for what otherwise appear to be specific

political and social campaigns. Thus for example it offers the environmentalists the possibility of decentralization and a check to the power of
large organizations, and to gays the prospect of a society of self-regulating
communities in which they could choose their own welfare services. The
need for such a generalizing political model has never been greater. It
explains how plural groups with different and competing values could co-
exist through self-governance, with the added protection that representative
central government and the law remain intact to offer protection against
groups that harm the interests of others.

Chapter 4 is included because it offers a clear critique of attempts to
make state socialism and political democracy compatible, and also because
it explores the limitations of the attempt to renew socialism through the
promotion of democracy on the part of leftist civic republicans. Inevitably,
as times change so do political solutions and the latter part of the essay,
which attempts to argue for an enhancement of democracy through corporatist representation, is now somewhat overtaken by events. Corporatist
solutions remain relevant where the institutional preconditions continue to
exist and where the bodies involved in the bargaining are representative
enough to be in the general interest. Such societal negotiated governance is
not rejected here, rather it is seen to be less and less effective. The reasons
for this have been outlined above, chiefly the diversification and decomposition of social interests. Political doctrines that are attempting to reason
from circumstances and from existing institutions have to evolve as
conditions change. I see that as no defect but a positive advantage. However,
it does mean that one has carefully to adjust one's institutional prescriptions
in terms of both core principles and the facts – a hard job in a culture that
tries to keep normative and descriptive statements apart.

The second part of the book also consists of four essays. Chapters 6 and 7
explore the notion of an organizational and postliberal society. Chapter 6
does so by trying to account for the growth of quangos in Britain – a vast
sphere of quasi-public governmental power. It does so by arguing that it is
not a mere matter of the ideology of the governing party but a response to
changing conditions of governance in which the British style of informality
and voluntarism in some institutions, and uniform centralized administration in others, has become obsolete. Chapter 7 outlines the problem of
postliberalism and outlines the possibilities of governance through civil
society.

Chapter 8 examines the response of an intelligent free-marketeer to the
problem of an unrestrained capitalist system's tendency to undermine its
own social foundations. David Green's espousal of voluntarism is admirable,
but his aim is a "civic capitalism" in which voluntary actions compensate for
the inadequacies of a minimal state.[13] The chapter points out in response
why in modern circumstances voluntarism and extended public governance

need to go together and that welfare needs to be public, although it need not be delivered by the central state. It also argues that in many ways the reforms of the 1945 Labour Government, seen by many on the left as the cynosure of social democracy, were in fact a false route. The postwar reforms in effect nationalized welfare for the working class, putting their entitlements at the mercy of government policy and subjecting their services to top-down administration. The option of reinforcing localism, municipal services and voluntarism by public support and public funding was never seriously considered, even though there were Labour Movement voices raised against appropriation of worker-controlled welfare by the state. Labour and the Conservatives in Britain have both been committed to statism and centralism, the latter in practice if not in ideology. Chapter 9 outlines the current crisis of centralized state welfare and briefly sketches the principles of an extensive system of public welfare delivered in the main through voluntary associations.[14]

The third part of the book moves to consider the international context in which an associative democratic system might develop. For much of this century associative democracy was inconceivable. It could not answer to the challenges of war and internal revolutionary threats in the way that a centralized hierarchical state power could. Few citizens wanted to be invaded and overrun by foreigners. Few in the industrialized world (including the majority of manual workers) wanted the uncertainty and civil strife associated with violent revolution, whether of left or right. The prospect of security was thus the most powerful legitimation for the state and the threat of totalitarian forces the best justification for the simplicities of plebiscitarian democracy combined with strong government.

These threats are no longer pressing. Western societies are neither threatened by invasion nor by revolution. Now social diversity and an open international economy limit the credibility of the "sovereign" state as the primary source of governance within a territory. Certain problems long ago evolved beyond the scope of stand-alone national governance – creating a stable order for world trade and a viable regulatory regime for the global environment being the two most salient examples. The moves toward complexity, flexibility and decentralization in business also favour more localized, more effectively informed authority. Centralized national governments find it difficult to be responsive to the demands of business for suitable collective services and specific support; for most purposes the era of national industrial policies is over. Regional governments have re-emerged as effective economic regulators in partnership with nation states. Thus we now face an emerging division of labour in governance between international, national and regional agencies. The nation state can no longer assert a monopoly over deciding who shall govern and how. The nation state is a vital but specific part of a complex system of governance. At both the international and the regional level associative relationships and institutions increasingly provide essential elements of governance. Voluntary bodies and non-governmental organizations are a vital part of an emerging international "public sphere", with the capacity to focus the informed publics of the world on salient problems. They also provide services and governance; acting in many cases where states are indifferent or incapable, providing solidarity between the rich and poor worlds. At the regional level bodies like trade associations, labour unions, charities and other interest groups contribute to local negotiated governance and the creation of networks to facilitate local public co-operation and discussion.

Clearly, associations cannot solve all the world's problems, but they are an important part of the new division of labour in governance. They help to democratize what would otherwise be a highly elite-centred system of international governance through intergovernmental relationships and supranational agencies. One must always be alert to the conversion of political ideas into pious rhetoric, especially as circumstances change. Chapter 10 is a critique of the central and eastern European 1980s espousal of "civil society", ideas that were exceptionally influential in the west. The notion of a citizens' coalition against the state made sense when the state was an authoritarian body dominating society and also the satellite of a foreign power. Once communist power dissolved, the notion that "civil society" could provide the foundation for a new non-confrontational politics based on dialogue was abruptly challenged. The countries of central and eastern Europe have returned to the messy politics of competing parties and conflicting interests. Inevitably, this critique had to await the demise of the *ancien regime* – to have challenged Václav Havel during the communist dictatorship would have been nothing more than siding with party stooges. The latter part of the essay explores why democracy is likely to be ineffectual in Russia for a long time to come and why government there is likely to face a political state of exception for the foreseeable future. As with most such pieces the essay is clearly a mixture of blindness and insight, it predicted a *coup d'état* but not its failure. No specialist, let alone an amateur, could have predicted that the plotters did not realize that they had to fight for power not merely assume it. The *coup* was symbolic rather than a ruthless bid for power. The plotters did not try to *seize* power because they were too deluded to imagine they had lost it. They thought the mere announcement of their rule would lead the whole populace to knuckle under; most of it did and some elementary precautions could have forestalled the dissenters.

I was emboldened to write about Russia despite my ignorance, precisely because the rapidity of change seemed to place knowledge at a discount. Subsequent events seem to have confirmed the analysis. The notion that Russia would become a western-style liberal society with a market economy and a representative government was always a fantasy, but one indulged in by the Russian reformers and their western advisers. Russia is a highly illiberal organizational society, dominated by the big interest cartels like the banks and oil and gas producers and by competing elites. It will remain in a state of exception for the foreseeable future. The question remaining is not will Russia evolve into a parliamentary democracy but whether the present form of elective dictatorship will survive and permit a measure of political openness, or if it will turn into an even uglier and more authoritarian regime.

Russia will not be a genuine democracy but that does not mean it will become a threat to the west or that we shall return to the political rigidities of the Cold War. If Russia does develop a form of ruling ideology rather than the present confused makeshifts, it is unlikely to be one suitable for export. The most likely option is a form of Slavophile nationalism. Russia has too many problems within its borders and difficulties in the Near Abroad to seek to become an aggressive world power once again. Thus Chapter 11 argues that it is in the west's interests both to placate Russia in respect of its regional concerns and to offer generous economic aid. The chapter also argues that western states are unlikely to intervene in conflicts that are not central to their economic or political interests beyond diplomacy and protest. This may seem to be contradicted by the US-led settlement in Bosnia. However, until the Croatian and Bosnian Government military victories changed the terms of the conflict, western intervention would have involved serious fighting to be effective. To oversee a brokered peace is one thing, to enforce it against an unbroken Bosnian Serb army is another. The point is that if western states are possessed of all the hardware necessary for self-defence, and if they are unlikely to intervene abroad except as low-level peacekeepers, then the need to retain a centralized state apparatus of the kind required for the total wars of the twentieth century has disappeared.

Chapter 12 is a criticism of Francis Fukuyama's view that there are no alternatives to the present world of plebiscitary democracy and market society. It is followed by three essays that attempt the difficult move of outlining what a future international order is likely to look like. The first, Chapter 13, is a robust critique of the fashionable concept of "global-ization". It argues that national economies are not being dissolved even though we have an open international economy with high levels of trade and investment flows between its major players. It also demonstrates that the international economy is not inherently ungovernable, and that a mixture of international governance and appropriate national polices can regulate and stabilize the world trading system. Chapter 14 uses a dense historical argument about the origins of the present system of states in the sixteenth and seventeenth centuries to demonstrate that effective state-level governance requires an appropriate international environment – it shows that sovereignty required not just mutual recognition by states but that the state's ability to gain control over its territory was made possible by the emerging convention that states did not interfere in each other's religious affairs. The final chapter outlines why the nation state remains important both in an economic context and as the foundation for the rule of law. Without democratically legitimated states capable of upholding international law the prospects for governance by international agencies and intergovernmental regimes would be grim.

Thus despite the advocacy of associative democracy as a vital supplement in governance, the role of representative democracy and of the state as the source and upholder of law remain central. Associative democracy aims to make existing forms of representative government less narrowly plebiscitarian, to add to the function of democratic legitimation greater and wider powers of popular input into decision-making. A democracy thus strengthened is likely to lead to a fairer and more equitable society in the advanced countries. If the populations of the world's richest nations feel more secure and more in control, they are less likely to fear and to discriminate against the poor and low-paid of the world. Thus greater democracy in the west is, at least potentially, not just self-serving, but a foundation for better international governance and a more equitable world order.

The criticism of the concept of globalization offered here is not intended narrowly to refocus concern on national issues, but rather to support a sustainable open international economy and to promote a determined effort to reduce the differences between rich and poor nations. Globalization rhetoric leads us to be frightened of international competitiveness, to see other countries as a threat and to see social solidarity within our own wealthy countries as a cost we can ill-afford. It promotes competition between nations and within them, advocating that we brutalize our own poor and undermine our own working conditions and labour rights to compete with low-wage countries. This is the most damaging vision, one that can only favour a wealthy minority. Associationalism, by contrast, is an attempt to defend and to further social solidarity. Solidarity is neither instinctive nor under modern conditions can it be imposed through state compulsion; it has to come from the intelligent choices of individuals. Individuals can realize their purposes in the main only by bonding together with others. The great advantage of associationalism is that it shows how individual choice and collective action are compatible, and how the specific solidarities of associations can contribute to building a sustainable and civilized social order.

Notes

1. The path-breaking analysis here is Piore and Sabel (1984).
2. See Power (1994) and Miller (1996).

3. Hutton (1995) is the most accessible critique of economic liberalism.
4. See Sabel (1991).
5. For examples see the advocacy of "Rhenish capitalism" against Anglo-Saxon models in Albert (1993) and Hampden-Turner and Trompenaars (1993).
6. See Lembruch (1997).
7. See, for example, Reading (1992).
8. For an up-to-date, balanced and intelligent assessment of economic governance in Italy see Locke (1995).
9. See Soskice (1996) for an argument that German institutions could not easily be grafted into British ones.
10. Sabel (1994, 1995).
11. See Hirst (1997) and other essays in this volume advocating the stakeholding concept.
12. For an argument as to why not see Hirst and Thompson (1996), especially Chapter 4.
13. See also Green (1996).
14. Hirst (1994), Chapter 7 lays out in far greater detail the model of the institutions of a decentralized welfare state based on voluntary associations and answers the major objection raised by critics to such a system.

Part I

Democracy and associative governance

2

Associative democracy

The conflict between liberal democratic capitalism and state socialism dominated political life for most of this century. Now the political arena is changing radically. The problem is whether we can develop political ideas to make sense of those changes and to guide political action. State socialism is finished as a credible political idea. But liberal democracy is almost moribund, too, something most celebrants of the collapse of communism have failed to notice. In fact the collapse of communism and the stagnation of liberalism are connected. Liberal democracy derived its most powerful legitimation from the threat of ideological dictatorships; whatever its limitations it allowed citizens to criticize and to change their government. Authoritarian regimes and the revival of religious fanaticism in the third world are too distant from us in the west to have the same effect. At the same time the western public is more and more confused about what government can accomplish and whether voting makes any difference.

We cannot rest content with a stagnant liberalism and the absence of any strategy for reform. Liberal democracy is inadequate precisely because changing political circumstances are making its institutions less and less able to cope. Unless it is supplemented by other ideas, it will fail to adapt to a changing political world.

There are three main reasons why liberal democratic institutions are failing to cope with the new challenges. The first goes back to the beginning of this century, when representative democracies embraced big government and interventionist bureaucracy in order to secure their societies against external threats and internal conflicts. War mobilization, the growth of welfare, and the regulation and support of big business all promoted the growth of large public and private hierarchical administrations. The result was that the institutions of classical liberalism, adequate to superintend a minimal state, were left in place to administer the bureaucratic states of today. Existing democratic institutions provide low levels of governmental accountability to citizens and of public influence on decision-making. And it is less and less evident that large bureaucracies, whether public or private, are efficient and that the public gains enough in competent administration to compensate for its loss of control over its affairs.

The second reason is that representative democracy has atrophied, has become more a means of legitimation of centralized and bureaucratic government than a check upon it, at the very time when expectations of citizens are rising. Mass higher education and individuation are creating large demanding publics, who are reluctant to have government intrude into their affairs. Western societies are less homogeneous than ever in their values, with ethnic, religious and lifestyle pluralism far advanced. Distinct communities have very different and often conflicting standards. This means that uniform national services are less acceptable to diverse publics. Modern societies are more and more difficult to govern because of this pluralism, and they are less able to overcome value conflicts through majority decision.

The third reason for the stagnation of liberal democracy is that it has been closely tied to the idea that the nation state is the primary political community. Liberalism evolved within the context of the sovereign nation state. For most of this century the role of the nation state has been strengthened. From the 1930s onward, through national macroeconomic management and redistributionist welfare policies states could ensure economic progress and social security within a market economy. Since the early 1970s however, the effectiveness of national economic management has declined dramatically. Faced with an internationalizing and increasingly volatile economy, in which competition between nations has intensified and growth rates are uncertain, national governments have proved unable to ensure the conditions for prosperity either by traditional Keynesian means or by the monetarist methods that became fashionable in the 1980s. States are by no means powerless in economic terms, but they no longer have reliable instruments of macroeconomic management that can sustain growth and full employment. If public bodies are now able to intervene effectively in the economy it is in their *political* capacity, by promoting co-operation between economic actors and by adopting policies that enable firms to create the microeconomic conditions for competitive success. Increasingly the public bodies able to perform these tasks are not conventional national states but regional governments.

With the end of the Cold War the military justifications for the nation state have weakened too. The world has not become conflict-free, but western societies no longer face direct military threats. The most serious problems facing western societies (be they economic, environmental, or social) cannot be tackled primarily at the level of the nation state. The sites of governance are shifting toward the supranational and the regional levels: to trade blocs like the European Community and to regional governments like the German *Länder* (substates). It is thus possible that by the early twenty-first century politics will have no "centre". Instead, political actors will be confronted with complex overlapping structures of government and social regulation, both public and private, at international, national, and regional levels. The classic institutions of representative government will be even less effective means of accountability than they are now.

Given such complex political structures, which will resemble the conflicting sources of authority of the Middle Ages, we will need a new theory of the distribution of power among these entities. A key task of such a new theory will be to find a means of subjecting transnational corporations to some form of public, democratic control. Liberal democratic theory does not have the resources, without supplementation, to perform these tasks. The institutions that it has become identified with – national parliaments, political parties, and the majority choices of the citizens of a homogeneous political community – seem less than effective means of organizing the new politics.

Liberal democratic politics is stagnant, and economic liberalism is in no better shape. It returned to popularity at the end of the 1970s because it promised renewed prosperity and greater freedom. The market was presented as a different form of democracy, based on consumer sovereignty. Markets, it was claimed, can register popular preferences better than political institutions do because they allow individuals directly to choose the goods and services they want. Such claims assumed that "free" markets would produce widespread prosperity because of their superior allocative efficiency. Yet, after more than a decade of conservative free-market policies, the negative results are obvious for all to see. The concept of the allocative efficiency of markets is purely theoretical and can provide no guarantee that markets will deliver the outcomes citizens want – full employment, sustained growth, and social stability. Economic liberalism has provided none of these. It is a doctrine that was bound in practice to favour the rich and the major corporations, under a cloak of rugged individualist rhetoric.

2.1 After socialism

Yet economic liberalism will rule by default in the absence of a new concept of economic governance. It appeals to the growing anti-statist sentiments among the successful in western societies, who do not want to be "administered" and who resent taxation to support collectivist welfare. State intervention was accepted when the bulk of the population were struggling manual workers, but social reforms and rising prosperity have created a society in which the majority perceive themselves to be "middle class", and wish to craft their own consumptions of services such as pensions or health care as much as possible. Re-emphasizing collectivism is thus no answer to the failure of economic liberalism. Keynesianism is too one dimensional as a doctrine of economic governance; it is confined to the state manipulation of macroeconomic aggregates to achieve full employment and economic growth. It has little capacity to change the behaviour of economic actors by other means. Keynesian policies can at best prevent a slump from accelerating; they can no longer deliver sustained growth.

There are committed democratic socialists who believe that the failure of economic liberalism and Keynesianism will create an opening for radical socialist policies. Some environmentalists also believe that increased regulation of resource use and tough physical planning by government are necessary if environmental catastrophe is to be averted. It would be premature to dismiss such ideas. However, they do face a problem in that such intervention has hitherto depended on the state, and nation states are now much less effective agencies of government.

Even if renewed socialist solutions are not possible, it is obvious that some new form of economic regulation is needed if stability is to be preserved. There is no such thing as a "market society", for the simple reason that the market is *not* a society. It is a mechanism of exchange that is embedded in other social relationships. In "freeing" the market, economic liberalism actually weakens those relationships. Societies will be unable to survive, and even to compete economically, if they just accept whatever results uncontrolled markets and international competitive pressures produce. If social control is to be restored over the economy it will have to be in a new way: the public powers and economic actors need to achieve a new form of co-ordination, based upon more localized forms of economic governance. Democratic control of the economy may be achieved by other routes than the policies of elected national governments, in particular by making companies answerable to a wider range of interests.

Is there a political concept that will address all these problems: that can restore the accountability of governments, cope with the new complexity of political authority, accommodate the plural values of diverse communities, satisfy the desire of the successful not to be regimented while meeting the needs of the poor, and provide new methods of economic governance? I contend that there is, and that it is called associationalism. It is, like modern liberalism and communism, a product of that great age of ideologies, the nineteenth century. However, the very reasons that led it to lose out to those competitors in the early twentieth century make it a suitable guide to radical renewal in the twenty-first.

2.2 Three basic propositions

Associationalism can be summed up in three basic propositions. The first is that the organization of social affairs should as far as possible be transferred from the state to voluntary and democratically self-governing associations. Associationalism seeks to combine the individual choice of liberalism with the extensive public provision of collectivism. The scale of direct state activity is reduced, but not at the expense of social provision. Associations would be publicly funded for functions such as health or education. This doctrine aims to strengthen government in and through civil society; thus civil society takes on many of the attributes of the public sphere. The effect would be to reduce the role of hierarchical organizations, both public and private, and to promote accountability through the democratic self-government of associations and the devolution of functions to the local level.

The second proposition is that political authority should be decentralized and perform as few functions as are consistent with its role. This is in direct opposition to a long-established trend toward centralization and state omni-competence. In this doctrine the state ceases to be a central "sovereign" body and the political structure becomes pluralistic as power is shared by a number of agencies. To call this structure "federal" risks some confusion, given the high degree of centralization in formally federal states like the USA. Associationalists have always supported the federal principle, but one in which the federation is like an association, the component agencies entering into relations of co-operation as necessity requires.

The third proposition is that as far as possible the economy should be organized on mutualist lines, that is, by means of non-profit financial institutions and co-operative firms in which both investors and workers have a significant say in their governance.

Associationalism has several intellectual sources: the English advocates of industrial and social co-operation, such as Robert Owen and George Jacob Holyoake; Pierre-Joseph Proudhon and the French mutualists; the English political pluralists Frederick William Maitland and John Neville Figgis, developing the ideas of Otto von Gierke; aspects of the French and German corporatist traditions, most notably the ideas of Léon Duguit and Émile Durkheim; and the two most important associationalist writers of this century, G.D.H. Cole and Harold J. Laski. Associationalism failed to have much political influence after the mid-1920s because the political forces on both the left and the right that supported state centralization and collectivism were better adapted to the conditions of the early twentieth century, and in particular the demands of total war. But conditions have now changed radically in the advanced western societies. If we consider the three propositions above, we shall see what associationalism has to offer.

I. The promotion of self-government through voluntary associations would address three major problems:
    1. How to ensure accountability in representative democracies?

2. How to cope with increasingly pluralistic societies with divergent values?

3. How to enable the successful to enjoy services that have all the benefits of being collective, without being uniform and compulsory, and without at the same time abandoning the poor?

The devolution of social functions to voluntary associations would enable the representative democratic state to become more like a minimal public power again. The state would fund and supervise, but would not be directly responsible for the voluntary self-governing associations that would deliver services in areas like health, education, and welfare. Citizens would choose to join these associations and would have certain entitlements to services, and the associations would receive public funds proportionate to their membership. The institutions of liberal democracy could then function as the agencies of supervision and accountability, unencumbered by direct responsibility for delivering services. Voluntary and democratically self-governing associations could be more loosely supervised than bureacracies are. In those areas wholly subject to the democratic decision of their members it is the members who bear the consequences. State regulation could be looser and simpler because an association's members would have the power to leave or press for change should any action of that body damage their interests. The state would not have to cover every contingency as it does when regulating large public and private bureaucracies, over which the members of the public have no direct control. Thus the laws could be both less extensive and less complex, making them easier to understand and thus promoting the rule of law. The current tendencies toward increasingly complex legislation lead, on the contrary, to the rule of lawyers and to the alienation of the ordinary citizen.

Voluntarism would also make social provision and social governance less conflictual. Communities would be free to establish their own services in conformity with their own values, subject of course to certain minimum common standards. Each subcommunity could craft the forms of education, health care, and so on that is desired. Each group would govern itself for its own purposes. Individuals would be free to leave and to join other associations, and the law would protect such freedoms. The clashes that now arise over state provision, where each group seeks to get the state to recognize *its* standards as universal, would thus considerably diminish. Different groups and associations would certainly have to get used to living side by side, each obeying its own rules and leaving others to do the same. Groups and associations would compete non-politically, by seeking to win the allegiance of individuals rather than by trying to impose common laws upon all.

Welfare states are in crisis throughout the advanced world. The well-to-do have become tax averse and less willing to accept the standard services that the state provides. The poor are seen, on the right, as victims of a dependency culture, and, on the left, as disempowered by welfare bureaucracies that deny them control over their affairs. Associational voluntarism would address the dissatisfactions of the affluent and the poor. It would allow the affluent to choose the services they please and to use their public entitlements to pay for them, at least in part. The poor will still only get the minimum entitlements – unless a radical change in attitudes takes place – but they could begin to deal with their own problems in their own way, to gain control of their affairs. Associationalism would enable organizations campaigning for the poor to use public funds to aid poor communities seeking autonomy and reconstruction.

II. The rejection of the "sovereign" state and the creation of a federal structure of authority based upon co-operation rather than hierarchy is now relevant, because the nation state is ceasing to be the primary arena for politics.

Associationalist and English political pluralist ideas can provide models for the emerging forms of governance that have no single authoritative centre. In a world dominated by states, English pluralism seemed counter-intuitive. Surely one body had to set the rules and stand above all others in a given territory? We can now see that many important problems are international, such as environmental pollution, and they can only be tackled by agencies that operate across the territories of states. The international arena is becoming crowded with such agencies (some are United Nations bodies, some intergovernmental, some part of an international civil society, like Greenpeace or Amnesty), and yet they remain outside the scope of our political theory. Consider an entity like the European Community (EC). It is neither a superstate nor is it simply an association of sovereign states; rather it is a multinational public power that has specific functions in which it takes priority over the member states. The EC has no armed forces and it has great difficulty agreeing on a common foreign policy. The great danger with institutions like this is that they will evolve blindly without clear political models, side-stepping the issue of accountability. The crisis over the ratification of the Maastricht Treaty showed popular discontent with technocratic government, but it has set back unification. Until the "democracy deficit" is tackled, the Community will lack legitimacy. A new federalism is the only way forward.

III. The third proposition concerns the construction of a more decentralized and mutualist economic system. Surely such objectives are now irrelevant in the face of economic globalization? I contend that the contrary is the case. Just as national governments are losing some powers to international agencies, they are also losing economic regulatory functions to subnational units.

The most successful of these regional economies, like the industrial districts of central Italy, provide models of economic governance based upon public–private co-operation. They achieve competitive success in two ways. Through the provision of collective services, they reduce the costs to firms of key inputs like trained labour and specialized equipment. And, through activities that range from collective marketing, to economic intelligence, to pooled R&D, firms gain from their co-operation with others. Industrial districts thus simulate the forms of voluntary co-ordination advocated by the associationalists. Some of the most successful manufacturing companies also mimic mutualist relationships: many Japanese firms have contrived a system in which workers are as committed as they might be in a co-operative, treating the company like a community of which they are members. However, these workers have few of the advantages of ownership or control.

The economies of the advanced nations are internationalizing. This threatens both the democratic control of the economy and the living standards of the less successful nations and regions. Economic internationalization threatens to centralize economic success in few nations and regions, deindustrializing other areas and diverting their financial resources away from domestic investment. Traditional methods of state intervention – protective tariffs, subsidies and regional aid – are unlikely to be effective in responding to such pressures.

The most effective response is to build up local and mutual financial institutions that are non-profit making but offer investors a guaranteed return. Such bodies would need to be legally protected and underwritten by public funds. They would enable regions to recycle their own capital – pensions, private savings, and so on – to create work and wealth within the region, rather than seeing both siphoned off halfway across the globe. Following from that, public agencies must aid and encourage small and medium-sized firms to overcome their reluctance to co-operate and their tendency to view other firms solely as competitors. Lastly, public agencies must promote worker involvement, the major source of high productivity. One way to do so is through broad-based training. Another way is to help set up mutualist firms that really do create a community at work, with employee ownership and authority. Such firms are likely to prove tenacious and efficient. The creation of industrial districts and mutualist firms may be a more effective response to international competition than, for example, trying to import Japanese techniques into US or European firms, where management continues to exercise its traditional powers and prerogatives.

2.3 Neither capitalism nor collectivism

Associationalism is neither capitalist nor collectivist; it embraces both co-operation and markets. Its aim is a regulated exchange economy that meets social goals through co-operation among economic actors and public agencies. The present trends toward weakly regulated markets and economic internationalization threaten to create a world that is ungovernable. In it the livelihood of all but a favoured few will be insecure, even in the advanced world, and the major beneficiaries will be major transnational corporations beyond effective political, let alone democratic, control. Associationalism offers ways in which these threats may be sidestepped, without placing too much emphasis on the weakening powers of the central state. It has the advantage over most economic doctrines in that it relies on the powers of citizens linked together in civil associations. It offers a route to economic revival that is consistent with the traditions of western liberalism. Most other routes either involve grafting Korean- or Japanese-style interventionism on to liberal democratic states, breaking their obligation to be neutral between one citizen or firm and another, or involve strengthening the autocratic powers of company managements.

One must be careful not to turn associationalism into a monolithic ideology. It is not the solution to every social problem, nor can associationist institutions be built overnight. The old advocates of associationalism were too ambitious and saw it as a complete replacement for both liberal democracy and socialism. However, it can only succeed in modern conditions if it is not seen as a way of completely supplanting such institutions, but as a way of restoring them to effectiveness by radical but practical reform.

Modern associationalism is not a utopian doctrine, nor would it involve the destruction of all other institutions in order to create a society consistent with its principles. It is best seen as a *supplement* to our stagnating political and economic institutions, not as a complete replacement for them. Thus, giving a greater role to voluntary associations, decentralization, and pluralizing political authority would help to restore legitimacy to liberal democracy.

The great advantage of the associative principle is that it can be used to a greater or a lesser degree, depending on political willingness to promote voluntarism and co-operation. Thus political change in this direction can proceed gradually as conditions dictate. Associationalism is also flexible enough to be adopted by a wide variety of social groups: it breaks out of the old left–right political spectrum. Thus environmentalists, feminists, ethnic communities, even conservative religious groups could benefit from an enhanced capacity to regulate their own affairs in civil society. Associationalism thus has the potential to be both practical and popular as a new doctrine of social reform and renewal.

Further reading

For an exposition of associationalism, see Hirst, (1993, 1994).

On English political pluralism, see Hirst (1989).

On the internationalization of politics, see Held (1991).

For the application of associationalist theory to the United States, see Cohen and Rogers (1992).

3

Associational democracy

Ideas can be compared to animal species: having lost out to the dominant doctrines and surviving in marginal niches, they may enjoy a new period of evolutionary advantage as selection pressures shift and their hitherto powerful competitors totter toward extinction. This may be the case with associationalism. This chapter outlines the contribution that associationalist doctrines can make to the reform of democratic governance and to the organization of economic affairs and welfare services in western societies.[1] Associationalism may be loosely defined as a normative theory of society the central claim of which is that human welfare and liberty are both best served when as many of the affairs of society as possible are managed by voluntary and democratically self-governing associations. Associationalism gives priority to freedom in its scale of values, but it contends that such freedom can only be pursued effectively if individuals join with their fellows.[2] It is opposed to both state collectivism and pure free-market individualism as principles of social organization.

3.1 New times for old ideas

Associationalism is the most neglected of the great nineteenth-century doctrines of social organization. It lost out to collectivism and individualism, and it lacked advocates who attained the political influence of Marx or the Webbs, Smith or Spencer. At the end of the twentieth century, however, associationalism may yet come into its own as a principle of reform and renewal of western societies. Centralized state socialism is clearly dead, and with it much advocacy of lesser species of socialist collectivism. The collapse of Soviet-style socialism has destroyed the credibility of this political model for a generation at least. Unregulated free-market individualism is also close to ruin as a political model. It has wreaked havoc on the societies that were foolish enough to follow those right-wing and Labour leaders who saw it as a principle of renewal: the USA, the UK, Australia and New Zealand.

One might think that left space for pragmatism. Yet that is hardly possible, for in the twentieth century "pragmatism" has generally meant some synthesis of liberalism and social democracy. Unfortunately, social democracy in the form of "Keynesian" national economic management and bureaucratically administered mass welfare is close to failure too.[3] Keynesian macroeconomic strategies are no longer effective in the new international economic conjuncture. Without full employment and sustained growth the costs of state-funded mass welfare raise serious distributional issues. Furthermore, bureaucratic welfare is all too often so inefficient and so demeaning of its clients that this lesser form of collectivism can hardly survive long as a model of social organization rather than as an administrative necessity in the absence of an alternative.

The distribution of economic success and failure since the end of the great postwar boom in 1973 shows that those societies that have fared best have managed to balance co-operation and competition, and have been able to draw on sources of social solidarity which have mitigated the effects of individualism and the market on the manufacturing sector.[4] Japan, with its construction of a capitalistic community within the enterprise and thick, quasi-corporatist networks between industry and the state, has achieved in a strongly business-orientated form, an effective simulation of the co-operative and co-ordinative economy advocated by associationalists.[5] That tends to indicate that associationalist institutions and relationships may prove highly competitive, if they can be developed. What was West Germany offers a similar business-orientated synthesis: between a responsible social democratic labour movement and a pragmatic, corporatistically inclined management; between an efficient manufacturing sector and the anti-inflationary monetarism of the *Bundesbank*.[6] Neither case, before or after 1973, much resembles the supposedly "classic" postwar combination of Keynesianism and welfarism, whether in its social-democratic British or "liberal" US variants. Japan and Germany are difficult models to copy, and in both cases they may be models on the verge of crisis. The "Anglo-Saxon" countries (the UK and the USA) have failed to develop or sustain these quasi-collectivist and corporatist forms of social solidarity. Given the failure of these formal structures of collectivist intervention, they have tried deregulating markets and have found that this has accelerated rather than checked decline.[7] Such societies need a principle of social renewal that does not trade on legacies of consensus they cannot renew or hardly possess, that is anti-collectivist while ensuring social welfare, and yet is consistent with strongly individualist values and an activist civil society based on voluntary associations. That principle is associationalism.

Associationalism began in the nineteenth century as a critique of a purely competitive market society and of the concentrated and centralized state power that was necessary to protect that realm of private transactions from foes without and preserve it from social strife within. In this task it was in competition with and was challenged by state socialism and reformist social engineering, and it was defeated by them. Associationalism had several distinct sources: the decentralist utopian socialism of Pierre-Joseph Proudhon; the English advocates of industrial and social co-operation like Robert Owen and George Jacob Holyoake; the English political pluralists John Neville Figgis and Harold J. Laski; and English Guild Socialism, whose greatest exponent was G.D.H. Cole.[8]

Associationalism failed not because it was inherently impractical and utopian, but because as a political movement it could not compete in given political conditions with collectivism and centralism. The great wars of this century stimulated both of these tendencies as the major states mobilized all social resources to pursue industrialized conflict. In doing so, they decisively reinforced the commitment of the European labour movements to statism. It is possible that in the west centralizing pressures are now lessening steadily. Western states no longer face major military competitors. Class war has for long been a vanished threat. With the lessening of the scope for national macroeconomic management by centralized agencies and the decline of hierarchical and centralized Fordist production organization, so too have the economic imperatives for large-scale concentrated administration lessened markedly.[9]

The main threats to western societies are no longer external and organized but internal and diffuse. They are nonetheless real for that, but centralized bureaucratic structures cope so badly with these more amorphous threats of crime and drug addiction, for example, that this can hardly provide them with a convincing *raison d'être*. The real problems stem from the failure to sustain full employment and from the side-effects of collectivist welfare. In the USA, in the UK, even in Germany we face the growing reality of a two-thirds versus one-third society. The notion of an "underclass" is both graphic and yet absurd, since its members will not accept their "place" at the bottom. A differentiated society cannot work if elementary freedoms of movement and association for all are to be preserved. Unless effective work and welfare are offered, in a way that both targets *and* empowers the members of this "class", then the way is open to an escalating conflict between crime and deviance and disablingly authoritarian measures which aim at the protection of the majority. The members of the "underclass" are not stupid. They know that wealth and success are in part capriciously distributed; that is, that they depend on the chances of social position and geographical location. Property will never be legitimate unless it offers real welfare – that is, a stake in society – to all in return. That is in large measure what Proudhon meant when he said "property is theft". The retreat to pure police protection of the property of the "haves" is ineffective and the theft of opportunity from the "have nots". They cannot overthrow society, but they can make it unliveable.

The only answer to this problem is a mixture of social crusading by those "haves" who care and empowerment of the "have nots".[10] That can only be achieved by effective and committed voluntary associations in partnership with the poor and excluded. Only by resourcing associations that help the poor to organize themselves and then funding the projects for trans-formation of ghettos and slums can the state help to reverse this corrosive process of social decline. Socialists have by and large written themselves out of this task, by identifying welfare with state provision for the better part of this century. Religious groups, community self-help groups and so on are the ones to see the need for activism and co-operation to create a "civil society" for the poor.

The Labour Movement and its political parties long ago retreated from this role. In the UK it gave up the hard and slow task of building socialism *in civil society* for the apparently quicker and more effective route of imposing it through the state. Friendly societies for welfare, co-operation in distri-bution and production, the voluntary principle and mutual aid as the basis for social organization, all were gradually discarded and diminished in favour of state provision and bureaucratic administration.[11] It turns out that voluntary relationships are tenacious and effective: they tend to endure as forms of social organization, where they are funded and supported by the right kinds of law and institutions. Bureaucracies are, by contrast, fragile and rigid; they easily lose impetus and their officials quickly lose *esprit de corps* in the face of crises of funding and function. Had the Labour Move-ment built socialism in civil society, alongside the efforts of other voluntary groups like churches, the disaster that has overtaken the health, education and welfare sector in the UK, for example, could never have occurred.

Centralized state power in the UK has allowed deregulation and privatization. It has also permitted rigid control of welfare institutions by a *Nomenklatura* committed to hierarchy, destabilizing "reform" and the appropriation of control by managers from "doers". Top-down management in welfare institutions is the creature of and the reflection of centralized state power. It is the enemy of all real welfare, of all real education, of all real healing. Each activity depends on the willingness of those who provide such services to act without strict reference to time and money. Each activity only survives as well as it does in the British welfare sector because there are still many such people who have not learned the calculus of utilitarian self-interest and who insist on keeping remote bureaucracies alive by acting on the principles of service and mutual aid.

Associationalism seems less incredible after the experience of the 1980s, when it is clear what tyrannical power over society is offered to the gov-ernors of apparently "liberal" states. We need a principle of renewal that will offer extensive and equitable welfare, but is prey to fewer of the authori-tarian dangers of collectivism. Whether power is held by the extreme left or

41

the radical right matters less than the existence of institutions that make such concentrated power possible. That is the real lesson of the 1980s, and one that many on the left failed to see because they were mesmerized by their traditional battle with the right.

The need for renewal is becoming apparent. The collapse of the Soviet system has produced an entirely new situation. Yet in the face of it, western triumphalism has quickly evaporated. In both the UK and the USA in particular there is deep and widespread dissatisfaction about both economic performance and the health of democracy. Conventional representative democracy has become little more than a plebiscite that chooses and legitimates the rulers of a big governmental machine that is out of control, in that it is largely unaccountable and cannot tackle major social problems. The crisis of citizen participation and of effective accountability of government to society is all too obvious. Democracy needs to be renewed. It needs to be more inclusive, to give voice not only to those who are excluded by poverty and discrimination but to many other citizens as well who see politics as a professional spoils system beyond their control and concern. With the end of the Cold War the rationale for defending the status quo in the west has lessened. It is no longer a legitimation of our flawed democracy to point out that it is far better than the system that produced Stalin and his successors.

The way is open for the advocacy of a programme of reform that would supplement and extend rather than destroy representative democracy. That supplement would involve a growth in the scope of governance through associations.[12] Associational institutions are in keeping with the fundamental principles of western liberalism; they are libertarian and consistent with fundamental human rights. Associational governance would lessen the tasks of central government to such an extent that greater accountability of both the public power and of the devolved associational agencies would be possible. The main political objective of modern associationalism is to decentralize and devolve as much of the affairs of society as possible to publicly funded but voluntary and self-governing associations.

Such associations are widely regarded in modern democratic theory as the social foundation for plural political interests, as the cement of the "civil society" that sustains the liberal state. Associationalism, however, treats such self-governing voluntary bodies not as "secondary associations" but as the *primary* means of organizing social life. In this doctrine, a self-governing civil society becomes primary, and the state becomes a secondary (if vitally necessary) public power that ensures peace between associations, protects the rights of individuals and provides the mechanisms of public finance whereby a substantial part of the activities of associations are funded. The activities of the state, central and local, are thus greatly reduced in scope. Large areas of governance of social affairs come to depend either on associations directly or on processes of co-ordination and collaboration between associations. In this way what the state does becomes more readily accountable. As its work is increasingly regulatory, so the legislature and judiciary rise in importance relative to the executive, reversing the strong trends in the other direction of this century in both the UK and the USA.

Representative democracy thus becomes viable, providing oversight of a government which is a guardian rather than a service provider. As the state ceases to be both provider of services and the guarantor of the standard of those services, it can begin to perform the latter role adequately. It thus inspects and oversees associations, and ensures their compliance with democratic norms in their internal governance and their conformity to commonly agreed community standards of service provision. Association-alism is thus eventually capable of accomplishing that reduction of the extent of the state's service provision activity that conservative anti-collectivists have sought and failed to achieve by means of privatization and the market. Unlike their efforts, associationalism attains this without a reduction in either the scope of social governance or the extent of publicly funded welfare, for neither of these domains is abandoned to unregulated market mechanisms. The scope of public provision is not reduced, but the form in which it is provided ceases to be directly administered by the state.

3.2 An answer to "Ottomanization"?

Associationalist ideas developed primarily on the left and on the part of religious social activists. Associationalism is not, however, a doctrine con-fined in its appeal to socialists or social Christians. It may be acceptable to groups far away in their beliefs from these intellectual origins, and whom the originators of these ideas could hardly have imagined. John Neville Figgis would find it hard to comprehend the gay movements in the USA, for example. This is simply an illustration of the extent to which western societies are subject to a process of pluralization of social norms and styles of life. This is most marked in the USA – where the divergence of ethnic, social, religious and lifestyle groups has produced a virtual process of "Ottomanization", in which plural communities co-exist side by side with very different rules and standards.[13]

One notices this most when such groups clash over the prevailing laws and mores: gays vs Christian fundamentalists, pro- and anti-choice cam-paigners on abortion issues, blacks vs Hassids in New York, and so on. The centralized state does not prevent and cannot check this process of pluralization. Indeed, it is hardly able to contain the violent antagonisms arising from it. Such tendencies toward divergence are almost inevitable in societies in which the range of social and personal choice is extended by mass affluence, by geographical and social mobility, and by the decline of prescriptive community standards in the face of the personal autonomy that the former factors make possible. At the same time, old and new foci of identity compete to bind individuals' choice of communities of association – religion, language, gender and ethnicity. For those left at the bottom these may appear as classes used to; that is, as communities of fate and resistance. For others, however "traditional" and communitarian they claim to be, old and new identities are reshaped to be sources of social solidarity around *chosen* standards.

Communities of choice and the associations representing them may be no less disruptive for being recent social constructs than are ancient feuds between "traditional" communities. Common national standards of personal conduct may be fewer and thinner, groups may have divergent mores and ideals of the good life, but most groups act in and make claims on the public realm in remarkably similar ways. Groups make similar claims to free-dom of action, seek to have their own chosen objectives made into "rights" and also seek to criminalize or deny public funding for behaviour of which they disapprove. This applies to both the born again and the politically correct.[14] In the end such antagonisms between groups and such attempts to annex the public power to their own exclusive interests are corrosive of the public sphere and of any common political life. This is exaggerated in the USA by weak and non-ideological political parties.

Surely in such circumstances associationalism is a cure that is worse than the disease, since it just endorses an entirely negative pluralism and permits groups to opt out of a common political culture? I believe the opposite to be the case. Associationalism offers the only clear way – in the absence of enforced "common" standards – to make such pluralism a going concern.[15] That way is to reduce intergroup antagonism by the acceptance of a substantial measure of self-regulation, at the price of mutual tolerance. No group could impose its vision on all, most groups could regulate themselves. Clearly, there would be limits to this process: a common morality is not that *thin* – paedophiles are not likely to enjoy rights of self-regulation, nor are rich white neighbourhood associations that exclude black residents. In other cases the likelihood of mutual tolerance is small. Pro- and anti-choice lobbies on abortion issues can hardly be expected to agree to co-exist, even geographically in separate states, any more than could slave and free states. Outside of such irreconcilable and competing claims to rights and moral regulation, the parallel and socially competitive social governance by associations would be possible more often than not.

In an associationalist society, given sufficiently varied and overlapping planes of social identity and cleavage, most conflicts between groups could be contained by being "parcellized". The co-existence of standards would enable the associations representing groups to regulate those who chose to join them and to remain. Most groups would have a strong interest in preserving the associationalist system because it would secure them the chance of public funding for their welfare activities, an enhanced role in social governance within their own sphere, and protection of their legitimate autonomy from predation by other groups, through the defence of group and individual rights by the public power. Laws regulating all persons and groups would remain, and so would certain common core standards. This core would be narrow but strongly subscribed to – the born again and the politically correct both abhor armed robbery, embezzlement of charity funds and child beating.

The advantage of a measure of localized regulation by groups and associational self-governance is that it would permit the reduction of the extent and complexity of the laws and regulations of the central public power. Framework legislation might be sufficient, if it set the goals of self-governance and the standards by which to measure it. This is true not only of associations in the social and moral sphere, but also, for example, of joint management–worker safety committees in the area of occupational safety and health. The result might be that laws might once again become almost comprehensible to the citizen, rather than filling kilometres of self-space. A society that spews forth more and more regulations, because its political institutions are centralized and purport to cover all aspects of life, does not attain comprehensiveness and uniformity in regulation – quite the contrary. Hence it may be just as well to accept the inevitable diversity that will come with self-governance. Provided the institutions in question are reasonably democratic and that there are protections for basic individual rights, such diversity can be healthy. A legal system whose rules are by their very bulk and complexity unintelligible to the citizens and whose regulatory processes often seem opaque to specialist lawyers is in danger of undermining the rule of law in its search to perfect it.

The essential checks imposed on such self-regulatory associations are that they must submit to certain minimum common standards of democratic self-governance and that they must not prevent exit by dissatisfied members.[16] Exit is not only a powerful solvent of oligarchy; it also limits the extent to which groups may sanction the loyalty of their members. There is no point in pluralizing the state only to create totalitarianism potentialities and authoritarian practices at the level of associations. Associationalism is a vital supplement to liberal democracy and *not* a substitute for it.

3.3 The politics of decentralization

Our discussion above is a negative thought experiment. It has envisaged an extremity of group divergence and value pluralism. In doing so it has drawn on tendencies that are evident in the USA. Other societies are more cohesive, but even in these there are strong reasons for decentralization and associational self-government, other than the dampening of intergroup conflict. Not the least of these reasons are the dangers of centralized state power and the failures of bureaucratic welfare collectivism I discussed at the beginning of this chapter. Moreover, even in circumstances of strong pressures toward group divergence, associational governance may actually *help* to rebuild ties between groups and facilitate the construction of national, regional or social foci of common identification. Associationalism hands over great powers and responsibilities to groups. But most associations will not be exclusive groups that enclose the whole of their members' social lives. A self-governing association cannot stand against all the world – if it did it would be a *de facto* "sovereign" state. Associational law, as we shall see, would limit certain acts as *ultra vires* – in particular, it would forbid trade unions to own firms directly and it would require associations (such as churches, welfare bodies and so on) to create special organizations for each domain in which they were in receipt of public funds (such as schools, hospitals and so on).[17] Thus the purposes and powers of most associations, and certainly the organizations they create for public welfare, would be limited – in the former case by their own choice in the main, and in the latter by law. The members of most associations would also be members of others. Moreover, for many purposes associations or their organizations would need to co-ordinate and collaborate with others in like spheres of activity – if only to build coalitions of mutual convenience when funds were distributed or common standards set. Associations might thus gradually create a network of formal and informal relations, which would enable society to enjoy both diversity in social governance and a substantial measure of co-ordination.[18]

As far as individual citizens are concerned, associational institutions might actually reduce the negative sources of identification with groups and dispose them to regard neighbouring groups in a more tolerant light. Greater democratic governance through voluntary associations means greater control over his or her affairs by the citizen. The possibility of diverse standards of social governance on the part of associations representing groups at least ensures that among those with whom one has chosen to live certain values will prevail. The combination of a reduction in powerlessness in the control of one's own affairs and the removal of the fear of being at the mercy of hostile moral legislators might well promote more widespread feelings of security on the part of citizens and a consequent lessening of hostility toward others. Fear of others' moral politics can be acute where the state is both centralized and claims a plenitude of power in the recognition and regulation of groups and their actions. In such a state moral minorities compete to control or influence power and then compel others to live in a certain way: the state is then either for or against gay rights, either militantly anti-clerical or the upholder of a compulsory religion.

Associationalism is an explicitly normative theory. It starts from the premise that voluntary self-governing associations are the best way of organizing human affairs that combines liberty with social obligation. But it is not merely a doctrine that makes judgements based on values; from this basic value premise, associationalist thinkers have developed powerful theoretical and practical criticisms of the centralized "sovereign" state, of bureaucratic collectivism and of the individualism of unregulated markets. They have also developed practical models of how to organize the economy and welfare on associationalist lines.

For this reason associationalism is the political theory best able to give effective expression to the feelings of unease that many have about contemporary social organization, but in a more coherent form than moral unease or protest. For example, associationalism provides a rationale for the decentralization of administration and a practical means of accomplishing it. Interest in decentralization, regionalism and "subsidiarity" is strong and growing right across the political spectrum: thus many conservatives genuinely want to roll back the state in the interests of greater accountability and not for mere financial advantage; Greens evidently want a less hierarchical and centralized economic system; and the left are desperately seeking some alternative to central planning. But this advocacy and aspiration lacks a coherent political theory; it is less effective as a result, and the different parts of the political spectrum are more conscious of their differences than of the means to hold their divergent aspirations in common. Decentralization and localism are strong and widely shared value preferences, responses to the remoteness and impersonality of big administrative machines, but they tend to be dismissed because they run counter to the apparent efficiency gains of large-scale organizations. Anyone who has seen the mess made by English local government since the 1960s by a series of centralizing "reforms" will know that these goals are more often promised than delivered.[19] Decentralization will accomplish little if the lesser units are as large and as bureaucratic as, say, London boroughs or English area health authorities. The need is to explain how and why things could be different.

Here English political pluralism is particularly valuable as a component part of associationalist doctrine. Proudhon in *Du principe fédératif* argued strongly against centralized power and defended the thesis that all power should be delegated *upwards* rather than the other way around, as is customary in hierarchical organizations. But he develops a utopian scheme in which communes give limited grants of power to higher bodies. Harold Laski is in this respect more practical and pragmatic, recognizing that centralized states will have to *devolve* power. In "The problem of administrative areas", he writes to persuade political leaders and state officials of the need to recognize functional agencies and to devolve power to them.[20] He is interested in a crafting of pluralism by reform, in which the state surrenders elements of sovereignty while exercising it. Like Proudhon, however, he starts from the premise that all power is by its nature federative. This is the case *de facto*, whatever the claims of the state *de Jure*. There are fundamental geographical and social divisions that must be respected in the organization of government. If they are not, then not only is liberty put at risk by excessive centralization, but also those wellsprings of association and co-operation that make a society truly efficient are threatened. Laski argued that the art of good government is to identify these discrete units to give them appropriate powers, and to respect the degree of autonomy necessary for them to function. He saw that they were both geographical and functional, and that both types should enjoy self-government: "the railways are as real as Lancashire".

John Neville Figgis argued that not only is good government decentralizing, but that the most effective form of government is the self-government of associations freely formed of citizens. The state should leave such associations to their own evolution by the decisions of their own democratic bodies. He argued that the claim of "sovereignty" – integral to the existence of centralized and concentrated state power – must deny this right to associations and treat all freedom of action of an agency as a concession sanctioned by representatives of the sovereign and revokable by legislation. Whether such "sovereign" power is democratically legitimated or not, it still has the potential for both tyranny and inefficiency. Indeed, being able to point to the support of a mass electorate made oppression easier. Figgis, in *Churches in the Modern State* (1913), well before the advent of modern totalitarian regimes, saw these dangers inherent in modern centralized state power, drawing the lessons from Bismark's *Kulturkampf* and French republican anti-clericalism. We can see the same lessons today, for example, in the abolition of the democratically elected government of London in 1986 despite widespread opposition by local citizens.

The autonomy of local and regional government is relatively well understood and respected in at least some states – Switzerland being the most notable example. Less well recognized still – and the English pluralist writings are all but forgotten – is the need for democratic self-government by *function*.[21] The problem here is that functional government can mean little if the great mass of economic affairs is conducted by privately owned and hierarchically managed firms, and the bulk of public services by state-funded and state-directed large bureaucracies. The space for real functional government is then tiny, within the existing voluntary sector and on the margins of social life. If these institutions persist unreformed, then the role of "democracy" is restricted in the one case to shareholders (at least

nominally) electing directors and, in the other, to citizens electing representatives who have nominal direction over the heads of public bureaucracies. Noberto Bobbio in *The Future of Democracy* (1987) remarks that
democracy has stopped short of "the two great blocks of descending and
hierarchical power in every complex society, big business and public
administration. And as long as these blocks hold out against the pressures
exerted from below, the democratic transformation of society cannot be
said to be complete".[22] The key test of democracy now is not " 'who votes'
but 'where' they can vote".[23] But the issue is not where in the literal sense,
but in what *kind* of institution and for what *kind* of authority.

The problem is that such hierarchical and large-scale organizations
cannot easily be democratized. Voting will change them much less than
might be supposed. Indeed, it will legitimate their governing elites if
hierarchy persists. Moreover, who is the constituency to vote in such organizations? Critics of industrial democracy have argued that the very idea of
self-government here acts against the accountability of such institutions to
society – it empowers the employees or providers of a service with a measure
of control over its delivery. This was the Fabian critique of administrative
and industrial syndicalism, for example – that it enabled the producers to
govern themselves at the expense of the consumer.

If such large hierarchical organizations are not readily democratizable by
the mere voting of their members, then the present situation remains highly
unsatisfactory; for large firms and bureaucracies are not well stewarded by
existing "democratic" mechanisms. The firm as a republic of shareholders is a
fiction; the management of firms is only notionally elected by and accountable to the shareholders (it is "answerable" to the stock market and to major
institutional investors, but that is another matter, and the economic
consequences are far from satisfactory). Large welfare bureaucracies are only
nominally accountable to ministers or councillors; for most practical purposes
senior officials make detailed policy and junior ones have a large measure of
administrative discretion with regard to clients. The concentration of
economic power in large corporations and the concentration of social welfare
and social control in large bureaucracies acts against that dispersal of social
power and influence that liberal democratic theorists have seen as essential to
the preservation of liberty. The sphere of civil society and secondary
associations shrinks in the face of bodies that are in effect compulsory (one
has to seek work, and large bureaucracies amount to a significant share of the
labour force; the unemployed are subject to welfare tutelage) and which are
not open to the *social* or *political* influence of the average citizen.[24] As a worker
the citizen cannot of right make company policy; at best he or she can only
disrupt the service the firm supplies by industrial action to modify that policy.
As recipient of state benefits or services the citizen has no political rights or
mutual ties in the capacity of claimant.

This is all the more absurd when one recalls that companies, while controlled by a few, are financed through the funds of the many – through insurance policies, pension funds, unit trusts and bank deposits.[25] The great mass of capital comes from the pockets of ordinary citizens, often in the form of necessary or compulsory saving. It is also absurd that while public welfare agencies are funded by citizens' social insurance and taxes (even by welfare recipients in the case of indirect taxes), citizens are treated like supplicants when seeking discretionary funds or actions from public officials.

3.4 Roads to economic democracy

The only answer to these problems is a long-term one: to restore the scope of civil society by converting both companies and state welfare service agencies into self-governing associations. This will be a long haul, and in the interim the most realistic policies are those which boost the co-operative economy and the voluntary sector in welfare. The need for the democ-ratization of companies is widely perceived. The most accomplished of modern political theorists, Robert A. Dahl, in his *A Preface to Economic Democracy* (1985) argues strongly for the development of a worker-owned co-operative sector as a way of checking the unhealthy concentration of corporate control over the economy that has grown up in the USA in this century. Democracy requires the diffusion of ownership. Revisionist socialists have espoused market socialism, an explicit model of an economy that marries co-operation and neoclassical economics.[26] The economic units are to be worker co-operatives and they are linked one with another and with consumers through market transactions.

The problem with views like the latter is that they treat the economy as if it were reducible to its component parts, to enterprises. Get ownership and control within the enterprise into the right balance, add to it an effective competition and anti-monopoly policy to prevent firms getting too big, and then the distribution of rewards will be fair and markets will also operate as efficient allocative mechanisms. Market economies, however, depend for their substantive outcomes on non-market social factors that the firm cannot easily create within itself.[27] Those factors are, for example, the achieving of an effective balance between co-operation and competition among firms that ensures an adequate supply of necessary "public goods" to firms (suitably trained labour, market information and so on), and the creation of a structure of publicly regulated financial institutions that provide a range of sources of investment finance at suitable rates and terms for the sustained development of the economy. These are but two examples of the ways in which successful market economies are embedded in a social context that the market cannot supply and cannot reproduce. The problem is that reformers focusing on one level, the enterprise, propose changes that make sense at that level, but at another level they ignore the ensemble of social conditions necessary to a democratic and decentralized society in which markets play a contained but constructive role.

Such balances between co-operation and competition are struck more satisfactorily in some national and regional economies than others.[28] But they may not be struck on terms that are favourable to openness, to democracy or to equality of influence between core economic actors and other parts of the society. This is why it is not possible to follow those wholly business-orientated commentators who advocate learning from Japan, even if we could manage to reproduce Japanese institutions.[29] The great advantage of associationalism is that it provides principles and concepts for assessing the range of institutions that make a balance between co-operation and competition possible, and for establishing which are most consistent with extended democratic governance in civil society. It does this in three ways. First, by insisting on the devolution of governmental functions to the lowest level at which they can be efficiently performed, it provides a *political* rationale for the tendencies toward local and regional economic regulation. Secondly, by emphasizing the principles both of organizing social activities through voluntary organizations and of voluntary co-operation between them, it provides political rationales for economic governance through open, inclusive bodies like trade associations, and for firms to co-operate in developing the industrial "public sphere" of a region or locality. Thirdly, by emphasizing the principle of mutuality, it encourages enterprises and other agencies to develop ongoing relationships and offer one another help in a range of ways (from the informal, such as the established customs of firms sharing work and information, to the formal, such as industrial credit unions).

The control of the concentration of ownership cannot be checked by state regulation alone, if, that is, the whole thrust of the economy is towards greater agglomeration of capital and if the operation of financial markets facilitates this. Associationalism would help to check concentration by strengthening the small- and medium-sized-firm sectors' capacities to resist, and by providing such firms with a supportive regional and local institutional context, a local industrial public sphere that makes such firms politically tenacious and economically able to share many of the benefits size confers on their larger competitors.[30] Associationalism would foster the development of, in particular, institutions to encourage the localization and regionalization of capital. Evidence suggests that where capital can be both generated and recycled within a region, the chances for that region to enjoy a measure of autonomy and economic success are greater if it is dependent on small and medium-sized firms. Combined with effective local economic regulation and strong patterns of association between firms, this factor helps to make localities into publicly aware and responsive entities that take charge of their economic fate. Local financial institutions and relationships of mutual borrowing and lending help to provide both the material means of autonomy and the foci of effective "intimate knowledge" of the region, which enable key actors to exercise strategic direction over its development.[31] In the case of the majority of British regions, concentration of ownership means that decisions about local firms are taken in London boardrooms or the City. Small and medium-sized British firms are isolated in purely competitive and market relationships. Local government is denied the fiscal and policy autonomy for local economic regulation by Westminster. The result has been economic decline, and the absence of local political and financial resources to combat it.

Worker-owned co-operatives are superficially an attractive way to ensure both the greater diffusion of economic ownership and economic democracy, through the diffusion of control. However, as the Guild Socialists like G.D.H. Cole were well aware (even more so than the Fabians, who favoured professional management in both public bodies and private concerns), industry is a service to society and this service is by no means ensured by giving its control of enterprises exclusively into the hands of their workers.[32] Guild Socialism, at least in its moderate version, was critical of syndicalism for this very reason. In *Guild Socialism Re-Stated* (1920), Cole outlines how this service would be organized through national guilds. This institutional design is clearly now obsolete in a world of international competition, rapidly changing technologies and shifting divisions of labour. But the need for extended accountability beyond the firm and for institutions that link firms in both the locality and the industrial sector are points that can be taken over from Cole into modern associationalism.

There are more stakeholders in industry than just the immediate producers. Economic democracy certainly requires that workers enjoy extensive rights of participation within a company, the right to acquire a share in its ownership and representation on its governing body.[33] But other interests have a right to be represented too – principally the providers of capital and the local community. Where the economy is regulated by regional or local collaborative and public institutions, where relations of capital provision are mutualized, then this tripartite relationship of stakeholders in company governance becomes credible. It also ensures that these three interests are each knowledgeable about business conditions and capable of ensuring that the firm is both competitive and profitable and yet provides a decent service. The creation of local or regional mutual financial institutions – local industrial savings banks, industrial credit unions for firms, and locally controlled pension funds – reduces the distance between capital providers and the company. Whether the capital be provided as shares, bonds or loans, whether the representation of capital as stakeholder takes the form of electing representatives through shareholdership or through interlocking directorships, matters less if financial institutions are local, accountable in diverse ways to the community and committed to the long-term success of the region or locality. Such patterns will develop differently as regions and localities evolve their own patterns of regulation, and this is preferable to prescribing one model in law. Local mutual institutions will be more effective stewards of citizens' money and more active stakeholder representatives on companies' governing bodies than are national or international absentee fund managers, who watch the stock market and little else.

In a similar way, the fact that companies are enmeshed in substantial local and regional relationships with other firms, trade associations and public bodies will make it much easier for them to choose for themselves or accept from outside representatives of the community-as-stakeholder. Assuming a tightly integrated and collaboratively governed local or regional economy makes it easier to see how one will find "community" representatives who are not mere nominees of either labour or capital, and who possess real knowledge and commitment to the firm and the local economy. Such tripartite representation in its governance helps to make the firm accountable to its members and to society at large: it has real stakeholders rather than the notional "shareholders" (who in the main are only interested in a marketable financial asset). At the same time, because the firm is embedded in society by this community representation and other links, the local community will feel responsible for it and will try to ensure that it stays in business to provide work and profit for local people.

A model of this kind that tries to balance co-operation and competition between firms, that tries to regulate as far as possible by means of trade associations, representative forums and mutually owned agencies, and that seeks to preserve the economic and social integrity of localities, is thus quite different from either the advocacy of collective ownership and planning or unregulated market individualism. Such a perspective, indeed, amounts to a relatively coherent concept of a "third way" between the two. Such a perspective emphasizes economic decentralization and explains how to get it through regional and local economies regulated through private–public partnerships. Not only does this associationalist theory encourage economic relationships of manageable scale, it also links to the political doctrine by showing how the firms involved in these relationships are easier to make accountable to employees and communities than are very large national and multinational firms. There is a great deal of evidence from studies of existing regional economies and industrial districts that such mutualist and associational economic relationships are possible, that they are not inimical to productive efficiency (quite the contrary), and that not all production and distribution need be conducted on a large scale in order to match national and international competitors.[34]

It should be obvious that such economies can only develop by genuine local initiative and co-operation, given a favourable institutional and fiscal climate that encourages such experiments rather than one which crushes them, as in the UK at present. Economic democracy must be built out of two kinds of partnership, one between employees, managers and owners within the firm, and the other between firms themselves and the locality. Modern associationalist economic doctrine accepts that the route to economic democracy is complex and that it cannot take the form of a single "industrial democracy" statute as envisaged by Labour radicals in the UK in the 1970s.[35] Company law must, indeed, be reformed and it must include strong inducements for firms to move in the direction of collaborative governance. Legislation that is permissive and incremental can then follow along these avenues of advance. Clearly, the idea of imposing "workers' control" by law is an absurdity and the statute would fall on the deaf ears of reluctant, ill-educated and often cynical workforces with low loyalty to their firms and poor motivation. Even if it were politically possible in countries like the UK and the USA, it would not be desirable. This may be a reflection of the policies of so many British and American firms' management, but it is an insuperable obstacle to the centralist and legalist conception of a single reform to impose industrial democracy – even if there were no opposition from business or unions. For workers in the majority of firms to be motivated to participate on an extended scale, a long period of human relations initiatives, training and worker capital acquisition incentives supportive of greater collaboration would be necessary.

The model of the development of an associational economy may not be at all like that envisaged by the Guild Socialists, in which it grew out of the efforts of the Labour Movement and was strongly worker-orientated. Rather, it is more likely to grow up from the coalescence of a series of concerns that concentrate on the preservation and construction of industrial districts and of local and regional economies. Classes used to be considered communities of fate; now for many people – including entrepreneurs, managers and skilled workers whose non-financial assets or labour are not easily relocated on national or international markets – it is the region that is a community of fate. It may well be that more collaborative relationships *within* firms, and the financial institutions necessary to find co-operatives, will develop from partnerships *between* firms, and between them and the local public agencies and organized labour. The Guild Socialists believed that the contest for political power was at best a diversion; society was to be changed by the Labour Movement pressing on capital and shifting the frontier of control irreversibly towards labour. This political naivety, which it shared with syndicalism, led to its political marginalization and to the disregard of such ideas by the Labour Party.[36] However anti-statist modern associationalism may be, it cannot ignore the reality of the modern state, and it knows that private initiatives must go hand in hand with – indeed, may depend on – public reforms. Legal and institutional changes would be necessary to facilitate the rapid growth of associational governance.

3.5 An associationalist strategy for reform

How might that happen? In the economic sphere one can argue that if industrial districts, organized regional economies, and collaborative relationships that balance co-operation and competition can survive competitive pressures from large firms, they can serve as a political model. The hope would then be of the gradual diffusion of localization and mutuality through its regional success stories, promoting both emulation from below and pressure for the reform of national laws to permit the diffusion of such developments. Similarly, in the welfare sector, the gradual growth of voluntarism as a remedy for and a supplement to state collectivism may create models to be emulated and diffused. Above all, what is needed is a *concept* that ties these various, often popular, ideas together and shows their practicality – political decentralization and governance through associations, new regional economies, and confederalism and voluntarism in welfare. That concept has been missing, not because it was not available, but because political activity and circumstances have only just caught up with long-neglected ideas. The only route to the success of associationalism demands a clear concept, because that will tie together organizationally and attitudinally separate efforts working in different localities and social spheres toward similar ends. Local unionists and the owners of small firms, Christian voluntary workers in the inner cities, ecological groups seeking both a more human scale and a sustainable environment may all profit from this knowledge.

The model of them all coming together in a single political party that attains power by persuading the electorate of the virtues of its programme, and then enacts that plan into the simultaneous reform of the whole society is quite inappropriate. That is possible as a dream for collectivists and for those who wish to decollectivize through deregulation and privatization – both accept centralized sovereign state power and do not wish to change it. Associationalists have to rely on the multiplication of diverse efforts. Associationalist relationships have to be built by citizens' initiative and bodies freely formed by committed individuals. Unless such relationships arise from genuine co-operation they will be of little value – the idea of being *compelled* to join a voluntary association for any purpose is an absurdity (but that is what a statutory "big bang" approach to an associationalist system of welfare would imply). The role of legislation must be permissive and gradual, not prescriptive and peremptory. Fortunately there is some hope that this process of diffusion of the associational model may begin to happen: if nation states continue to become less effective loci of economic regulation, if highly concentrated corporate power becomes less legitimate to citizens as it seems less and less the only route to industrial efficiency, and as the secret of supply-side success comes to be seen as a diffuse set of public and private commitments to the effective functioning of firms, networks and supportive public institutions. The ultimate legitimations of large scale are now economic; if they falter, then the case for more decentralized institutions will grow in strength.

But it would be foolish to talk ourselves into a process of transition to an associationalist wonderland – the substitute object for the workers' father-lands of yore. The associational principle can democratize and reinvigorate societies as a supplement to and a healthy competitor for the currently dominant forms of social organization: representative mass democracy, bureaucratic state welfare and the big corporation. Not all economic activities can be carried out by co-operative small and medium-sized firms (however efficient), nor can all economic regulation be collaborative or regionally based. Some elements of public welfare cannot be entrusted to voluntary agencies (however sophisticated the mechanisms for devolution of functions and funding): in the last instance, rights of entitlement, standards of service and principles of equity must be maintained by the public power at the federal level. National states and international agencies of a regu-latory nature (world public powers) will remain necessary and, in the latter case, will become more important. No serious associationalist imagines that global warming or third world poverty can be tackled (if they can be tackled at all) solely by voluntary agencies.

It is best to envisage associationalism not as "the society of the future", a system complete in itself, but as an axial principle of social organization; that is, as a pattern of organizing social relations that can be generalized across sectors and domains of social activity, which is not a localized institution or pattern of customary action. In this it resembles the market and bureaucratic administration. Such principles compete for dominance in modern societies: a mixture of the prevailing social conditions and the availability of a credible and effectively presented conceptual model decide whether a principle will play a major or a subsidiary role in a given period. In each case part of the role of a conceptual model is to show how the axial principle in question can be elaborated as the practical and credible basis for social organization. Such models as Smith's *The Wealth of Nations* or the Webbs' advocacy of bureaucratic collectivism have proved efficacious in aiding the spread of the market and state welfare principles. Associ-ationalism needs a similar elaboration to show its widespread applicability and effectiveness. What it has too often had are "blueprints", turning models into utopian actualities. Whether associationalism can act as a supplement to our failing institutions now depends not on restating the principle, but on working out the detail of credible models of associational governance in the economy and the welfare sectors. That is now the main task of associationalist theory.

Notes

1. I have tried to examine in greater detail elsewhere the theoretical case for associationalism and political pluralism: see Hirst (1990), chs 1, 4, 5 and 6, and (1989), Introduction, pp. 1–45. This chapter concentrates more on the current political situation and how associative democracy may contribute to democratic renewal than on expounding associationalist political theory. That theory is most usefully developed by working out the institutional framework of associationalism in sufficient detail to show how such relationships would work as one of the main means of social organization. Space prohibits trying to do this here: I have developed a model of an associationalist confederal welfare state in which voluntary service provision agencies are publicly funded but in which there is extensive consumer choice, and yet the system relies very little on either central administrative discretion in allocating funds or on markets: see Hirst (1994).
2. "Unless groups are allowed free development the self-development of individuals will be hindered." Figgis (1913), p. 12.
3. On the limits of Keynesian strategies today, see Piore and Sabel (1984), and Scharpf (1991). On the constraints of the failure of Keynesianism for welfare, see Cutler, Williams and Williams (1986). As an example of left dissatisfaction with collectivist welfare and of alternative market-orientated thinking, see Le Grand (1990).
4. On the mechanisms whereby co-operation and competition are balanced, see Hirst and Zeitlin (1989), and Sabel (1990).
5. On Japan, see Dore (1986b).
6. On the former West Germany, see Scharpf (1991), especially Ch. 7.
7. On Britain's failure to develop a collaborative and interventionalist system of economic regulation, see Marquand (1988), and for the USA, Thurow (1980).
8. For selected writings of Cole, Figgis and Laski, see Hirst (ed.) (1989). For Proudhon, see Vincent (1984), and Vernon (1979). For R. Owen, see Taylor (1982), and for G. J. Holyoake, see Holyoake (1891), and Gurney (1988).
9. See Hirst and Zeitlin (1991), and Piore and Sabel (1984).
10. This may sound like nineteenth-century philanthropy. Actually nineteenth-century voluntary action has been largely misrepresented: working-class mutual aid within voluntary agencies (outside the Labour Movement) was very important and there was substantial popular financial support for voluntary causes. Hence one should not assume charity was a "middle-class" imposition on the poor or that it was a failure: it appears to have contributed greatly to relieving distress and it was less demeaning and disabling of its recipients than much modern state welfare. For a major reinterpretation,

see Prochaska (1988).

11. A great deal of this switch from voluntarism and mutualism in the British Labour Movement occurred very late on in the twentieth century. In the 1920s, employers, unions and state officials still preferred a voluntary and employer-based system of welfare to a uniform state system. Beveridge was still strongly in favour of the voluntary principle in his 1942 Report: see Williams and Williams (1987), Ch. 5.

12. Arguments for democratic renewal are numerous. Examples of arguments to make interest-group representation more inclusive through institutional reform are Schmitter (1988), and Cohen and Rogers (1992).

13. This refers to the devolved structure of communal self-governance in Ottoman cities. See Davidson (1983).

14. On competing rights claims with reference to the abortion issue, see Kingdom (1991).

15. This strategy of plural self-governance does not stem from the premise that all value standards are relative. On the contrary, a pluralistic associational society requires a limited common core of widely supported beliefs and standards and, moreover, there must be strong grounds for those beliefs that the community feels it can justify: see Hirst (1990b).

16. Hirschman (1970).

17. Hirst (1990d; 1994, Ch. 7).

18. See Streeck and Schmitter (1984).

19. See Rendell and Ward (1989).

20. This essay is to be found in Laski (1921), pp. 30–103.

21. See Knight (1990).

22. Bobbio (1987), p. 57.

23. *Ibid.* p. 56.

24. See Belloc (1913/1977).

25. On the dominance of institutional investment, see Thompson (1990), Ch. 6, pp. 144–6.

26. See Le Grand and Estrin (1989), especially Ch. 2.

27. On the balance between co-operation and competition and the failure of the market to secure this, see Piore and Sabel (1984), and note 4.

28. On the significance of industrial districts and regional economic regulation, see Sabel (1989), and Zeitlin (1992).

29. For a stinging critique of Japanese institutions, a necessary if overdone corrective to Japan-worship, see Wolferen (1989).

30. For the concept of an "industrial public sphere", see Hirst and Zeitlin (1989); for the benefits of co-operation to secure the equivalent economies of scale, see Brusco (1992).

31. "Intimate knowledge" is a concept used by Alfred Marshall in *Industry and Trade* (1919) to describe a crucial part of the "industrial atmosphere" that made traditional industrial districts function. See Beccattini, (1990).

32. On this aspect of Cole, see Hirst (1990c).

33. For attempts to show how workers might establish a substantial measure of ownership and control by gradual change, see Matthews (1989), Ch. 3; Cornford (1990); and Turnbull (1991).

34. For studies of two modern industrial districts, both of which have proved strongly competitive in the 1980s, see: for Baden-Württemberg, Sabel *et al.*

(1989), and Schmitz (1992); and, for Emilia-Romagna and Italy generally, Brusco (1982), and Trigilia (1992).

35. For a criticism of those *dirigiste* Labour proposals of the 1970s, see Hirst (1986), Ch. 6.

36. On the failure of Guild Socialism, see Glass (1966), and Carpenter (1922).

4

From statism to pluralism

The future of socialism is often debated as if socialism had a single past. In the 1980s the radical right have tried to bury socialism. One of their best tactics in doing so has been to identify socialism with the authoritarian states and failing economies of the communist world. Western socialism can then be presented as a lesser version of this greater failure, but sharing essential features of authoritarian collectivism and economic stagnation. Socialism is defined by the right in terms of the triad of collective ownership, state intervention and centralized planning, and it is still defended by some of its supporters in those terms.

The vast majority of socialists, however, recognize the need for a more libertarian political creed compatible with an open society. Some radical revisionists think it necessary to go outside the socialist tradition altogether in order to do so. They embrace the free market and redefine socialism in terms of liberal democratic theory. This is to behave as if there are no *socialist* sources for a libertarian socialism. In fact certain important socialist doctrines have been strongly anti-collectivist and opposed to centralized public ownership. They have also been strongly anti-statist, advocating reliance on the self-governing activities of freely associated individuals. Associational socialism is the most valuable alternative to the undiluted individualism of the free-market right and to the centralist and authoritarian trends in modern society.

4.1 Associational socialism

Associational socialism, which flourished between the 1840s and the early 1920s, was a third force in the history of socialism, distinct from both Bolshevism and social democracy. It embraced a variety of movements and ideas, including Proudhon and the mutualist and syndicalist traditions in France; William Morris and the Arts and Crafts movement; and G.D.H. Cole and the Guild Socialists in the UK Associational socialism often won the battle of ideas, only to lose out to other socialist movements which relied on the more effective means of either electoral or insurrectionary politics. In an era of world wars, big government and highly concentrated industry, associational socialism came to seem an irrelevancy. Its stress on self-government and local autonomy ran counter to a period in which there were strong imperatives to central control. Because it believed in the virtue of voluntary action in civil society, it neglected the forms of political action necessary to create a state sympathetic to such voluntary activity and also failed to compete with other political forces to influence the existing state. The associational socialists were pushed aside by the 1920s. Yet the view of the associational socialist tradition as utopian and unworldly is quite wrong. Associationalism was not inherently impractical, rather it required the right context in which it could become practical politics.

The major wars of this century promoted centralization and bureaucratic control; tendencies inimical to the autonomy of self-governing associations. The wars also gave the political rivals of libertarian socialism the conditions in which to flourish. However, in the 1980s the international environment has changed radically – and perhaps irrevocably – with the end of the second Cold War. The tranformation of east–west politics, the pace of reform in eastern Europe, and the prospect of at least partial demilitariz-ation, all weaken the imperatives for centralized and secretive state security institutions to dominate national politics. A movement that seemed naive in the 1920s can profit from the liberalization of great power politics in the 1980s.

Associational socialism may also benefit from recent economic changes in the west. The imperatives towards the large scale in industrial organization have been perceived to be closely connected with standardized mass production for homogeneous mass markets. However, since the OPEC oil price shock and the consequent world depression of the early 1970s markets have both internationalized and differentiated. The reasons for this are ably explained by Michael Piore and Charles Sabel in *The Second Industrial Divide* (1984). Markets have become more volatile, product ranges have dif-ferentiated and firms have now to contend with changing demands for a more varied range of products across a series of national markets with specific characteristics. This undermines the relevance of "economies of scale" and encourages firms to change their production methods to permit more flexible output.

In such an open international economy, in which the major industrial nations trade manufactured goods ever more intensively one with another, there is less scope for purely national regulation. The social democratic strategy of using Keynesian measures to boost national consumer demand and thereby sustaining mass markets has given way to more complex strategies for preserving the local manufacturing base, particularly at the regional level. In such a competitive and rapidly changing industrial environment the scope for a central state-directed industrial policy is much reduced, thus undercutting the traditional socialist advocacy of "planning". The two major forms of active state intervention, Keynesian macroeconomic management and *dirigiste* planning, are thus both weakened as socialist answers to the problems of economic policy.

In this new environment both regional economic regulation and small-to-medium scale firms have grown in importance. But at the same time, other, quite contradictory tendencies have developed and these are most marked in the USA and the UK. If the logic of *industrial* concentration based on economies of scale in production has weakened, the purely *financial* pressures towards concentration of ownership have accelerated. The divorce of financial operations from the direct investment in new industrial plant and processes, conjured up in the phrase "casino capitalism", has led to the concentration of ownership of industry based almost solely on stockmarket opportunities. The acquisition and takeover of firms is often devoid of manufacturing or marketing logic. In this context, top management becomes ever more powerful and yet more remote and unaccountable. The operations of subsidiary firms will thus tend to suffer from such remote control. It can hardly be a matter of chance that it is the UK and the USA that have shown the greatest import penetration and consequent deindustrialization. These countries have participated least in the recent changes towards flexible specialization in production and the regional regulation of manufacturing sectors.

The financially based conglomerate holding companies lack a *raison d'être* in economic necessity; they are not essential for the organization of manufacturing. They are beyond the control of the formal machinery of share-holder representation and are unaccountable to their employees. Industrial concentration without economic rationality turns large-scale firms from a source of economic strength into a very real weakness. It represents a form of pure ownership increasingly divorced from managerial necessity. Traditional socialist remedies such as nationalization do not offer an answer to such concentration, since the component parts of such conglomerate companies make little industrial or administrative sense when gathered together. Decentralization and the promotion of economic self-government offer the best prospect of a form of industrial organization in which the major contributing interests – the providers of capital, management expertise and labour – have an active interest in the continued manufacturing success of the firm.

This need for democratization and decentralization is where associational socialism becomes relevant; because it stresses above all that economic units should be co-operatively owned self-governing associations. The tradition undoubtedly needs to be modernized. It is also true that traditional associational socialism was highly workerist and emphasized manufacturing industry, and it could hardly cope with today's complex division of labour within the enterprise or with the increasing diversity of occupations in the wider society. However, G.D.H. Cole's stress on organizing society on the basis of voluntarily formed self-governing associations was basically correct.

4.2 Battlefield

The left has been mesmerized by statism. Even moderate democratic socialists have constantly advocated giving more and more tasks to the state. The result, when such advocacy is successful, is to give more power to the state and less to socialists, and this in turn drains socialism of creative energy as a *social* movement and diverts it from constructive enterprise in civil society. We have built socialism (or rather tried to) through the agency of the state and encouraged passivity in the recipients of state services. Yet we wonder why socialism is no longer a mass movement.

The more tasks that are given to the state, the greater is the stake in controlling it and the more the state can take away if control changes hands. We have learnt that lesson through our experience of Mrs Thatcher, but we have hardly adapted to the fact that we need to devolve activities from the state to civil society as far as is possible. Socialists in the west, just as in the east, have seen the need to "capture" the state, to make certain changes in policy "irreversible". Yet such a vision is hardly compatible with a pluralist society, in which there are other groups and social projects than socialism. It rests on the belief that socialists have a natural majority in society and, therefore, a right to a monopoly of effective political power. This belief has been widely held by democratic socialists; it is not a peculiarity of the authoritarian left. This belief is almost inevitable if the state does come to control more and more of the affairs of society. Democracy becomes a battlefield; the only issue, who shall control the levers of power?

As the state has directly provided more services, so the individual has enjoyed less and less liberty in determining *how* they are provided. The recipient of collectivized services administered by officials, the individual is also increasingly likely to work for a large private organization in which she or he has little or no say. The growth of state activity has not checked the growth of big business: often it has actively promoted it. The result is to place much of the affairs of "civil society" into the hands of unaccountable private governments that dwarf many pre-twentieth-century states in size.

If socialists could accept the idea of a state that facilitated the work of democratically run associations in providing work and welfare, then they might have some chance of finding a more secure future for socialism. Democratic socialists seek to encourage co-operation, mutual assistance, fellowship and the greatest measure of equality attainable. They are not necessarily tied to particular social institutions like state ownership or central planning in meeting these objectives. Understood in this wider sense socialism can co-exist with a society of plural organizations and differing objectives. It could build its institutions of co-operative work and mutual assistance alongside other active groups of citizens and their projects: religious groups, ethnic communities, lifestyle communities. A socialism committed to a pluralist society and to concentrating on organizing social life through self-governing associations in civil society would pose less of a threat to others than a statist socialism, and might therefore expect to command more support. In particular it would be more open to Green conceptions of social organizations and to co-existing with Green associations.

A challenge to statist socialism does not mean a return to the Marxist illusions of "smashing" the state. On the contrary, even if as many social activities as possible are devolved to self-governing associations in civil society, there will still be a need for a public power to regulate the actions of these associations and to ensure that they have the resources to carry out their tasks. A pluralist society with diverse social projects needs a public power to ensure order, but that public power need not be a "sovereign state": that is, a state claiming the exclusive control of power, asserting its primacy in every social domain, and imposing itself through a single centralized hierarchy. A pluralist state – as conceived by such English political pluralists as J.N. Figgis, G.D.H. Cole and H.J. Laski – would be based on a quite different principle: that the state exists to protect and serve the self-governing associations. The state's powers would be limited by its function and such a state would recognize the inherently plural nature of all free social organization. Pluralism requires that distinct locally and functionally specific domains of authority should have the autonomy necessary to carry out their tasks. This pluralist conception of the state is essential to a libertarian society, for "decentralization" and "devolution" of power will accomplish little if all they do is to recreate centralized authorities at lower levels.

Traditional state socialists raise two major objections to such a society of self-administering associations. The first is that while self-governing firms may give employees more say within the workplace, the wider economy remains anarchic and at the mercy of the "laws" of the market. This, however, is to treat the market economy as if it were a single self-sufficient system divorced from control by the wider society. There are no "laws" of the market; rather there are specific markets with diverse social conditions and consequences. Markets are embedded in social relations, and it is these relations that play a major role in deciding how markets work. Moreover, there are other ways of organizing an economy than centralized planning. Associational socialists like Cole always stressed the important role of voluntary co-ordination between associations at national industry and local levels. Some of Cole's conceptions of how to accomplish such co-ordination were naive, but this does not diminish his general point. There is much evidence that those national and regional economies that achieve such patterns of co-ordination, that provide for the effective consultations of social interests and that support firms with a surrounding network of social institutions which provide essential services, are the ones that have been most successful under modern conditions of manufacturing competition. West Germany, Italy and Japan offer excellent examples of different patterns of such co-ordination. It is the most unregulated "free-market" economies in the west, the UK and the USA that have done least well.

Centralized state planning is, moreover, no answer to the supposed inherent anarchy of the market. Planning produces its own anarchy, its own distortions of economic behaviour and its own corruptions. This brings us to the second objection. This is the claim that a system which assigns most welfare tasks to voluntary associations must produce inequalities in provision, benefiting some households and localities at the expense of others. Yet this inequality is just the result that centralized bureaucratic welfare systems have managed to accomplish. Nothing, moreover, prevents the state in such an associationalist system from enforcing minimum standards on associations in receipt of public funds or from providing its own welfare safety net.

4.3 Cats' homes

In such an associationalist society there would be public funds raised by taxes and there would be capital markets to provide investment resources for firms. Voluntary associations would not finance all social activity through flag days. The state could, for example, collect an "associational tax" as a substantial percentage of total tax revenue, and allow taxpayers to nominate, say, about 25 per cent of their associational tax payments to a limited number of organizations (perhaps five to ten). That would prevent all revenue going to cats' homes and the like. The state would then distribute the bulk of the remainder of the associational tax according to the registered membership of associations and retain a reserve for meeting shortfalls. Such a system would ensure funds would flow towards the more popular associations. Moreover, industrial finance would become a mutually owned sector. Firms would establish credit unions: pension funds, insurance companies, etc., would lend to industrial banks and buy industrial associations' bonds. Self-governing firms would thus have access to external sources of capital and would be subject to the disciplines of borrowing at interest on organized capital markets.

Such a society is administratively and organizationally feasible. It is not a utopia, nor does it – as most utopias do – make unwarranted assumptions about human stamina and motivation. Self-governing associations need not be participatory democracies nor need they be small scale: representative elections and a professional management answerable to a democratic governing body may well be sufficient for most purposes. Many voluntary associations at present are of this nature, and providing they perform their tasks well enough, members are happy to subscribe and do no more than vote for the existing council. A society of self-governing associations leaves people free to choose the extent of their involvement. It does not compel endless hours of voluntary service above the demands of home and work.

But how to create a society of associations? How to tackle the current big corporations? How can one seek the greatest measure of equality possible when top tycoons are paid up to £1 million a year? Clearly, big business would regard the conversion of firms into self-governing associations with horror and would resist it root and branch. But if the public could be persuaded of the virtues of democratically accountable business, top managers would find themselves in the predicament that they are relatively few in number and that even executives in their subsidiary firms might welcome a reform. The 1988 British Social Attitudes survey shows that the British public are anything but enamoured of the motives and performance of top management.

If a reforming government tried to convert existing firms into self-governing associations, what would that involve? First, making management accountable to the relevant interests represented on a supervisory board of a company – let us assume that shareholders, employees and community interests have equal importance and that they should each elect one-third of the board. Secondly, creating a single membership status – *all* permanent employees to have the same rights and conditions of service, from the managing director to the lavatory attendant. Let us assume that inequalities in income will be flattened, to create a ratio of no more than 1 : 8. Thirdly, instituting a comprehensive system of co-determination, participation and consultation at all levels within the firm.

This is not so radical as it might appear. West German firms have comprehensive industrial democracy and co-determination measures, while many Japanese firms have single employee status, and in the period of most dramatic Japanese growth many companies had very low salary differentials. Nevertheless, it would be very unpopular with top management in Britain.

Measures likely to be unpopular with influential people need to be practical. How could these changes be applied to big conglomerate firms? While many aspects of industrial concentration may be economically unnecessary there are many cases where large-scale organizations are essential. How can these organizations be effectively run by democratic methods? The simple answer to this is that if we believe *states* can be made democratically accountable to their citizens to some significant degree, then companies surely can. But let us accept that the structure and operations of a complex company may be difficult to understand and therefore difficult for representatives to govern. There are then two answers: unscrambling into their component parts those companies where size has little economic logic, and creating different organizational structures for those companies where large-scale operations are necessary.

First, large size can be attained by partnerships of semi-autonomous subunits: firms that share work and contract one with another; firms that subscribe to marketing networks; firms that create collective bodies to represent their common interests or to provide common services such as training. These links can be by interfirm co-operation alone or through linkage with and co-ordination by public bodies. In such cases firms enjoy all the advantages of scale, without the participating units becoming too large or complex to be democratically governable. These relationships are already common in the most successful regions of the western industrial economies, and, far from being pie-in-the-sky, are widely identified as a key source of industrial efficiency, as many contributors argue in my edited collection (with Jonathan Zeitlin), *Reversing Industrial Decline?* (1988)

Secondly, large firms can be stripped down to a "core" of absolutely necessary activities that must be under direct control. Such a core might well be strategic management, R&D, and some crucial manufacturing operations. To get down to this core firms would follow a strategy of "internal privatization": sub-contracting non-core activities to co-operatives, promoting labour/capital partnerships and management-worker buy-outs of peripheral activities. For labour-intensive core activities the firm would contract with a labour co-operative on a fixed term deal. The result would be an economy of modestly sized units, capable of operating in combination on a very large scale. None of them would justify vast differentials of income, since firms would be smaller than the conglomerates of today and their internal hierarchies would be flatter. The overpaid top managers could be bought out as their positions were abolished by reorganization.

How could one prevent such contracting out to labour co-operatives giving rise to iniquities as great as the conditions of gang labour in the Durham mines in the nineteenth century? Surely, management would exploit such changes to dump liabilities upon labour? But two ready answers present themselves: that the state requires compliance with a law regulating contracts with labour co-operatives and that trades unions remain to police and protect workers' interests.

Such a process of turning firms into associations and stripping them down by internal privatization would create an economy based on manageably sized and internally accountable units. It would offer an end to the servile state, in which most people earn their living as employees without either a stake in or a measure of control over their workplace. It would also create a genuine "enterprise society" in which there would be scope for individual initiative and responsibility. Mrs Thatcher's conception of an enterprise culture is one in which choice is offered to individual consumers through the market. But confronted with an economy dominated by big corporations, the individual's choice as employee or consumer is severely limited. This is exacerbated by the Conservatives' ruthless trimming of the countervailing power of the unions in defence of employees, and their indifference to the need to extend further the role of law and regulatory agencies to protect consumers' rights. As J.N. Figgis argued persuasively in *Churches in the Modern State* (1913), it is difficult for individuals to pursue freedom except by freely associating with others. In an enterprise society based on self-governing associations, individuals have both opportunities for choice and the power to make those choices stick. Such a society permits a wide range of competing associations, and therefore choice based on genuine pluralism, and all the advantages of large scale where necessary, without unaccountable hierarchy. Through associations, such a society offers to its citizens unparalleled opportunities for individuation and freedom.

4.4 What about the workers?

I have tried to indicate the ways in which the economy of self-governing associations would be possible and defensible against the hostility of management. But what about the unions? Surely, they have as much to fear from the growth of self-government at work? What would be the place of unions in such a scheme? The answer is: stronger certainly than in either state socialism or corporate capitalism, and more constructive than in either of them.

In an economy of self-governing associations the majority of workers would still receive the main part of their income in wages. Therefore, wage determination would remain important and would need to be institutionalized. Wage determination would take place at three levels:

1. National bargaining between the major interests – the state, associations and unions – leading to a fixed-term accord for overall norms.
2. Regional councils in which public bodies, associations and unions operate arbitration machinery to settle disputes about the application of norms to groups of workers in particular firms – at this level unions would also co-operate to ensure the provision of collective services such as training for firms and workers in the region.
3. Unions would ensure the firm's compliance with laws governing labour contracts and ensure that wage norms were democratically arrived at.

There would be a positive right to strike, but the combination of internal self-government in firms, and the unions' participation in comprehensive measures of collective wage determination would be designed to make strikes measures of last resort. The system of self-government in firms would be based on free votes of individual employees rather than through the union branches, thus maintaining the unions' independence and also preventing them from taking control of firms' internal decision-making procedures. Unions would therefore remain voluntary bodies to which individual workers could choose to subscribe. Like every other association they would be required to meet minimum legal standards of democratic self-governance. They would have the power to enforce fair contracts for employees: firms could not create "labour rackets" under the cover of self-government.

In an associational welfare system the unions could greatly extend their role as providers of welfare and other services compared with their position today. Unions would be eligible to get funds under the "write-in" provisions for 25 per cent of the associational tax, to receive funds proportional to membership and to bid for projects from the reserves. Unions would potentially control very large funds to use for the benefit of their members. They would also contribute to training policy through co-determination machinery and control training funds and offer training themselves. The benefits of belonging to a union would be very real for members. Unions would provide benefits as associations in civil society and directly organize welfare. Socialists in combination with the unions would directly carry out policy instead of campaigning for it to be done by the state, and they would be directly responsible to their own membership for the success of that policy. They would have to compete with non-socialist associations like churches in providing welfare.

Unions would not, however, directly organize or own production (such activities would be *ultra vires* under associational law). Thus associationalism would be quite unlike syndicalism. Workers would be free not to join unions and the self-government procedures of firms would be independent of the unions. Workers, therefore, would not be compelled to be part of a rigid corporatist structure, and unions would have to win and keep members to ensure influence. Workers would have the union to protect them if for some reason a firm became riven by factional strife or dominated by a management clique. They would also have unions to ensure that their job rates, skill classifications and training were protected. Unions would have an interest in and would help to maintain labour mobility and, therefore, the liberty of the worker.

Because it can be adapted to large-scale industry and permits a complex division of labour, associationalism is one of the few nineteenth-century social doctrines that remains fully relevant today. It combines liberty with effective management, and decentralization and self-action with profession-alism and efficiency. It offers a radically greater range of choice than most other social doctrines: greater consumer choice than state socialism and more real choice for the worker than corporate capitalism. Associationalism also allows diverse groups to choose their own form of social organization: it offers possibilities of self-action to religious and other groups as well as to socialists. Because it avoids the authoritarianism of a socialist society fit only for dogmatic socialists, associationalism may appeal to enough groups in society for them to tolerate it and work along with it. It is the only socialist doctrine of which this can credibly be said, and therefore it is, in the long run, the only practical socialism.

5

Democracy: socialism's best reply to the right?

Socialist critiques of the New Right and economic liberalism more generally abound, and this essay will not add to them. Rather it is concerned with the half-way houses into which modern revisionist socialists are frequently driven, positions intended to salvage socialism but which all too often put its very coherence as a political idea into question. On the one hand, the new revisionists are, rightly, strongly opposed to the new economic liberalism, but on the other hand, they are, rightly, in full-scale retreat from the prevailing twentieth-century conception of socialism based on the triad of collectivism, public ownership and state-controlled centralized planning. Commonly, they imagine that a commitment to democracy will both save socialist strategy, providing a road to political power, and also save the substantive content of socialist ideology, making the struggle for socialism coincident with that for the democratization of state and society.

The paradox is that such socialists are generally strongly opposed to economic liberalism because of its formalism, that is, the view that the free market shall determine through its operations alone, and with minimal legal or institutional check, the shape of both economy and society, and yet they seek to counter it with an equally radical formalism, democracy. Democracy is a political mechanism as abstract to substantive social outcomes as is the market as an economic mechanism. Democracy is a general concept for a class of decision procedures. Such procedures determine, for example, by elections and the principle of majority decision who shall occupy certain posts of authority or, less frequently and less effectively, what policies shall be pursued by those who occupy such posts. But democracy is a formal power of majoritarian decision. In its most radical plebiscitarian populist version it advocates "put the issue to the people". In itself such a decision procedure can be no more certain to set certain particular and substantive policy goals or to pursue certain values than the free market. A democratic decision is an open either/or. The "people" can choose Christ *or* Barrabas, to ban foxhunting or to outlaw homosexuality. Democracy can no more guarantee "good" decisions than unregulated markets can guarantee full employment or balanced growth.[1]

Modern democracy is an idea of roughly the same vintage as economic liberalism. Both are products of an eighteenth-century radicalism that challenged the political and economic order of the *ancien régime*. Economic liberalism challenged mercantilist state economic policy and a society in which economic capacity depended on status. Political democracy challenged the restriction of political decision-making to privileged positions and a society in which fixed orders of rank stood in the way of the formal legal and political equality of all citizens. Economic liberalism and political democracy both challenged the absolutist state of the *ancien régime* and yet they were its creatures. Without the creation of an absolutist public peace, the tendency toward passive social levelling that went with it, and the absolutist project of administrative reform that sought to create a homogeneous space of state power, neither doctrine could have had the conditions to appear credible. In the era of religious sectarianism the idea of democracy was tantamount to the advocacy of civil war. Both economic liberalism and democracy suppose public peace – both in the sense of a state monopoly of the means of violence and the absence of fundamental conflicts over values. Both ideas appear in the aftermath of the religious civil wars, conflicts silenced by the absolutism that the economic and political radicals opposed, and they appear before the "social question" threatened to wreck both the free pursuit of wealth in the market and the safety of letting the people determine their rulers or their laws.[2]

Economic liberalism and political democracy are doctrines that appeared prior to the questions which socialism sought to resolve. Those questions were the governance of great industry for the benefit of its workers and the removal of the social problems created by the instability of employment and the poverty of a large section of wage workers. Those questions radically increased the stakes of political reforms which introduced democracy based on universal adult suffrage. As Carl Schmitt showed, liberalism and democracy are in conflict, and this includes economic liberalism.[3] Classical liberalism rested on a society in which certain fundamental areas of life were "depoliticized", notably religion and economics. Religious toleration and a market economy make belief and the pursuit of wealth "private" matters, matters to be confined to the sphere of civil society.

The essence of parliamentary liberalism for Schmitt was that parliament was an arena in which decisions could be made by "discussion", because of the fundamental consensus created by "depoliticization". Once this "depoliticization" breaks down then everything once again becomes political, as in the era of the religious wars. Democracy then becomes a boundless power of popular decision, actually a power of party politicians legitimated in office by a plebiscite. As such it can unmake the limits of the liberal era, both civil and economic liberties, in the interests of a majority party will. In this respect economic liberalism – a formalism in the sphere of economic affairs

– is committed to a politically substantive set of values: that the fundamental rights of enjoyment of property – to buy and to sell, to trade abroad, etc., without let or hindrance – are secured by law. Hence the equivocations of Hayek, the most rigorous economic liberal, when confronted with the *political* formalism of democracy.

Socialism has, on the contrary, generally embraced democracy but has sought to surpass both representative democracy and parliamentary liberalism. The commitment of democratic socialists to the prevailing forms of western democracy has been perceived by those most committed to radical and thoroughgoing socialism as a betrayal and a compromise with the existing order. Radical socialists could embrace both democracy and rapid socialization only on the basis of certain assumptions. The two main assumptions are both dubious and in contradiction with one another.[4]

The first assumption is that the working class form the enormous majority of the population and will, as capitalist society develops, come to be unified around the political aim of socialism. The development of genuine universal suffrage in a bourgeois democratic system will, therefore, assure the victory of the socialist cause. This was the position that both Marx and Engels in later life and also orthodox social democrats like Karl Kautsky adopted. But a working-class democratic victory is only the first stage in a process of political transformation. Orthodox Marxists in the west generally remained convinced that some form of revolutionary action would be necessary to cement a working-class electoral victory, and that the aim of socialism was to go beyond the limitations of existing forms of "bourgeois" democracy. Kautsky, for example, retained this radical objective even though he sought to attain it through governmental action legitimated by mass electoral support and conforming to the rule of law (e.g. 1909, 1918). More radical revisionists like Eduard Bernstein (1899) saw that electoral democracy and the rule of law were inconsistent with revolutionary objectives. Non-revolutionary democratic socialists, like the British Fabians and Labour Party, rejected the aim of surpassing "bourgeois" political institutions.

The second and more radical assumption is that because of the fundamental political unity of the working class, parliamentary forms of democracy based on multiparty elections will become obsolete. The people have a single interest and a plurality of parties is no more than an obstacle to its realization. But the Marxists who advocated such a new form of democracy, notably Marx in *The Civil War in France* (1871) and Lenin in *The State and Revolution* (1917), did not envisage a dictatorship based on a single party. Bourgeois democracy was to be replaced by forms of popular democracy and the direct participation of the people themselves in decision-making: the "dictatorship of the proletariat" was to be the rule of a *class* not a *party*.

These two assumptions may have been necessary to square radical socialization with democracy, but their political effects were disastrous. The first assumption was modified and split-off from the second by those who entertained the illusion of a "parliamentary road" to socialism. Wherever and whenever socialists were successful enough in competing in elections and pragmatic enough to remain within the limits of the liberal order, parliamentarianism came to take precedence over the notion of a socialist "road" to revolution by means of democracy. The commitment to liberalism was as much a condition for the electoral success of the revisionist parties as was their espousal of socialism. That commitment to the liberal constitutional order was a fundamental brake on the pace and scale of socialization, but also a condition of political survival. It trapped parties like the German Social Democrats in the contradiction of a pragmatic current practice and illusory long-term revolutionary goals. In practice the more liberal a party and the more displaced the long-term aim of thoroughgoing socialization the more successful it was electorally – as was the case with the British Labour Party. Liberal "socialist" parties succeeded electorally because they could be trusted politically. They were tolerated as democratic competitors by their opponents and permitted to form governments because those opponents were willing to take the risk that the constitutional order would be safe in their hands. Socialist parties were willing to accept liberal restraint on the boundless power of democratic decision, to accept the placing of obstacles in the democratic "road" to socialism. This bowing-to-the-limits liberalism placed upon democracy was inevitable if parties were to survive in the prevailing forms of parliamentary political competition. The potential vote for revolution in a stable parliamentary system is always that of a containable minority. Moreover, the opposition parties would never accept the legitimacy of a revolutionary party should it succeed by an "accident" at the polls – its success would create a state of emergency in which the threat to the constitutional order justified the suspension of the liberal rules of the game in defence of that order.

Parliamentary socialism was thus confined to a social democratic political practice. It was imprisoned within the constraints of constitutional liberalism and the liberal collectivism of the welfare state and the management of a mixed economy. But the more radical of the democratic socialists constantly chafed against such constraints, for they confined socialism to the status of purely formal party commitment to an ultimate and ever-receding goal. Hence they returned to the dubious assumption of a majority socialist working class. They survived on the hope of a decisive and massive electoral majority for radical social change, that ultimately the working class would turn to its objective interests. This illusion has been a constant of radical democratic socialism from Karl Kautsky to Tony Benn. It simultaneously sustains parliamentarianism and disparages the social democratic commitment to remain within the rules of the game.

The second assumption led to a different and far worse kind of disaster wherever socialists captured state power without the constraints imposed by powerful "bourgeois" opposition parties and without being committed to the liberal constitutionalist "rules of the game". Popular democracy has never been a credible doctrine of governance of large and complex states. The absence of any better and more pragmatic doctrine of governance for a socialist society within Marxism has led revolutionary socialists to create more or less oppressive forms of tyranny. The boundless formalism of majoritarian democracy and the commitment to revolutionary socialization have gone hand in hand in justifying change forced through by unrestrained and centralized state power. To call these forms "People's Democracies" or "Socialist Republics" is to mock any notion of democracy whilst endorsing its boundless formal power of change.

Democracy and liberalism are potentially in contradiction. But the twentieth-century experience of pitiless tyrannies claiming to act in the service of a higher form of democracy than mere "bourgeois liberalism" has breathed life into constitutional liberalism. It may restrain democratic change but it is better than forms of ruthless change claiming to represent new forms of democracy, whether that of the "democratic dictatorship of the proletariat" or the "*Führer-Prinzip*". Hitler and Stalin have become the best legitimations of parliamentary democracy and liberal civil rights. Nazism is a vanished abomination, but the political legacy of Stalin is still with us. *Perestroika* will have to proceed far before Stalin's spectre and that of all the lesser but still brutal contemporary tyrants like Pol Pot or Ceauşescu ceases to blight the prospects of all but the most timid parliamentary socialism in the west.

The history of socialism's relationship to democracy is thus both compromised and fundamentally compromising. This above all else has confined its political appeal. But the other core component of twentieth-century revolutionary socialism, centralized economic planning, has proved to be an equal obstacle to socialism wherever electorates have had a political choice. Centralized economic planning was claimed by revolutionary socialists to offer both an end to the "anarchy of capitalism" and to permit forms of technical change and economic modernization more radical than even those of capitalism itself. But such planning has proved to be neither economically efficient nor consistent with political liberty. Centralized planning requires the concentration of decision-making power in certain state apparatuses and has failed to deliver levels of popular consumption and prosperity comparable to capitalist economies. Hayek has prospered as the leading apostle of economic liberalism largely on the strength of his long-term and unequivocal denunciation of such planned economies and because he has identified all lesser forms of intervention as no more than way-stations to full state control of the economy. Hayek (1944) argued that *any* attempt to substitute for the free workings of the price mechanism would lead to the authoritarian and inefficient corruption of economic rationality by administrative allocation.

But curiously this critical stress on the irrational intervention of authority hides the fact that the socialist commitment to central planning involves a parallel if different economic formalism to that of economic liberalism. Both are at one in seeking the greatest possible production of utilities by the most efficient means. Both seek to subordinate economic institutions to the logic of economic calculation. For central planning to work, enterprises must follow plan targets and indicators, just as firms must follow market signals. Moreover, enterprises are as much a convenience of economic decision-making in such a socialism, a consequence of certain plan priorities and the resource allocations coincident upon them, as is the firm in free-market economics. Planned resource allocation and market allocation both regard the whole structure of the economy and the enterprises in it as the malleable substance of calculation, up for grabs if planners or entrepreneurs so decide.

Central planning is thus in many ways as formalist with regard to the society and institutions under its sway as is the classic conception of the perfectly competitive market. Indeed, planned economies have always been seen as agencies of radical transformation and modernization, and never as the defence of given rights and privileges, the stabilizing of institutions and the preservation of certain forms of social order. The end to the "anarchy" of capitalism could only be achieved by total and unimpeded economic change. Yet such defence and stabilization is often what attracted workers to socialism in the west; it offered an end to uncertainty, unplanned change and economic insecurity. The fear of unemployment, of the loss of skill, of the destruction of traditional social surroundings, are powerful sources of support for socialist and labour parties, but they imply a conservatism fundamentally at odds with the boundless goals of economic and social change implied in socialism. Socialists have been inconsistent in this matter – Karl Kautsky's *The Class Struggle* (1892) at one and the same time castigates the uncertainty and change inherent in capitalism and offers a planned and ordered socialist future. That the latter involves changes as vast and unsettling as the former escapes him.

This socialism cannot stand in opposition to free-market economies in the way the economic liberals would have it – as if the latter pursued economic action based on formally rational calculation and the former did not. Actually both theories of formal economic rationality are far from the institutional complexities of capitalist economies and socialist "centrally planned" economies. Western economies are as far in practice from the model of a perfectly competitive market as Soviet-style economies are from the model of an efficient centralized plan that substitutes for the free working of the price mechanism. The success of western economies – their greater GDP per capita, productivity, and consumer satisfaction compared to the Soviet system – has many causes, and the existence of perfectly competitive markets is not one of them. "Centrally planned" socialism has generally been implemented in economically backward areas and has been used as the lever of economic modernization and industrialization at the expense of consumption and the traditional rural economy.

That economic liberalism involves a commitment to the free market is a commonplace. But free markets are defended for a theoretical reason in that they are claimed to provide a power-neutral and quantitative information system to the rational economic agent. They permit calculation by independent economic agents of the most rational use of resources, and that rationality is expressed in comparative prices and profits. Ultimately, therefore, the free working of the market as a price system is a precondition for the formal rationality of the calculating agent. The entrepreneur and the consumer are both such agents and neither of them has any substantive commitment to any particular production process, method of working or product. The search for the greatest profit and the cheapest price will lead both of them to revolutionize the existing state of affairs, if need be. The social organization of the economy and all institutions directly supporting it must be potentially fluid and subject to change. Formal calculation requires a social order willing to tolerate any amount of social, occupational, technological and locational change necessary to economic rationality. The social order is at the behest of the calculating agent. Economic liberalism thus proposes a state of economic permanent revolution based on the free market, but a revolution which operates within a stabilized political and constitutional settlement in which political liberalism sets substantive limits to the formerly boundless power of democracy as a decision procedure. The free market is claimed to benefit the great mass of consumers, but it requires those consumers as workers or producers to accept ceaseless social and technical change; ultimately they will benefit from the economic insecurity of the free market permanent revolution.

Such a view has always been subject to intense criticism from those who have seen the economy as necessarily embedded in relatively stable social institutions and who have argued that unrestrained change at the behest of sovereign calculating agents could only undermine the very foundations of ordered economic life itself. The names of Karl Polanyi and Emile Durkheim spring immediately to mind.[5] Similarly, countless economic critics have pointed out that such ceaseless change in pursuit of the individually rational goals of economic agents leads to results that are unacceptable in aggregate: that such a system cannot secure full employment, avoid large-scale poverty and gross inequality, and prevent the damaging of the environment. These criticisms are familiar and they cut little ice with hardened economic liberals because they see the defence of given institutions and patterns of occupation, and the substantive goals that go along with them, as a dangerous brake on economic growth and technical progress. Moreover, the mixed economy and the welfare state do not merely reduce welfare, in addition the public sector serves as a base from which socialism can slowly and insidiously advance until it has suffocated the free market. The road to serfdom is paved with the good intentions of the welfare state and the mixed economy.

Accumulating social rigidities and the protection of existing producer interests lead to relative economic failure and this is exposed by international competition. However embedded in social institutions the economy may be, a nation that defends the existing structure of production by protecting employment and output in given enterprises is doomed to failure in the face of more flexible international competitors. Expanding public sectors and large nationalized industries provide the political base for such imposition of limits to market action and technological change. There is an element of truth in this, as the success of Mancur Olson's *The Rise and Decline of Nations* (1982) shows.

But *all* it shows is that the accumulation of powerful interest groups with the capacity and the desire to defend given institutions and privileges will lead to a block on change. It does not show that societies that promote technical change and productive efficiency either rely on a free market to do so or actually change the social institutions which sustain the economy in order to promote change *in* the economy. In fact the best arguments against economic liberalism are not those relating to employment, equality or pollution. The economic liberals have no answer to mass unemployment, large-scale poverty or environmental crisis, but it would be a rash socialist who honestly believed that they had an answer. What economic liberalism cannot guarantee are the two things central to its claim to economic rationality: technical innovation that promotes productive efficiency and the levels of investment necessary to resource it. There are good reasons to suggest that weakly regulated markets and the close interaction of different markets lead both to a short-term view of profitability and efficiency, and to a steady drift of profit-seekers toward activities where market information alone is sufficient to economic action (markets in securities, national currencies, commodities and property are obvious examples).

There is good evidence to suggest that those regions of those states which have proved economically most successful in the more uncertain, more competitive and rapidly changing international economy of the later 1970s and 1980s are those in which strong continuity of institutions and enterprises has precedence over the free market.[6] Technical change and productive flexibility are more likely to be sustained and accepted where they can be contained within appropriate institutions and thus not disorder the whole ensemble of social relationships. Thus societies like Japan which accept rapid technical change, do so on the basis of a deep *social* conservatism. This conservatism in Japan may involve the wholesale reinvention of tradition after the debacle of 1945 but it is nonetheless real and effective. Central to conservatism in Japan are the family and the enterprise, which cushion their members against change and make them more adaptable at work. The system of guaranteed employment for core workers and the perception of the enterprise as an ongoing collective body in which all members have a stake, provides a certainty and security that permits flexibility in terms of tasks undertaken and working methods. Management and workers are linked by frameworks of common commitment and trust.[7]

In industrial districts in Japan, Italy and West Germany, such as Sakaki, Emilia-Romagna and Baden-Württemburg, firms coalesce and co-operate in complex networks.[8] These networks depend on relationships of trust and mutual commitment and not simply market and contractual relationships. They are sustained by ongoing social institutions, which mix the public and the private sectors into a common "public sphere" for the industry or region in question. Firms not only compete but also co-operate, they share information and certain common services. Such dense networks of mutually supporting firms and institutions are resilient and flexible in the way firms isolated in purely competitive relations with others cannot be. Consequently they can take what appears from the standpoint of a purely competitive market culture as unacceptable risks, that is, to adopt a long-term view, to invest in new products and processes which involve anticipating the market, to invest in upgrading the skills of their workers and to share their knowledge with other firms to enhance their role as partners or subcontractors.

Those societies most wedded to the economic liberal view of firms striving in competitive markets to best one another have failed to understand or respond to the international competitive success of such regions – the USA and the UK being the prime examples. Firms isolated in purely market relationships with others are forced to carry the full cost of any innovations or investments they make. Economists who unhesitatingly accept the notion of economies of scale tend to see them in terms of a single plant or firm, rather than in terms of regional networks. But the very different economies gained from such networks are real if they are subtle, and confer competitive advantage on the whole region and not just the individual firm. By contrast the dis-economies of competition are less obvious, but nonetheless real. They are not merely or even a matter of the duplication of resources, but involve losses that stem from the absence of security, trust and information, and which by increasing the risk to the isolated firm lead it to avoid the taking of risk in matters of investment and new techniques.[9]

Trust makes change possible and trust involves the certainty that relationships and the expectations they involve will continue to exist. Trust is not merely an attitude, it is an institutionalized relationship. Trust between workers and management within the firm, between one firm and another, and between firms and the public agencies through which they co-operate all serve to make forms of technical and organizational change possible, which in the absence of trust will be resisted.[10] It is only when institutionalized in definite patterns of common action – co-operation, communication, bargaining to set common goals – that trust can endure. A society that answered to the needs of the formalism of a perfectly free market would lack such relationships: in it technical change would prove more risky to entrepreneurs and would be more actively resisted by workers precisely because they are isolated in purely market and contractual relationships.

These patterns of regional and intraenterprise co-operation have analogues at the national level, particularly in those small states like Austria and Sweden that have relied on technically advanced export industries as the core of their economic strategy of adapting to the world market.[11] Here patterns of corporate bargaining and interinterest co-operation in setting and sustaining macroeconomic policy objectives have ensured the stability that makes investment in the long run and in technical change possible. The consequences of such change for workers are met by training and labour-market policies supported by industry, labour and the state. Larger states like West Germany have less intense and co-ordinated but still effective variants of this corporatism.

Economic liberalism and modern ideas of democracy are alike formalist in that they both oppose the fixing of society by a network of institutions and non-contractual relationships. The reason is that they both originated in a body of ideas which sought to sweep away the status-ridden social order of the *ancien régime*. The regulated economy of mercantilism and the society of fixed status groups represented an obsolete and tenacious combination of economic and political substantivisms – hence the formalism of both economic liberalism and political democracy against the fading institutional order of a quasi-feudal society. If we now turn from the limitations of economic liberalism that stem from its formalist conception of the economy to those of the democracy that many modern revisionist socialists wish to use to reinvigorate the socialist project in the west we find analogous problems.

It is interesting how widespread is the commitment to democratization as the core of socialist strategy. It is also interesting that this commitment covers a very broad political spectrum. Cautious defenders of the necessity of liberal democracy, constitutionalism and the rule of law like Noberto Bobbio seek to add to the central parliamentary institutions the wider democratization of industry and other social institutions.[12] A mainstream pluralist theorist like Robert A. Dahl advocates an economic democracy based on co-operatives as a necessary compliment to political pluralism; without this economic pluralism corporate capitalism subverts pluralist democratic influence.[13] Both Bobbio and Dahl are clear that there is no choice between socialism and liberal democracy; if the two come into conflict then the latter must be supported without hesitation. Better a liberal polity and political freedom at the cost of economic inequality than the loss of such benefits in the dubious pursuit of socialist economic and social goals. Non-democratic socialist societies are neither noticeably more efficient nor more egalitarian than democratic capitalist ones.

One then passes to a spectrum of more radical views: Bowles and Gintis, Cohen and Rogers, Keane, Laclau and Mouffe, Rustin and Walzer. This socialist commitment to democracy has also given rise to political groupings like Charter 88, committed to the reform of British democracy and the development of a constitutional state.[14]

What is striking is that this widespread conviction about the need for democratization on the part of socialist intelligentsia in the west is greeted with a wall of silence by professional politicians and electorates alike. In neither the UK nor the USA, the two main centres of such advocacy, is political change in the mainstream political agenda. Democracy appears to be a vital and at the same time pragmatic issue to the intelligentsia, unlike the tried and rejected advocacy of a centrally planned society it offers socialism the hope of realism and relevance. But strikingly democratization is no nearer to being a popular objective than is socialism in its traditional guise.

Why is this so? It is no part of my case to argue that democratization is not needed in the west or that the criticisms made of existing institutions are not valid. Indeed, I have made similar points myself (Hirst 1986) and supported the proposals for political change of Charter 88. The reason for the indifference of electorates is complex but certainly not that their dissatisfaction with the existing political system has not been recognized or has yet to find a focus. The widespread indifference to and under participation in elections – most marked in the USA, even for Presidential elections, but also evident in local authority elections in the UK – are a problem for a believer in a democracy based on active and aware citizenry. But they are not a sign of active concern about the political process by the electorate. In fact most citizens in the UK and USA believe they live in a perfectly adequate democracy, whether they vote or not. Most people put their private concerns first, and provided they are secure and prosperous enough, confine political interest and participation, if at all, to a vote in periodic national elections.

Central to the ideas of the new democratic socialists are the need for active participation, for the expansion of the idea of citizenship and the creation of a "new republicanism" centred on a view of the polity as a means of attaining what the citizens deem to be the common good. The radical socialist advocacy of political reforms proceeds at two levels: the proposal of specific institutional changes, like PR or legally guaranteed civil rights in the UK, and the proposing of very general and abstract views about common citizenship. What is missing here is a doctrine of government that addresses the problems of modern representative democracy and proposes a solution to them. Without such a doctrine constitutional changes tend to become isolated panaceas, and the advocacy of citizenship turns into little more than legitimatory rhetoric for the British Labour Party that needs new grounds for justifying traditional collectivist strategies.[15]

Between the panaceas and the rhetoric is a considerable vagueness about the actual institutional changes that are necessary to make modern government more democratic and more effective. This vagueness of many of the democratic socialist authors is a consequence of what we call the "republican-citizenship" standpoint itself. The new republicanism found in authors like Walzer (1983) or Mouffe (1988) is an attempt to revitalize the concepts of common citizenship, civic virtue and active participation by individual citizens in the public sphere. It draws on an old tradition of republican thinking which it modernizes to adapt to new concerns.[16] That tradition is part of the core of the modern democratic critique of absolutism, the ideas of Rousseau and Tom Paine being central.

The experience of mass democracy in the radical republicanism of the French Revolution showed the limits and illusions of this revived classical republicanism. It is only in terms of a conception of "civic virtue" and of the fundamental homogeneity of a "people" that a mass democracy could appear tolerable. In practice the revived republican ideas of the eighteenth century predated and were contradicted by modern mass electoral democracy, designed for small republics these ideas were unsuitable for mass nation states. Political virtue is always in vanishingly short supply, and a large state cannot give rise even to the illusion of a homogeneity of interest that Rousseau's small, poor and virtuous republics presupposed. Mass democracy could only work if mass political participation were limited, if the conflicting interests were represented in explicit political parties that offered a check one to another, and if the professional political actors subscribed to certain fundamental liberal norms that made electoral competition and succession of the majority party to office tolerable.

In short, republican democracy was defeated and the advocacy of modern democracy turned into support for political reform which created representative governments with mass electorates. The basic assumptions of the republican tradition predate and cut across those of modern mass democracy. That is because modern democracy has sought to limit two features of classical republicanism – the active and direct participation of citizens in government and the boundless power of a democratic majority decision. Carl Schmitt was certainly right that democracy and liberalism are always potentially in conflict. What he recognized less clearly is that the workable forms of modern democracy would be tempered both by liberalism and by devices that took account of both the heterogeneity of the people and the need to check the scope of democratic decision by effective powers of opposition. Modern democracy is successful to the extent that it does not single-mindedly obey the logic of majority decision. Republicanism thus returns us to the radicalism and formalism of eighteenth-century doctrines of democracy confronted with absolutism: for the eighteenth century nothing could gainsay the majority vote of a virtuous and united people, its boundless power of decision was legitimated precisely because of its capacity to sweep away absolutism and feudalism.

The new republican current is successful with dissatisfied intellectuals but can hitch itself to no effective major reforming interest because it tends to set itself against certain consequences of modern mass democracy. One reason is that it tends to ignore the pluralism of organized interests which is the foundation of modern democratic political influence. Hence it advocates an activism and a participatory ethic that address all citizens alike and therefore nobody. To the extent that they have influence modern citizens are members of specific organized interest groups, and citizenship as such confers only limited and minimal rights of political participation. The citizen body is decomposed into plural and competing organized interests.

The main reason why the criticism of the new republicanism cannot bite beyond the intelligentsia is that it is advocating "democracy", which most people believe they enjoy anyway. The dominant political idiom identifies democracy with the prevailing forms of representative government. It can do this because it can point to the disasters which follow forms of *unrepresentative* government seeking to replace obsolete multiparty electoral democracy and parliamentary institutions. Generally such attempts to replace "bourgeois" democracy on the part of fascists and socialists appeal to a higher true majority interest of the "people" – a decisive political will which is denied expression by the petty complexities of the party contest. The popular experience of dictatorships and single-party states make the identification of democracy with representative government and multiparty elections credible.

For this reason, the direct criticism of representative democracy and the advocacy of its replacement by some other form of democracy is not merely dangerous, it is suicidal. The advocates of the new democratic socialist republicanism aim to be political realists, so they are careful not to advocate any system other than a plurality of political parties competing for the popular vote in periodic elections. Despite all the problems modern democracies have encountered, the legitimacy of representative government remains unshaken and people are terrified by the advocacy of alternatives to it. Even 20 years of Mrs Thatcher are unlikely to change that in the UK. But the dominance of representative government poses real problems for the new republicanism centred on a democratization involving more active participation and a heightened civic consciousness. It cannot but accept the prevailing forms of democracy, but it wants to add elements of a tradition that is alien to representative government, and which harks back to a republic of fully participating citizens.

Representative democracy with universal suffrage involves both the mass participation of ordinary citizens in elections and a minimal contribution by them to active politics. The voters in such a mass democracy cannot be, as individual participants, either very influential or very involved. Activism is the choice of a minority, who are activists in political parties and issue organizations. It is difficult within the representative ethos to recreate the "civic virtues", because these virtues stem from a classic republican tradition of active participation in government.

The advocates of citizenship and republicanism necessarily tend to be hostile to such minimalist forms of political participation and yet are unable to supplant the institutions that give rise to them. Parliamentary and representative democracy is seen to be in need of renewal, and yet the actual forms of real public influence on and control over government outside of elections in a mass democracy are generally downgraded by the new republicanism. These forms are organized social interests and the processes of lobbying and corporatism that go along with them. Individual citizens can pursue their specific interests only by associating with others, and interest organizations involve far more citizens than political parties – trade unions, local bodies, pressure groups, and so on. On the one hand, the new republicans recognize that organized interests spring from an active civil society independent of the state, which is good for democracy. On the other hand these interests threaten to undermine participation on the basis of active common citizenship, which is seen to subvert the common good. Organized interests cut across the common civic sphere, breaking political influence up into the self-seeking interests of particular groups. Organized interests are influential to the extent that they achieve their own ends, which are different from a notion of the collective sovereignty or common popular will of all citizens. Eighteenth-century republicans, such as Jean-Jacques Rousseau, always argued against the influence of intermediate associations and sought to abolish any organized political bodies other than the state and the participating individual citizens. Modern republicanism does not go this far, but it has a strong suspicion of corporatism and lobbying and of the privileged political influence it gives to major organized interests.

That western electorates are apathetic and indifferent to the issue of political reform is exactly what we would expect in a reasonably affluent and stable mass-representative democracy. People want a chance to vote out the government but are willing having elected it to leave it to get on with the business of governing while they get on with their own affairs. In consequence, reform will only become part of the mainstream political agenda if it can piggyback on the concerns of citizens in their private life, notably economic concerns.

In fact the best analysts of the workings and the limitations of modern representative democracy are generally not of the republican persuasion. We can ignore anti-democratic writers here. It is social theorists rejected by the Marxist left, like Weber and Dahl, who show *why* minimal level of mass participation is inevitable in a modern democracy. Weber saw that competition for a mass vote implies organized national parties and that such parties tend to be hierarchical and bureaucratic. Parties get in the popular vote by encouraging voters to identify with the party's political image and its leadership; they simplify the voters' choice. The function of democracy is what Weber calls "plebiscitary" – the electorate endorses a party and legitimates the rule of a party government by giving it the mandate of a majority vote. Representative mass democracy is therefore a justification of governmental authority and not itself a form of rule by the people. The influence of citizens is confined to endorsing one party government rather than another.[17]

Dahl in his *A Preface to Democratic Theory* (1956) stresses the limits of democratic voting, trying to minimize expectations of what can be accomplished in the way of popular control by means of elections. He stresses that modern democratic rule is the rule of *minorities*, of parties that have no more than a large fraction of the electorate (like Mrs Thatcher's 43 per cent in 1983 and 1987). He emphasizes that the health of democracy depends not just on elections but also and more importantly on the political competition for particular influence on government policy by non-state associations. Mass democracies can only make simple choices between parties and the actual business of detailed policy-making depends upon a party government being open to influence by a wide variety of associations. Societies are democratic not merely because they have universal suffrage and multiparty systems, but because influence is widely diffused and is organized by a large number of competing organizations independent of government.[18] In terms of this view, Mrs Thatcher's government is breaking with the spirit of modern mass democracy because it uses its "mandate" from a plebiscite to drive through policy by state action and has deliberately chosen to ignore the claims for influence of many of the non-state interest organizations. Indeed, it has chosen to act against some of them, like the trade unions.

If the analysis of thinkers like Weber and Dahl is correct then it is virtually impossible to introduce a republican ethos into modern democracy, to create an active and involved citizenry participating in common core political institutions. "Citizenship" in this sense is what modern democracies discourage. Critics of the left and right who saw this wanted to replace representative democracy with another system. In the case of the Marxist left with a direct democracy of soviets or workers' councils, in which all members could themselves participate in the work of government. Such an idea has failed absolutely to attract western publics. If we seek to enhance citizenship and active public influence on government then we can go one of two ways: either we must frontally challenge representative democracy and pay the price of political exclusion, or seek a different form of citizenship and public influence which is compatible with representative democracy, and which has sources outside of the republican tradition.

"Democracy" is a formalist political doctrine in the sense that it does no more than advocate that certain mechanisms be used for deciding certain issues. Direct democracy, in which the people participate in legislation and administration, and representative democracy, in which the people elect politicians to do those things, both involve the majoritarian principle. A majority, however, is first and foremost an arithmetical fact and is not a social agent with a given specific character. As such neither of the main forms of democracy can guarantee political outcomes. The Marxist left advocated soviets and direct democracy because it believed the working class was a social agent with a specific character, and one which formed a homogeneous overwhelming majority. It ignored and denied the pluralism of social interests, groups and values: the basis of any society in which power and influence are relatively widely diffused. The modern democratic socialist left advocates a more ambiguous form of "democracy", one that does not seek to displace representative government, because it believes that greater accountability of government to the citizens will lead to certain desirable outcomes. In order to make that accountability credible it is driven to advocate the new republicanism based on "citizenship", because only if the people are citizens with the appropriate virtues can anything like that begin to happen. As with the Marxist left, the outcome of the decision procedure is smuggled in with the hypothesis the nature of the deciding agent. It is the virtues of citizenship that turn the people and the majority from an arithmetical fact into a social force.

But as we have seen, a workable mass-electoral democracy implies just the opposite. A majority conceived as a social agent may be formally "democratic" but it can act in an anti-pluralist spirit. Such a claim to majority would actively legitimate the dominance of one set of interests. Modern representative democracy, if it is given the major role in the political system, serves to legitimate the ruling party government. Such a government can also act as if it were a majority social agent, and in a way that works against the plural influence of organized interests. No form of democracy can be so devised as to secure certain substantive outcomes. Something more than a majoritarian principle and certain core political institutions is needed to do that – that something being networks of social relationships analogous to those which we discussed when pointing to the formalism of economic liberalism. Representative democracy has definite limitations but it is the only form suitable for large-scale societies. The problems of modern politics cannot be solved simply by substituting one form of democracy for another.

How then does one advance the cause of greater democracy without a frontal attack on existing forms of representative democracy? First, one must start by accepting that modern representative institutions cannot be supplanted, they can only be supplemented. The experience of authoritarian leftist and rightist governments leads mass electorates in the west to cling tenaciously to the vote, and to its deciding who shall govern. Although electoral democracy limits participation, it does offer the real check on authority of the possibility of vetoing a party government at elections. Moreover, electorates tend to be conservative in supporting the electoral system they are familiar with; they tend to identify it with democracy even if it has severe defects. At the last general election in the UK over 75 per cent of the electorate supported the parties that accept the current first-past-the-post electoral system, that is the Conservatives, and Labour. Socialists and democrats must also face the fact that a majority of voters, over 60 per cent, still fear Labour as a single-party government more than they do the Conservatives. Many electors still see electoral reform and electoral pacts as stalking horses for a Labour victory and are likely to be suspicious of them in the future.

The only available answer to the general problem of democratization is a long-term one: to seek to strengthen the role of organized social interests in influencing government and to democratize the internal governance of those interests themselves. It is to see the future of democracy in building a more effective pluralist system of political competition.

In the UK it is therefore necessary to demonstrate how Conservative Party government undermines this real pluralist foundation of our democracy. Constitutional changes are secondary to the commitment of ruling parties to be open to a wide range of associations' influence. To do this, and to make this pluralist influence more democratic, the range of interests with influence needs to be extended beyond powerful "lobbies", like the road haulage industry or the farmers, and the process of that influence needs to become more open. Organized interests need to be more inclusive of their potential memberships and impelled, by bargaining, to take heed of other organizations and interests. This is not an exclusively British problem, and this reform of interest bargaining has been proposed for western countries generally by Phillipe Schmitter (1988). It is to advocate open corporatism, and corporatism has often been perceived by both right and left as a threat to parliamentary sovereignty. Corporatism is also widely perceived by Conservative Government and many trade unionists to have failed in the UK and to have been part of an era of consensus politics that led to economic decline. This is a superficial view; if corporatism did "fail" in the UK it is because it was never practised properly nor persisted with in a sufficiently disciplined way for long enough to work. Something which upsets not only Mrs Thatcher, but the right- and left-wing trade unionists Eric Hammond and Ron Todd respectively, shows that corns are being trodden on – that open corporatism may undercut both authoritarian party government and self-interested powerful lobbies.

A corporatist supplement to our representative democratic polity is not something that has to be sold directly to the electorate. It is not the stuff of a single party's legislative programme but of a wider social pact. It needs to be sold first to enough of the political class and to enough of the leaders of the major interest groups. Such a supplement does not require radical and formal constitutional change in the first instance.

If the corporatism of bargaining by organized interests is the best way to secure influence on government and for government to attain its objectives without compulsion, then the processes of bargaining need to be inclusive, formal and open. Why corporatism has had such a bad press is because these conditions have often not been met. The Italian fascists advocated corporatism, by which they meant in practice the mobilization of associations and occupational groups by a single-party state to its own ends. Corporatism has also meant the private influence of exclusive interests, a narrowly competitive interest-group struggle for particular benefits. The politics of private-interest lobbying in the USA offers a good example of the triumph of highly exclusive groups seeking purely selfish benefits from the state.

Modern societies cannot give rise to a "general will" in the way that the eighteenth-century republicans hoped for. The nearest such complex societies can get to a general will is a social pact between the major economic and social interests to further certain common and bargained goals. Such a pact requires a governing party coalition strong enough to act as a social leader, but not so strong as to dominate associations through the state and inhibit real bargaining. This is a difficult balance to strike but it is not impossible. It requires a source of leadership capable of proposing and negotiating a social pact. Typically this will be a political party with the drive and popular support to make the process credible and attractive enough to the major social interests.[19] If the British Labour Party sought to act in such a leadership role, and to sell the need for an ongoing and disciplined pact to its own associated interest group, the unions, then it would be a large part of the way toward credibility with the electorate as a party government. Labour is more likely to get back into office if it acts as the party of more than one group of interests. In a period of rapidly diverging major party objectives, then for one party to succeed another implies a radical shift in the preferences of the electorate. We are no longer in a period when the common ground between the parties made switching votes a relatively easy matter for many voters. Labour is unlikely to get back as a *labour* and pubic-sector party, but might do so as a party creating a new kind of cross-interest consensus. It will not get back as a weak copy of the Tory Party – better a strong dose of the real thing in many voters' minds. Labour has to outflank the Conservatives with a new strategy if it is to compete with them in elections, and central to that strategy is to act out of office as something more than a potential single-party government.

A democracy strengthened by processes of inclusive corporate bargaining between associations enables social interests to be mobilized effectively to secure common commitments to economic performance. This the Conservatives have failed to do, their rule has benefited only part of the UK. It is the extension of electoral democracy and party government by formalised and inclusive bargaining that has sustained the economic success of states like Austria and Sweden, and to a lesser extent West Germany. It has enabled them to achieve these results with a low degree of coercion. Successful corporatism links the demand for greater democratic influence and the needs of social mobilization to secure economic growth. It is a progressive form of what David Marquand in *The Unprincipled Society* (1988) calls a "developmental state". Britain has lacked such a state, it has suffered in consequence a less democratic and more coercive polity, and a less successful and more divisive economy.

An important feature of such a corporatist supplement to representative democracy is that it allows for a more complex and qualified form of decision-making than a simple either/or. No decision procedure can guarantee that all the decisions made by means of it are the right ones, but, as we have seen, democratic procedures involve a radical simplification of the issues such that they can be determined by a majoritarian principle: one candidate rather than another in elections; yes or no to a proposition in a referendum. Complex issues of social and economic policy are not such – the relevant issues may not be proposable in an either/or form. Moreover, the majority preference, in terms of those issues, may leave a strong and unreconciled organized minority interest unwilling to comply with it or actively to co-operate in making it work.

Corporatism offers a quite different set of processes of reaching decisions: the bargaining of policy objectives and implementation by a plurality of organized interests, the consultation of such interests by government in making policy, the orchestration of influence and lobbying to modify decisions, and the seeking of the co-operation of the bodies involved in the implementation of decisions. Corporatism involves both a continuous process of exchanging information and provides channels of communi-cation and co-operation between public bodies and the organized interests represented in corporatist forums. This in essence is what Emile Durkheim meant when he defined democracy as a process of communication between the state and a civil society of professional associations in his *Lectures on Civic Morals* (1957). Corporatism is another way of conceiving democracy in terms of communication and influence. Typically an effective corporate bargaining process involves processes of concession and intermediation of interests in which a common course of action or a mutually agreed objective is the result. Such processes have often been condemned as leading to muddled compromises, but that is generally because they are viewed in terms of a majoritarian, "winner takes all", concept of policy. On the contrary, where such bargaining meets the conditions for effectiveness, plural and potentially opposed interests can be accommodated in a course of action that enjoys common consent and in terms of which organizations agree to seek to deliver definite forms of compliance from their members. This makes for consistent and sustainable policies, which can be accomplished with a relatively low degree of state-enforced compliance. Such corporate processes of policy-formation or analogues to them have been crucial to the success of "developmental states" in following long-term policies for economic growth.

It is the possibility of serious economic difficulties – as the Conservatives' one-sided push for economic modernization reveals its partial and inadequate nature – that provides the best prospect for introducing a corporatist supplement to representative democracy in the UK. The Conservatives have reduced social pluralism and promoted economic division, without assuring sustainable growth. Labour is more likely to be taken seriously by voters as the Conservatives' "economic miracle" unravels if it shows itself capable of functioning as the orchestrator of a "one nation" social pact. It is the possibility of a new social strategy for economic development that will justify incremental political change in a corporatist direction. Politicians and the public may suffer political change if it offers a sustainable regime of economic regulation. Corporatist bargaining offers both more public influence through inclusive organizations and a new regime of macroeconomic control to replace Keynesian mechanisms of state-controlled demand management as the basis for an expansionary policy.

A purely political argument, and one which involves radical changes in existing democratic institutions, is unlikely to capture the politicians or the electorate. There is no doubt that the changes advocated by radical intellectuals in the UK, for example Charter 88, in challenging parliamentary sovereignty and seeking to counter it by a strong and institutionalized form of the rule of law, that is a written constitution safe-guarding fundamental civil and political rights, amount to a revolution in the traditional doctrines and practices of the British state. Such revolutions are not to be had merely because they are desirable: they presuppose a fundamental political crisis and a disruption of the continuity of the existing institutions of state. Radical political and constitutional changes are almost always the result of war and revolution. Defeat and occupation, and revolution as the result of war, are the ways in which the continuity of existing states has been broken in the twentieth century. Peaceful revolutions in political affairs sanctioned by electoral victories are rare. Social pacts in periods of economic crisis to secure economic performance but which lead to greater democratic influence are more common – Sweden in the 1930s is the classic example. If political change is to happen in the UK we must hope that Labour comes to see the need for such a social pact and to recognize that it can develop best as the leading party in a developmental state.

In the latter part of this essay I have tried to illustrate the general discussion of the issues of how to democratize western societies further and the relationship of such democratization to socialism by considering the example of how the British Labour Party might find a road back to political power. That "road" is quite unlike the concept of socialism as the "democratization" of core political institutions involving the participation of an active citizenry. It is also unlike classic Marxist revisionist conceptions of a "parliamentary road to socialism". It rests on certain substantive and widely shared concerns to promote economic performance. Whilst general doctrines of democracy, whether direct or representative, can be discussed in the abstract, forms of corporatism designed to ensure the more effective influence of a plurality of organized interests can only be discussed in a specific institutional and economic context. Corporatism is a general term for a wide range of particular relationships adapted to producing specific substantive outcomes.

As in the case of manufacturing, so in the case of the influence of organized interests, there is as yet no adequate and widely accepted body of theory to specify these networks, patterns of co-operation and forms of bargaining. Or, at least, no body of theory like, say, neoclassical economics in its role as a justification for economic liberalism. Traditional socialism would also appear to have little place for these relationships, if it is taken to mean either Fabian state collectivism or the Marxist advocacy of centralized economic planning. But *other* socialisms have been closer to such relationships in the institutional orders they have proposed. Proudhon's ideas are interesting in this respect because they were drawn from a context – nineteenth-century France – in which industrial districts continued to function and in which manufacture was embedded in precisely such networks of co-operation and mutual assistance between artisans, firms and municipalities.[20] Again, the solidarist tradition, strongly informing the sociologist Emile Durkheim's conception of politics and the governance of the economy, drew on a continuing French body of institutions and attitudes, far removed from the "free market".[21] English Guild Socialism and political pluralism were both strongly anti-collectivist and proposed a system in which self-governing groups of producers and associations would play the major role.[22]

Socialism has always been a complex and diverse body of ideas, and, given the failure of central planning and state collectivism, and the fact that fashionable market-socialist alternatives appear to them to be little more than economic liberalism without capitalists, then there is a need to draw on the socialist sources closest to the patterns of co-operation in manufacturing and the forms of corporate bargaining that offer routes to both economic success and social stabilization.

But it will not do merely to pull Proudhon or G.D.H. Cole out of the hat: as if everything acceptable to contemporary socialists had to have a fully fashioned traditional socialist pedigree.[23] Modern socialists also need to learn from and adapt to the patterns of co-operation in industrial districts and the forms of corporate bargaining in national economies that exist today. That certain regions and societies have been economically successful is not the issue, it is *how* they have been successful. Socialists have other goals and standards than GDP per capita and the balance of trade in manufactures. The argument is that such networks of co-operation and such practices of corporate bargaining not only promote manufacturing efficiency and economic stability but allow for a more mutualist and less coercive society, one closer to certain fundamental socialist values than either collectivism or market socialism. That raises the issue of what can be done to adapt such institutions and practices not only to other, less successful, societies and regions, but also to other problems and spheres of social life.

Many socialists have sought to redefine socialism in terms of democratization, but, as I have tried to show, democracy is a doctrine which is both formal and without specific social content; also, there is no evidence that western electorates are either interested in democratization or can be made to behave like "citizens". The advantage of the forms of corporatist supplement to representative democracy proposed here is that they do not depend on such mass active participation and they are directed toward goals citizens do approve of, notably that of improving economic performance.

Notes

1. For an explication of democracy as a "political mechanism", see Hindess (1983), Ch. 2; for the limits of representative democracy and also its status as the dominant political idiom in the west, see Hirst (1990a) Ch. 2.
2. For an insightful account of the role of absolutism in ensuring public peace, and the crisis of absolutism faced with the criticism from "civil society" in the eighteenth century, see Koselleck (1988).

3. For his critique of parliamentary democracy and analysis of the conflict between democracy and liberalism, see Schmitt (1985); see also Ellen Kennedy's helpful introduction to her translation. On Schmitt's political theory generally, see Hirst (1990a) Chs 7 and 8 and Schwab (1970).

4. See Dahl (1948), which remains the best and most considered short exploration of Marxism's inability to come to terms with majoritarian electoral democracy and the competition of free political parties necessary to it. See also the papers by Hindess, Jessop and Jones in Hunt (1980).

5. Polanyi's most relevant works here are (1944) and (1971); for Durkheim see (1893) and (1957).

6. See Piore and Sabel (1984) for an analysis of the social and political context of regulation sustaining the postwar boom, the interaction between the institutions sustaining the mass market, and standardized mass production; this work also explores the concept of an emerging form of manufacturing responding to the conditions of the 1970s and 1980s, "flexible specialization", and the social networks which sustain it. See also Hirst and Zeitlin (1988).

7. For a useful analysis of Japan's social institutions which sustain its manufacturing performance, see Dore (1986a) and (1986b) and Friedman (1988).

8. For an account of these industrial districts, see Sabel (1989).

9. For an account of the dis-economies of competition and the role of a "public sphere" in promoting co-operation in industrial districts, see the Introduction to Hirst and Zeitlin (eds) (1988) and Hirst and Zeitlin (1989).

10. On trust relationships and patterns of co-operation between firms, see Lorenz's comparative study of Lyons and the West Midlands (1989).

11. For an account of corporatism in small states in western Europe and its role in macroeconomic stabilization and manufacturing success, see Katzenstein (1984) and (1985).

12. See Bobbio (1987) and (1988).

13. See Dahl (1985).

14. See Bowles and Gintis (1986); Cohen and Rogers (1983); Keane (1988); Laclau and Mouffe (1985); Mouffe (1988); Rustin (1985) and Walzer (1983).

15. Most of the writers considered above define citizenship in terms of active political participation, but there is also a Marshallian use of citizenship in terms of the social rights that all members of society should enjoy by virtue of their common belonging and to have the minimum conditions necessary to independence. T.H. Marshall defined this concept in his "Citizenship and social class", in Marshall (1963) and it has been taken up, among others, by Plant (1988). This conception tends to fit better with traditional Labour Party collectivism than the more activist republican versions of the concept.

16. For accounts of republicanism in the eighteenth century, see Pocock (1975) and Venturi (1971).

17. See Weber (1919/1948).

18. For a more elaborate account than *A Preface to Democratic Theory* see Dahl (1982), and also for a defence of pluralism as a theory of political competition and an attempt to argue its consistency with corporatism, see Hirst (1990a) Ch. 3.

19. For an attempt to develop this concept of a party as a "social leader" in a process of bargaining leading to a social pact, see Hirst (1989).

20. For Proudhon's ideas and also the social institutions in terms of which they were credible, see Vincent (1984); for industrial districts and institutions of economic

co-operation in them, see Sabel and Zeitlin (1985).

21. For Durkheim and the solidarist tradition, see Hayward (1960).

22. For English Guild Socialism, see Glass (1966) and Wright (1979); for English political pluralism, see Nicholls (1975) and Hirst (1989b), Introduction.

23. For an attempt to adapt the associationalist socialist tradition to modern conditions and to link it to received forms of corporatism, see Hirst (1990a) Chs 5 and 6.

Part II

Democracy and civil society

6

Quangos and democratic government

Assessments of how democratic a country is concentrate on the degree to which government is accountable to the people and the effectiveness of the means of ensuring accountability. For a government to be properly accountable its decisions and actions must be transparent, and the people and their representatives must have ready remedies with which to sanction poor governmental performance. Quangos must thus be, almost by definition, a matter of concern for anyone committed to democratic accountability, for they place public money and government functions in the hands of unelected persons whose links to the elected bodies that supervise government are tenuous at best.

For this reason quangos have been an issue of public concern in Britain since roughly the mid 1970s. This concern has two peaks, the late 1970s when it was expressed by the right, and the early 1990s when it came from the liberal left. In the 1970s it was Conservatives who saw such quasi-state bodies as the Manpower Services Commission as a symptom of a rapidly developing corporatist state and thus a danger to the power of elected governments and the sovereignty of Parliament.[1] Conservatives feared that such quasi-autonomous bodies made both public policy and public expenditure difficult to direct and control from the centre.

Despite promising to cut back the tentacles of the quango state the Conservatives have done nothing of the kind. They have curtailed the role of corporatist representation and abolished some organizations (like the National Economic Development Office (NEDO)) but have greatly expanded the scale and role of quangos. Thus in the early 1990s concern was voiced about the enormous growth in government through unelected bodies. The issue now was not the power of organized social interests as against elected representatives, but of new market-orientated and managerially run institutions that substituted consumer responsiveness and bureaucratic hierarchy for political accountability. It is the Conservatives who have created a new and much larger quango state on the back of the one they strove to curtail in 1979. The key issues are the sheer number of such unelected governmental bodies, the scope and scale of the public functions they perform, the high proportion of public expenditure that they administer, and the unrepresentativeness and political bias of their personnel.

John Stewart focused this concern in his telling phrase the "New Magistracy", raising the spectre of an unelected quangocracy ruling the country like the old Justices of the Peace.[2] He charts the shift from a prevailing conception of public accountability being realized through political mechanisms, such as elected local governments, to the very different and much weaker conception of accountability through the market satisfaction of consumers and through contract compliance, an accountability in the hands of accountants. Likewise Weir and Hall (1994), editing the Democratic Audit of the United Kingdom, in its survey of quangos, *Ego-Trip*, catalogued the vast scale of extra-governmental bodies (EGOs) performing public functions, and outlined the constitutionally ambiguous position of these institutions in terms of accountability to Parliament.

The public discussion of quangos thus focuses on the issue of "accountability", and specifically accountability to elected bodies and through them to the people. The danger in the rhetoric of the growth of "unaccountable" government is that we tend to fall back on existing forms of political accountability as if they were unproblematic. There is now a serious issue about the degree to which representative institutions can render government in general accountable and not just quangos. The issue at stake is not merely whether the policies of the Conservatives since 1979 have led to deviation from the norm of accountable and representative government, but whether there is a viable *status quo anti* to which we can return. We must extend the question of accountability beyond quangos and question the current effectiveness of traditional mechanisms of accountability. The growth of quangos is just one, unimaginative and undemocratic, solution to a general crisis of representative government and to a specific crisis of government in the UK.

The main themes of this essay are as follows:

1. That the core institutions that ensure representative government originated in the eighteenth century and were developed in the nineteenth, whereas since the beginning of this century the scale and scope of state functions and public administration has expanded beyond the capacity of such institutions for competent supervision.
2. That the UK has suffered particularly from this general problem. Because of its unwritten Constitution, the obsession with preserving parliamentary sovereignty, and the growing concentration of power in the executive, the UK has found it difficult to create a stable and well-defined relationship between central and subsidiary governmental powers and also between the state and the public institutions of the wider society.[3]

3. That the solutions to the general problem of accountability and its specifically sharp form in the UK require that the traditional institutions of representative democracy be supplemented by new institutions that give greater powers to citizens and that re-draw the boundaries between public authority and civil society.

6.1 The limits of representative democracy

Quangos must thus be placed in a wider framework if the problems of accountability they pose are to be fully understood. The crisis created by the growth of quangos should lead us to reconsider the foundations of our democracy and renew them. The basic institutions of modern representative government are now quite old, they have been with us since the 1780s. Democratic franchises were gradually added to these institutions and in most countries fully democratic electorates were only created well into the twentieth century. These representative institutions, and specifically the supervision of the executive by the legislature, were designed for small governments, with a limited range of activities, and outside of the armed forces, a small number of personnel. Thus these institutions superintended what were in effect "nightwatchman" states and substantially self-regulating societies. The relationship between government and parliament was intimate and could rely primarily on informal knowledge, and the role of legislation was limited, with Bills relatively few in number and simple in content.

Modern omnicompetent public service states and the large official bureaucracies that go with them were superimposed on these institutions of representative government. The combination of eighteenth-century constitutionalism, nineteenth-century liberalism, and modern big government and mass democracy worked well enough for most of this century and only began to pull apart quite recently. The reason for this relative harmony between very different types of institution is that most of the new public services were collectivist. They were uniform in administration and universal in provision, with the result that they could be administered through stable bureaucratic hierarchies and fixed rules.[4] These were relatively straightforward to supervise. Moreover, the common people (who formed the democratic publics of the new collectivist and industrial states) were happy enough to be protected from common contingencies, like sickness or unemployment, or offered standard basic services, like elementary education or public housing. Democracy could appear to be a matter of voters choosing between parties in terms of their promises with regard to such services.

The state's ability to protect citizens from the vagaries of the market and yet not exercise excessive administrative discretion helped both to maintain the arm's-length relationship between governors and governed necessary to a liberal society and to simplify the task of democratic supervision. Keynesian macroeconomic management in the UK preserved both the autonomy of private property and the structures of liberal government. A small elite of civil servants controlled the level of economic activity through relatively traditional policy mechanisms and under the overall policy supervision of ministers. Moreover, to the extent that government dealt directly with industry, it was assisted by the fact that employment and output were highly concentrated in a small number of mainly nationally owned firms.

These saving features of the relationship between big government and liberal democratic accountability have diminished rapidly and radically, especially since the early 1970s. In western industrial states the great postwar boom promoted a growth in public spending and the range of public services. The public sector rapidly outgrew the old collectivist security state, leading to a system of such complexity that it is difficult to control by traditional mechanisms of political accountability. Moreover, modern publics have become more demanding, better educated and less differential. Their attitude to public services has changed from one of gratitude to a consumer consciousness. They demand higher quality and also more diverse services of greater complexity. Whereas they were once satisfied with elementary education and payment of the doctor's bill, the majority are coming to expect things like higher education or organ transplants as a right. They demand legal and administrative protection from a far wider and more differentiated range of contingencies, particularly in the environmental field. As the expectations of the majority have risen, so the willingness of a core constituency of the successful to accept and pay for the old basic collectivist services has declined. Those old simple and standard services succeeded in their own terms – they enabled people to escape poverty and insecurity. But as they did so the needs and attitudes of the majority of recipients of the services changed, and they created a demand for a more complex and differentiated public service state.

The majority of the population are no longer the struggling unskilled manual workers and their families that they were at the beginning of the century. Yet as a large part of the population has become more prosperous and more demanding in its expectations of what it will pay the government to provide, massive constraints have been placed on public expenditure and provision in the UK by successive economic crises and mass unemployment. Thus economic stresses have produced renewed demand for basic welfare services at the same time as the demand for enhanced services has risen. This has made administration more complex, has placed constraints on public expenditure, and has made it difficult to determine the main direction of policy – providing basic services like income support and social housing that sustain the poor, or providing differentiated high-quality services for those who are prosperous enough to protect themselves against basic contingencies.

Secondly, from the 1973 oil price crisis onwards, the economies of almost all the advanced industrial countries have changed in ways that have made economic governance by the national state much more difficult. These economies have internationalized even further, being severely constrained by the outcomes of international financial markets and also facing intensified foreign competition in trade and manufacturing. These economies have also become more diverse and complex internally, generating features such as the following that made government regulation more problematic:

1. Technological change has accelerated to a point where a centrally directed "industrial policy" that attempts to manage change and "pick winners" has become all but impossible.
2. The population of firms has differentiated in size, structure and management style; large firms no longer enjoy an inherent competitive advantage (as the examples of US Steel and IBM show), the result is that governments have to deal with a much more complex business sector and, in particular, have to pay attention to the conditions that enable small and medium-sized enterprises to prosper.
3. Divisions of labour have changed out of all recognition and labour markets have differentiated, making the working population less homogeneous, and creating new problems for training policy, labour market policy and workers rights.
4. Centralized corporatist structures based on large firms and stable industrial labour forces have lost some of their salience, thus weakening co-operative economic governance between industry, labour and the state.[5]

The upshot of all these international and internal changes is that modern economies cannot be directly and quickly changed in their performance by the macroeconomic policies of the medium-sized nation states.[6] Such economies are less "national", so that governments have less control of the economy and so the success or failure of their policies is more difficult to judge and hold to account. The two most effective methods of economic regulation – Keynesian demand management and economic co-ordination through the co-operation and bargaining of the central organized economic interests – are no longer readily available. Instead, if governments are to intervene they require more complex and localized knowledge. If they are to promote successful economic performance they need to be able to tailor policies toward difficult areas like industrial training, collective services for manufacturing, and local investment.

Many countries have been aided in coping with these problems of changing mechanisms of economic regulation by having effective regional governments that have the local knowledge to aid industry, and also well-structured industrial districts that can provide collective services to industry through public–private co-operation.[7] They have also benefited from extended dialogue between the organized interests at local level and thus the possibility of wider co-operation that can survive the demise of highly centralized corporatist bargaining. In general the scope for top-down bureaucratic control, whether public or private, is now much less. Most large bureaucracies lack the high-quality local knowledge and the responsiveness for effective responses to a complex and rapidly changing economic environment.

The UK, lacking regional governments, having allowed its industrial districts to decline into insignificance, and having set its face against dialogue and co-operation between management and labour because it smacks of "corporatism", has found itself ill-placed to cope with the new demands for public intervention in the economy.[8] It has continued to pursue centralized and highly ambitious macroeconomic policies – behaving as if the only thing obsolete in the post-Keynesian era is Keynes himself. Where it has tried to deliver services to industry it has done so in top-down forms through quangos like UDAs and TECs that do not really involve the full range of local interests or give them a say in policy. This combination of macroeconomic ruthlessness in Whitehall and undemo-cratic quangoism in the regions is a major contributing factor to the failure of UK manufacturing and the poor performance of the British economy.[9]

Thirdly, in the Anglo-Saxon states in particular (though the tendency is observable throughout the advanced world), publics have become more tax averse. This is partly because the participation of the majority of the population in direct taxation is a relatively recent phenomenon but also because they have competing demands for the private provision of enhanced services. Low growth has constrained citizens and governments alike. In the USA for example real incomes for the bulk of the employed population are stagnant or have fallen since the 1970s. In this context governments find it difficult to avoid constraints by generating additional public funding out of growth. States also now enjoy less autonomy in fiscal policy in an internationalized and highly competitive world economy.

The result has been that demands for high-quality responsive public services that are necessarily expensive have rocketed, and yet governments have faced severe constraints on their ability to pay for these services either out of the consumers' own pockets or by borrowing. The result has been to put immense pressures on the public sector, both in the simple form of expenditure cuts, and in the more demanding form of needing to deliver high-quality cost-efficient services. In the past basic services were sufficient and/or additions could be paid for out of an expanding budget. Now the pressures towards quality and efficiency demand responses that traditional bureaucracies and the old forms of accountability that went with them find difficult to provide. Public sectors throughout the advanced world have faced a period of intense turbulence and have sought new models of funding, organization and service delivery.

The result of these changes has been to put a strain on the relationship between government and accountability. Government has become complex and increasingly diverse. Far from being stable it has been involved in a continuous process of experiment to cope with the demands and constraints under which it operates. The scale and scope of legislation has grown. Societies are anything but self-regulating, nor can they rely on big bureaucracies (public and private) efficiently to manage their own internal affairs. Citizens' demands for protection against risks have grown. Societies have become less uniform and less easy to regulate by general rules. The result has been an explosion of legislation against multiple and changing contingencies, forcing frequent changes in rules and a proliferation in their provisions. Legislatures throughout the advanced world have become virtual law factories, churning out rules and sanctioning powers of administrative regulation at a rate that makes detailed scrutiny almost impossible.

These are problems that are common to almost all advanced countries. The tasks of government have become more difficult, the satisfaction of citizens with government has become less as the expectations they have placed upon it have become greater, and the capacity of representative institutions to supervise administration, always threatened by the rise of big government, has diminished to the point of crisis. Legislators and elected officials are marooned at the centre of states that have finally grown beyond the capacity of nineteenth-century representative democratic institutions to supervise.

If this problem has become general and acute in the last 20 years, it is at its sharpest in the UK. The reason is that the UK has had an under-developed version of the liberal democratic constitutional state, it has long put pragmatics and policy at the heart of democratic politics rather than a formal architecture of constitutionally ordered political institutions. Indeed, the very features that have made British government effective in the past and enabled it to make rapid decisions – that is, the concentration of power in Whitehall and parliamentary sovereignty – are now liabilities when more decentralized, open, and responsive forces of power have become necessary.[10] The defining features of the British system of government – an unwritten constitution, the absence of codified and entrenched citizens rights, the dominance of the executive over the legislative through prime ministerial power and the disciplines of the party system, the loose doctrine of ministerial responsibility, and the relative underdevelopment of a system of administrative law – mean that the UK's mechanisms for the supervision and restraint of government are very much at the mercy of government.[11]

The massive growth of quangos can be seen as a response to the general problems of government outlined above within the context of the UK system of highly centralized power and attenuated accountability. Undoubtedly the extensive use of quangos owes much to the Conservatives' mistrust of local government and to the belief that government can be reinvigorated by private-sector practices and personnel. It is also true that English local government was ill-adapted to take on and manage the new tasks of government and also that many British institutions like the nationalized industries and the NHS were in a state of advanced bureaucratic sclerosis. However, the extent to which the quango model has been used exceeds explanations based on either ideology or previous administrative failure. Quangos have penetrated not only into every area of government, but their influence extends throughout the wider society and to an extensive range of non-state institutions. One of the reasons for this spread of quangos is that not only were the institutions of central and local government ill-adapted to the changing environment in which they had to operate, but that the relationship between the state and the wider society in the UK had become extremely problematic by the time Mrs Thatcher came to power.

6.2 Democracy and civil society

Quangos have not only come to undertake functions hitherto directly performed by central and local government, they have also intruded into the state's relation to the wider society and have come to exercise governance functions in relation to public bodies, voluntary associations and private firms. The growth of the quango state has significantly transformed the relation of government to public (but non-state) bodies like the universities, and to private bodies of some consequence to public policy (like housing associations).

Every society has a political constitution that defines and limits the power of the state, but it also has what we may call a "social constitution", that is, a complex of laws, practices and procedures that defines the ways in which the political institutions and the wider society interact. This social constitution is more diffuse and less formal, but it is nonetheless real, and its effective working is crucial to the health of democracy in the wider sense, as government balanced by an open and pluralistic society. The relation of the state and those activities that it regulates is normally thought of in terms of the concept of "civil society". Civil society is frequently thought of as a private sphere composed of individuals and their associations – as a spontaneous order that should be independent of the state in a democratic country. The problem with this traditional liberal view of civil society is that in emphasizing the independence of society from government it tends to ignore the fact that many of the components of this wider society are not spontaneous. Rather "civil society" is made up of institutions, associations and corporate bodies whose powers are defined and regulated by the state. Modern industrial societies do not just include the state and private individuals, they are also made up of many large and complex organizations such as professional bodies, broadcasting networks, major charities, trade unions, and so on. How the state defines the powers of action and the forms of internal governance of such associations and organizations, the degree to which it intervenes to affect their workings, is central to the workings of democracy.

The issue here is that a democratic state must ensure that such organizations do not violate the rights and interests of its citizens, but also that such organizations enjoy an appropriate measure of decision-making autonomy and self-government. Many of the institutions can be regarded either as private, or as non-state but public, agencies of governance of an area of activity; they are of political consequence in the widest sense. This is especially true if they are in receipt of public funds and/or perform roles the government has delegated to such agencies. Thus citizens can expect that charities receiving public money for public purposes are accountable and regulated, or that self-regulating organized markets like the Stock Exchange deal fairly with the public. The issue is how this is done, whether government is too intrusive or too lax in its regulation.

I would contend that the UK's social constitution is now as problematic in its workings as is its unwritten political constitution. A good part of the reason is that government is either excessively interventionist, for example, in the way government departments and quangos control charities in receipt of public funds, thus bureaucratizing the voluntary sector, or excessively non-interventionist, for example, allowing too lax a self-regulation in the financial services sector. The use of quangos in relation to the non-state sector has grown considerably but it has neither increased democratic – as opposed to managerial – accountability, nor has it directly empowered citizens in their dealings with such bodies and associations. The general tendency of government (with significant exceptions in the financial and business sectors) is to increase its direct and indirect control over such bodies, whilst failing to protect and enhance forms of democratic self-governance within such bodies.

Until the early 1960s in the UK, the general response across the political spectrum would have been that the relationship between the state and the wider society – the social constitution – was reasonably satisfactory. The social constitution at that time had three main features:

1. Control by an Establishment
2. Self-regulation and voluntarism
3. An arms'-length relationship between government and the major public but non-state bodies.

These features were seen to have several advantages: they minimized the need for formal regulation; they ensured, through the common presence of like-minded personnel, a measure of consistency in the way the different institutions behaved; and they achieved a balance between public funding and the autonomy of public but non-state institutions.[12]

The interlocking elites of the Establishment meant that central government, big business, the media, the universities, the Anglican Church, and so on, shared common perceptions and followed broadly similar unwritten codes of conduct. Self-regulation and voluntarism allowed major social activities to be governed with minimal state intervention. Thus limited companies were regarded as little republics of their shareholders, investors being protected by their rights under company law to participate in company governance. The Stock Exchange was in essence like a club, its rules being made and policed by its members. Trade unions were purely voluntary bodies, but were given the privilege of certain legal immunities from damages arising from trade disputes. Institutions like the BBC, the Arts Council, and the University Grants Commission made it possible for the state to fund activities like the arts or higher education whilst leaving it to the appointed members of such bodies to make decisions about policy and the distribution of resources without overt intervention by Ministers or civil servants.

Why did this very particular and extremely British pattern of informal social governance develop? The main reason is due to the nature of the UK's central political institutions as they evolved from the eighteenth century onwards. The UK, unlike many continental states, did not bring the majority of its major social institutions within the public realm or subject private activities to close legal and administrative regulation. The reason is less to do with Britain's ancient traditions of liberty than with the limited scope for such developments within the unwritten constitution. Because of the legislative sovereignty of parliament, because of the considerable discretionary power of the executive centralized in Whitehall, and because the unwritten constitution excluded the entrenchment of rights and powers, it was almost impossible to create a system of constitutionally ordered lesser authorities and public but non-state bodies. Except for the dominant core political institutions, all other bodies, public and private, had to be constitutionally makeshift and to exist at the central states' fiat.[13]

Hence the attractions of the voluntary, the quasi-private and the informal governance of social affairs. Self-regulation was a way to escape from inclusion within the state or from legal regulation without constitutional protection. The unions, for example, preferred to be voluntary bodies rather than accept a system of positive labour law that would be subject to the changing whims of a sovereign parliament. What they wanted from parliament was legal immunities, not active regulation.

105

Lastly, many British institutions developed before large-scale industrial and social organization became the norm. In a world of local and face-to-face commercial and social relations, informality made good sense. Lloyds grew out of a coffee house and provincial stock markets from the private and informal meetings of traders. Voluntarism was attractive in this period because the alternative had been the privileged monopoly corporations established by Act of Parliament, favouring the few and excluding the mass of traders.

These facts underlay and helped to sustain the notion of the continuity and exceptionalism of British social institutions. Like the unwritten constitution they were a uniquely British inheritance. Until very recently the traditions of voluntarism and self-regulation were seen as assets, as part of a viable and distinctly British way of doing things. However, by the 1960s questions were beginning to be raised about aspects of this relatively stable pattern of social governance. In particular many politicians and commentators, Conservative and Labour, thought that the unions needed more formal legal regulation. But in the main politicians and informed opinion remained happy with the informality and self-regulation characteristic of the social constitution, much as they did with the major political institutions and the unwritten constitution.

The same could hardly be said today. The unwritten constitution survived so well because its practices and conventions compensated for the fact that the UK's formal political institutions were obsolete by international standards. The gradual collapse of shared understandings among politicians that began to be a serious problem in the mid 1970s undermined the supports for the existing settlement. Mrs Thatcher's tendency in office to treat the unwritten constitution as if it were written, stretching the limits of convention to party political advantage where practices were not explicitly prohibited, gravely damaged the old system.[14]

The social constitution worked well enough for similar reasons but it too began to come under pressure at about the same time. It worked and had some definite advantages, provided four conditions were met. First, that governments accepted the practice of voluntarily limiting their intervention in the affairs of public but non-state bodies like the BBC. Ministers generally recognized the need for bipartisan appointments to governing bodies and the need to let institutions make policy, refraining from imposing explicit agendas or extending central government control.

Secondly, this system was tolerable when private self-regulating institutions controlled activities that were primarily the concern of their own members, where those members were willing to bear the risks involved, and where others who were affected were prepared to defer to such informal governance. The London Stock Exchange developed as a self-regulating body, for example, at a time when private investors were the norm. But by the 1970s the main investors were financial institutions trading in order to generate financial assets for members of the public who had taken out insurance policies or pension plans. Informality would seem an inadequate protection for such indirect and unrepresented stakeholders.

Thirdly, informality made sense when the elites were small and their members shared a common background and, in the main, abided by the unwritten rules. The Establishment was overwhelmingly public school and Oxbridge educated, and to a considerable degree our elites still are. What put paid to such cohesion was internationalization – for example, the entry of foreign banks and institutions into UK financial markets on a large scale, and also domestic social mobility, producing less a change in personnel at the top than a lessening of the willingness of those below them to practice deference and trust.

Fourthly, social governance through informality worked when tacit and essentially local knowledge was adequate to ensure members' effective participation and when insiders' perceptions were an effective check on adherence to informal codes by the majority of those involved.

Britain could not remain the clubby self-enclosed society its elites had shaped and simultaneously remain an effective competitor in dynamic internationalized markets and accommodate the modest measure of social mobility created by the post-1945 welfare state – in particular its broadening of access to education. Informality could only survive on the basis of parochialism and exclusivity. However, the wider world was less inclined to accept the amateur and private government of institutions like major financial markets, nor would the new educated middle classes continue to defer to the Establishment forever.[15]

In the later 1960s and the 1970s economic and social turbulence shook many established institutions to their foundations. Conservative and Labour administrations tried to modernize Britain, but without changing the fundamentals of its social constitution. This is a major reason why they failed. Both major parties experimented with corporatism. Labour in particular tried to reform economic governance with quasi-state bodies like the Industrial Reorganisation Commission and the Manpower Services Commission. The result was an incoherent compromise. Britain became corporatist enough for organized labour and the representatives of big business to have tremendous influence. It did not become corporatist enough to ensure genuine and ongoing co-operation between the major organized economic interests. It was, therefore, unable to achieve effective economic regulation through co-ordination of action between industry, labour and the state. Both individual firms and unions clung to voluntarism and self-regulation. Employers' organizations and the TUC were unable to enforce collective discipline on their members or make sure that top-level bargains would stick, as was the case in countries like Germany or Sweden.[16]

Governments of both political colours remained committed to Westminster executive discretion and exclusive party rule, refusing to concede a sufficient degree of joint and collaborative control over economic policy to the social interests or to obtain the co-operation of non-ruling parties. Mrs Thatcher's victory in 1979 after the disastrous collapse of government–union collaboration in the "winter of discontent", and her conviction that the corporatist state needed to be demolished, ended any remaining chance that the UK would evolve in a continental Social or Christian Democratic direction.

Mrs Thatcher's Government was also committed to the thoroughgoing internationalization of British financial markets and to ending the rule of a cosy bipartisan Establishment. In theory, therefore, the Conservatives ought to have reformed Britain's social institutions on a coherent neoliberal programme. Yet Thatcher, no less than Wilson or Heath, failed to comprehensively modernize Britain's institutions of social governance. The Conservative governments of the 1980s failed to remodel the public but non-state and the major private organizations in a coherent and democratic way. A market-based but well-regulated, transparent and meritocratic neoliberal system remained a matter of rhetoric.

Three tendencies have prevailed in Conservative policy in reshaping the social constitution since 1979. The first is to centralize power and to subject to active government intervention public bodies like the Arts Council, the BBC and the universities that had been perceived internationally as the success stories of the arm's-length approach. Moreover, the government extended its influence over and active management of voluntary bodies and charities, using the lever of public funds. Bodies like the Housing Associations or the Citizen's Advice Bureaux were forced to managerialize themselves and to accept Whitehall imposed agendas.

The second (as we have noted above) is that, far from abolishing quangos as promised in 1979, the Conservative governments have multiplied them and given them central roles in the provision of services and the regulation of activities that might have been assigned to or remained with more accountable public but non-state institutions. The top management of such quangos has been selected in the main on a highly partisan basis, creating a vast new domain of government patronage. Those affected by quangos' activities have been given no say over their policy and no means of democratic challenge, short of electing a non-Conservative government at Westminster. To take one example out of the vast number of these quangos that give cause for concern, the Urban Development Agencies have extensive discretionary powers, are independent of local authorities, and are not accountable to local residents.

The third tendency has been that central elements of the old system of self-regulation have been left undisturbed. This is the case even though in the financial sector the institutions in question handle billions of pounds of British citizens' and foreign investors' money. Lloyds, the London Stock Exchange, and the pensions and insurance industries have been left to govern themselves, despite pressing needs to meet international standards of public governance and disclosure. The government continues to treat as "private" matters for company managements, issues of major public concern such as the sale of Rover to BMW. In these cases the continuation of informality and self-regulation is indefensible and will ultimately undermine the UK's reputation for reliability, and therefore, its competitiveness in major international industries.

The central flaw in this approach to the governance of non-state institutions and publicly consequential activities is that it has been shaped by no coherent model of how an advanced democratic market society should be run. Standards have been inconsistent and no explicit public debate about how to proceed has been encouraged by the Conservatives. Inconsistency is the rule, and *ad hoc* action and secrecy too often the norm. The Conservatives have been strongly interventionist in certain sectors and yet indulgently tolerant of continuing self-regulation in others. Powerful and undeclared vested interests, changing prejudices and fashionable theories, and the tendency of Whitehall to seek ever greater control, have all had a part in shaping the outcome.

The inconsistency of devising means for the governance for the whole of civil society by an exclusive party government elected on a minority of the votes cast and consistently minded to act in a highly partisan spirit should be all too obvious. To be effective such forms of governance of public and private organizations need to be widely agreed, to follow clear and common models, and to be easily understood by those involved. The old informal system had at least the advantages that it was consensual and well understood within the key elites. If the majority of the British public was excluded by the clubbyness of the old system, it is no less excluded by the complexity, haphazardness and insider dominance of the new. The new insiders are slightly different from the old – less cohesive in origins and more committed to managerialism. But they are no less members of an exclusive and unaccountable elite.

This is not just an issue of domestic political concern. How well British institutions work is also a matter of the country's long-term international competitiveness. This is obvious in the case of foreign investors, who want a well-run and secure financial system, but it is no less a matter of concern, for example, that British universities are seen to be free of unwarranted government interference if they are to gain a growing share of the market in foreign students. Building up democratically accountable social institutions is part of being a modern open society, a necessity in an internationalizing world where social efficiency is one of the key sources of competitive advantage. Complex, closed and capricious institutional cultures are both inefficient and a deterrent to foreign investors, consumers, and internationally mobile talented professionals.

This latter point is reinforced in its saliency because Britain is a member of the European Union. The Union is continuing to evolve common legal standards and regulatory practices that will have a major impact on British companies, organized markets, quasi-public institutions, and the voluntary sector. Just as the unwritten constitution makes it difficult to assess the impact of political change on Britain coming from the EU, so the incoherence of Britain's civil constitution means that it will be in danger of importing a great deal of standards of social governance piecemeal and without public debate. The UK can have little chance of a coherent policy on this issue whilst its social institutions remain in such a mess. It will have little idea of what to promote among its European partners, or what it wants to resist at all costs becoming the European norm.[17]

Some of the UK's traditions of voluntarism and informality are genuinely valuable. Strictly voluntary associations, charities, and clubs have played an important part in its social life and it is healthy that they should continue to do so. The point is not to insist that everything be legally regulated and bureaucratized, quite the contrary. Power, whether state, public, or private must be clearly defined, its workings be transparent, and its exercise accountable to those affected by it. Voluntary organizations in particular cannot prosper in a highly centralized state where power is concentrated in unaccountable government institutions, and in quasi-public and corporate bureaucracies.

To achieve this transparency and accountability requires the categories of state, public, and private institutions to be clearly defined and their powers circumscribed. The present system allows government and other powerful actors to play fast and loose with the categories of public and private. For example, monopolies and mergers, takeover rules, the operation of organized markets, and company governance generally, can all be presented as "private" matters when it suits the government to do so. Similarly, the autonomy of quangos can be emphasized when the government wishes to avoid awkward issues, blaming job losses in the NHS on trust managements, and yet as paymaster and standard-setter it can direct the affairs of trusts when it wishes. This gives government the discretion to intervene when it wants to and to let decisions happen by default when it does not. This is advantageous to ruling politicians and insiders, but it can hardly be in the interests of the public.

The UK has not resolved the conflicts that have arisen once the old informal system of self-regulation and elite control became obsolete. To do so will require more than tinkering and piecemeal reform. To resolve those conflicts will require extended public debate and the development of a model of how an advanced, open and democratic society should be run that is acceptable to a large part of informed opinion.

6.3 How can democratic accountability be enhanced?

The foregoing argument has made two points. First, that it is not a wholly effective response to the overuse and the excessive powers of quangos to reassert an established norm of representative democratic accountability. Quangos are part of a strategy, however ineffective it may be, of responding to these major problems of modern governance that also make democratic control by elected representative increasingly difficult. Secondly, we cannot treat the issue of quangos on its own, as if it were merely a matter of an ill-conceived policy on the part of the recent Conservative governments. Quangos are part of a much wider problem of the relationship between the state and civil society. Despite nostalgia for the UK's old social constitution, its informal arrangements and unwritten understandings were no longer adequate in a world that demands openness and has rejected defence.

To raise the issue of the weakness of representative democratic account-ability is to enter dangerous ground. Too often in the past the deficiencies of representative government were raised in order to argue that it be replaced by some other system that did not rely on multiparty competition for the votes of all adult citizens. Obvious examples are the Marxist and radical advocacy of direct non-party democracy. Direct democracy has never been a viable option for democratic accountability in large and complex states and societies. For the purposes of giving all citizens power over their governors and of conferring legitimacy on core governmental institutions there is no realistic alternative to representative democracy. However dissatisfied we may be with present forms of accountability, we shall have to adapt and supplement the institutions we have.

If radical direct democracy is no solution, then recent "quick-fix" attempts to involve citizens in government through electronic referenda or citizen's juries are hardly a satisfactory solution either. The basic limitation of such solutions is that while they may involve citizens in some high-profile decisions and may involve the public in consultation on the formulation of some policies, they cannot superintend the regular workings of modern large-scale government. Furthermore, electronic democracy is likely to be only partially inclusive. It will leave many citizens uninvolved and uncomprehending, especially those who currently underparticipate in politics. The problem would be especially acute if these quick fixes were added to the present highly centralized state as a palliative, for it could just as likely enhance the power of the governors over the governed as it would increase democratic input. It could supplement government power with the gizmos of electronic legitimacy, enabling politicians to mobilize consent on certain key issues whilst leaving others unaddressed.

If the objective of reform is to be to renew democratic accountability then we need to begin to tackle the problems of the current scale and complexity of government at root. Undoubtedly short-term measures to make quangos more politically accountable in conventional ways and their personnel more broadly representative are necessary; the sheer size of the quango state means that it can hardly be transformed overnight. But the way in which and the level at which governance functions are performed also needs to be changed, and this would be necessary even if a strategy of increasing existing powers of central government bodies had been followed instead of combining that with quangoism.

How might such reform be undertaken? Space forbids more than an outline here. The essential task is to simplify government and devolve its powers so that the existing institutions of representative democratic accountability can begin to function somewhat as they were intended to do in the nineteenth century. The aim must be to simplify the core institutions of government and the role of legislation, without abandoning governance functions or reducing the public services or welfare provision that are essential to a well-managed modern industrial society.

This problem was perceived by the right in the 1970s in terms of governmental overload; their objective being to reduce the scale and scope of government by having it shed facilities and provision. This programme relied on giving publicly provided services and regulatory tasks to markets. The market was seen as *alternative* to government as a means of co-ordination and control in and of itself. The economic liberal diagnosis was partially correct; big government is unaccountable and unresponsive to citizens, even if the free-market remedy was inappropriate. Weakly regulated markets cannot substitute themselves for the functions of government; they tend to undermine that minimum of social solidarity and economic security among citizens necessary to a cohesive and active democratic society, and, worst of all, they tend to undermine the long-term capacity of the economy to promote investment and infrastructure.

The solution lies not with less government but with the restructuring of the state and the redrawing of the relationship between the public and the private spheres. This involves three distinct but complimentary strategies of reform. The first is relatively conventional, if radical, in so highly centralized a state as the UK. That is political decentralization – devolving powers to elected regional governments with legislative and fiscal powers. Regional governments are effective means of promoting local economic governance, as a great deal of international comparative evidence demonstrates that they are likely to have effective local knowledge and are able to promote consent and involvement through dialogue with local representative bodies like trade associations, unions etc., in areas like collective services to industry and locally relevant education and training.

Regional governments are large enough entities to effectively take over many of the functions of economic regulation, social provision and planning currently performed by central government. Current local authorities are too small to do more than provide a limited range of local services. Regional governments could take over the responsibility for rendering key quangos like UDAs and TECs more accountable. If local democracy is to be restored, the chances are that regional governments are a better bet than existing local authorities. If they acquire major functions of central government then they are more likely to attract the attention of voters; because they are bigger and more diverse they are less likely to become single-party "rotten boroughs" (especially if they are elected by PR), and as they will be of some consequence they are more likely to attract high-quality politicians than existing local authorities.

The second is radical and unconventional, that is, to devolve functions to self-governing voluntary associations and to assist them by the grant of public funds proportional to membership. Quangos are undemocratic organizations in receipt of public funds. In many cases they and government departments are pressing the voluntary sector to become more bureaucratic and managerial, more externally "accountable" and less internally demo-cratically accountable as a result. The voluntary sector remains one of the success stories in the UK – it is popular with and responsive to its members. The advantage of promoting the performance of governmental and public functions by voluntary associations is that they both reduce the admin-istrative load on government institutions and they can be directly account-able to their members – increasing the decentralization of democratic supervision. A radical shift in this direction would simplify the tasks of government, reducing its performance of now contradictory roles – that of service provider and that of overseeing the services provided.

The third solution is directly to democratize many quangos, like NHS trusts, higher education corporations, locally managed schools, HATS and so on, involving both their personnel and their service consumers in their boards of management, thus returning institutions to those involved in them rather than having them controlled by nominees who often do not use the services in question or know little about them.

If we accept that civil society is not just composed of private individuals, but also consists of institutions of relevance to the public and that receive public money, then we can see that "publicizing" civil society, by creating forms of democratic self-governance under the general superintendence of representative institutions, is a better solution than managerializing it and reducing the involvement of citizens in their services and institutions. This redrawing of the boundary between public and private, accepting democracy in civil society, also enables us to see a way of simplifying the scale and scope of legislation. If citizens are responsible for making their own rules for those activities of direct concern to them, then legislation need deal with fewer contingencies and guard directly against fewer risks and abuses. Legislation can be simpler if citizens have more remedies in their own hands. It can concentrate on protecting citizens from a more limited range of harms and act as a means of appeal, rather than as an initial remedy or all-purpose source of regulation.

Quangos are a means of farming-out government functions based on distrust of the public, the belief that they are best left as passive consumers, and a belief that administrative accountability through management procedures is preferable to democratic control. Reform of the quango state offers a chance to enhance democracy by giving greater say back to citizens, thereby both increasing the scope for active involvement and countering the widespread feeling of alienation from politics, and making the institutions of representative democracy more effective by reducing the scale of the government activities they superintend.

Notes

1. See, for example, Hailsham (1978).
2. "A new magistracy is being created in the sense that a non-elected elite are assuming responsibility for a large part of local governance". Stewart (1992).
3. See Marquand (1988).
4. See Mulgan (1994), Ch. 8.
5. For an account of these changes, see Piore and Sabel (1984).
6. It does not follow, of course, that national states are powerless in the face of globalization.
7. For the role of regional governments see Sabel (1989), and on industrial districts, see Zeitlin (1992).
8. On why industrial districts have disappeared in the UK, see Zeitlin (1994).
9. See Hirst and Zeitlin (1989).
10. See Barnett (1994), Introduction.
11. See Barnett, Ellis and Hirst (1993).
12. See Sampson (1962) which conveys this informal elite culture very well.
13. See Marquand (1988).
14. This approach is nowhere better conveyed than in Young (1989).
15. Hence the concern of intelligent economic liberals to have a written constitution in order to protect a market society, see Vibert (1991).
16. See Hirst (1991).
17. This is one of the reasons why intelligent Conservatives are concerned with constitutional reform, see Mount (1992).

7

Democracy and civil society

Democracy in modern times has always meant more than just a measure of popular control over the personnel and decisions of the state. A democratic state is widely held to be inconceivable without a democratic society. Hence the major modern political doctrines that have claimed to be democratic have all insisted that democracy involves a definite relationship between the state and the wider society. The doctrines in question – classical liberalism, democratic socialism and corporatism – have seen this relationship in different ways.[1] However, they have done so in relation to a shared conception of the modern state as a compulsory organization that claims a monopoly over the right to determine the forms of governance within a definite territory. However, in the late twentieth century both the state and the relationship it has to the wider society are being transformed as a result of profound social changes. This necessitates a radical rethinking of the role and scope of democratic governance, and the mainstream political doctrines are at best poor guides in this rethinking, and at worst obsolete.

7.1 The changing character of the state

The main changes altering the nature and position of the state are twofold. The first concerns its capacity to legitimate its powers of compulsion, to make claims on the lives and property of its members. In the era of total wars and savage internal social struggles these claims were supported because threats to political survival and social stability were very real. Citizens feared invading enemies and domestic attempts to seize power. With the collapse of the Soviet bloc as an external adversary and the disappearance of internal revolutionary movements, most advanced western societies no longer face serious enemies that require large-scale political and economic mobilization to counter them. Hence the territorial integrity of states in itself matters less to citizens and claims to state compulsion can no longer be founded on such genuine and shared fears.

The second main change concerns the growing dispersion of the capacities of governance to agencies "above" and "below" the nation state. The internationalization of economic and social relations has lessened the ability of the state to impose distinct "national" economic programmes.[2] For at least some of the "haves" this is a valuable form of liberty. Companies and citizens can use the international financial markets as a sanction, voting with their capital and their savings against state policies they see as imposing excessive costs. States have lost some of the economic coercive power over citizens they had in the era of punitive import duties and exchange controls. At the same time as some of the powers that national governments have claimed to possess over the economy have weakened, so many regional governments have become effective sources of economic regulation. Major cities and industrial districts are increasingly becoming social and political entities in their own right and national governments are, willingly or not, ceding powers to them. States are losing their monopoly over who governs in their territories; nation states are becoming just one (albeit vital) part of a division of labour in governance and the nature of that division is no longer under their exclusive control.

7.2 Classical liberalism and civil society

Given the eclipse of state socialism and the current generalized acceptance of markets as the main means of economic distribution, it follows that most practical politicians are in fact liberals of one variety or another. Thus it is necessary to begin our account of the contemporary relationship between state and civil society with classical liberalism. Central to liberalism is the distinction between the public and the private spheres. The public sphere is based on representative government and the rule of law; its purpose is both to govern and to protect the private sphere. The state's primary tasks are to protect private property and individual rights. Laws should be general norms, applicable to all citizens irrespective of status. The state is the public and political sphere, limited in its scope and functions. The private sphere is that of individual action, contract, and market exchange, protected by and yet independent of the state. Lawful association in civil society is a "private" matter.

Thus, since its inception liberal political theory has regarded its main objective as the preservation of an extensive sphere of private action independent of the state, and has seen this as an essential complement to and support of the formal political institutions of representative government. Modern pluralist theory, developing classical liberalism, argues that a society comprised of a wide variety of active "secondary associations" provides the basis for that diversity of interests and opinions that makes multi-party democracy sustainable in the primary association, the state. In recent years, adding to and developing classical liberalism, the concept of "civil society" has been redefined and become fashionable both in eastern and western Europe. It is seen as a source of authentically democratic social movements separate from and oppositional to the totalitarian or the bureaucratic business-oriented state.[3]

What all these positions have in common is a conception of the private sphere or civil society as a spontaneous order independent of and separate from the state. Modern libertarian radicals and the free-market right have a major common objective, that is, to protect civil society from encroachment by the state and hierarchical bureaucratic administration. They fear that either the spontaneous order of social life or the free market is being displaced. The right fear big government, and libertarian radicals fear both state bureaucracy and big business. Economic liberals like Hayek and post-Marxist radicals like Habermas seem unlikely bedfellows, but they share the belief that civil society is a spontaneous order. Hayek feared not just a state socialist command economy as a threat to freedom, but the steady process of bureaucratic encroachment on the market in the interests of welfare and regulation in a formally democratic society. The market can only function adequately if it is autonomous, and therefore spontaneous. The task of government is to guard it against excessive governance. Likewise, Habermas, for all his long and sophisticated reflection on the public and private spheres in modern society, fears that spontaneous substantively oriented interaction, the life world, is threatened by the domination of the formal bureaucratic rationality of the system.[4]

The problem with such views is not that excessive bureaucratic control over individuals by political and social institutions does not pose a threat to liberty. Rather, it is that this classical liberal legacy of conceiving civil society as a spontaneous order separate from government actually undermines the devising of effective remedies to the growth of unaccountable hierarchical power in both the public and the private spheres. The issue is no longer usefully posed in terms of either the autonomy of civil society from government or the restriction of the scope of public governance. In fact both state and civil society are made up of large complex organizations, and the boundary between the two is not all that clear. Seeking to preserve individual freedoms in and through civil society treats it as if it could be purely a realm of individual choice, contract, and voluntary association. The issue is better conceived as the freedom of individuals within institutions and the autonomy of institutions within their legitimate sphere. And thus how to achieve effective democratic governance of both public and private institutions.

If civil society is conceived *non-politically*, as spontaneous, private and prior to politics, then it will become an ever more marginal sphere. It will be those aspects of social action that are left over, that large public and private institutions do not organize. It would be what remains when the corporate economy, bureaucratically organized public services, and compulsory state regulation are subtracted. The answer is, of course, not much. The nation state may be losing certain capacities and some legitimacy, but this does not mean that the scale and scope of compulsory authority and top-down control are lessening in modern societies. Indeed, the relative weakening of the control of the state over certain domains, like national economic policy, may lessen its ability to check other organizations, like major companies, in the interests of democratic accountability and individual liberty.

Economic liberals have favoured deregulation and privatization as a means of reducing the role of the state, thereby restoring the power of markets. If anything this has worsened the crisis in the relationship between state and civil society. In privatization and deregulation, control and social power are not ceded to markets based on equal competing individuals, but to large hierarchically controlled organizations: to privatized utilities, to quangos and to private companies contracting out services. These bodies are not in the main voluntary associations, and in respect of them the citizen as employee or consumer mostly has little choice and less control. Typically such organizations are bureaucracies, which means that they subject their employees to imperative control and compulsion and they deal with the recipients of their services through standardized procedures. The lower ranks in such institutions obey orders from above and have no countervailing powers: they are subordinates. The recipients of services or customers depend for what they receive on administrative decisions beyond their control; the best they can hope for, if they are lucky, is that they can switch to buying from another unaccountable body that offers a better deal.

7.3 Confronting the organizational society

It is difficult to see how a political democracy can survive if individuals "private" lives are so controlled by undemocratic authority. The scope of democracy becomes limited and citizens have little experience of it. They become subordinates or consumers, and even their leisure time is dependent on the offerings of large business corporations. States may no longer have such well-founded grounds for the more draconian forms of coercion, but, in the absence of a new democratic political settlement, this does not alter the prosaic, day-to-day powers of most major social institutions, public or private. We have become habituated to a thousand minor but very real restrictions of our liberty, each trivial but as a whole making most of us less than fully free. Most people have little choice but to work for large organizations and to accept services and to buy products from them. We take the power of such institutions for granted, whether it be a private company telling its employees how to dress or how often they may go to the lavatory, or a Job Club determining how many letters an unemployed person must write in a week, or some blatant piece of insolence that undermines the dignity of the consumer and is justified as "company policy".

That such institutions may be notionally accountable – to their shareholders or to parliament – does not alter the compulsory and coercive character of their day-to-day workings in respect of individuals. On the contrary, such attenuated accountability merely legitimates such powers without giving those directly subject to them any control. Top-down hierarchical administration is at best a necessary evil in a free society. In a society that truly valued individual autonomy it would be justified only when there was no option – where no other or less coercive form of organization was available or sufficiently efficient for the activity in question. In a society where state coercion and compulsion have fewer objective justifications, the powers of major institutions proliferate. To restate the paradox with which Rousseau begins the *Social Contract* in a form appropriate to modern times: "citizens are told that they are participants in a free and democratic society, yet at every turn they are subject to the constraints of hierarchical administration without significant opportunities for control and consent".[5]

Rousseau asked, having posed his paradox, what could make it legitimate? The contemporary answers as to how to overcome our paradox are not encouraging. Positions derived from classical liberalism are inadequate to deal with these more complex issues of accountability because liberalism was designed to protect society *from* the state, rather than deal with the problems of liberty in a state and civil society dominated by large hierarchical institutions. In a period when statist and socialist solutions have become ineffective and politically unviable, we are left with a rhetoric of individual rights in politics and the advocacy of market principles in society. Trying to return to an idealized nineteenth-century relationship between state and civil society, as the most extreme economic liberals do, is evidently impossible – we cannot recreate a society of perfectly competing small traders and manufacturers in open markets. To recognize this is not just an issue of the economics of competition, it is also a problem for governance. The hegemony of liberalism means that most attempts to counter or meliorate weak economic regulation and social accountability are half-hearted or ineffective. Hence the weakness of communitarian rhetoric as a substitute for liberalism, its failure to confront the reform of institutions and its urging of consensus on deeply divided societies with plural and competing values.

If core activities of central concern to the life of the citizen like welfare, public services, and economic production are not to remain dominated by top-down administration, and if policy is not to become the prerogative of a managerial elite, then the whole of society and not just the state needs to be viewed politically, as a complex of institutions that requires a substantial measure of public and popular control over leading personnel and major decisions. That is, civil society must no longer be viewed as a "private" sphere, it needs to take on elements of "publicity" in the original sense of the term. We require a constitution for society as much as we do for the state. Once one recognizes that society is dominated by large-scale quasi-public and private institutions possessed of powers that dwarf those of many premodern states then the issue of their accountable governance becomes inescapable. We currently have an "uncivil" society: that is, one dominated by managerial elites, not one controlled by constitutionally ordered associations. The existing forms of governance have become threadbare – accountability to parliament for public services and to shareholders for the actions of managers in private firms. These forms of liberal accountability fail in the face not just of big government but also of an organizational society. Thus the major "private" institutions – for example, firms, media networks, major charities – need to be made accountable in some direct way to the major constituencies involved in or affected by them. Public or quasi-public institutions – for example, hospitals, schools, universities – need to give voice and choice both to service providers and to recipients. This is not an easy matter, especially when some of the most powerful private institutions are multinational, but a political discourse circumscribed by classical liberalism has no space in which to begin to pose this issue constructively.

Noberto Bobbio, seeking to advance democracy beyond the limits of classical liberalism but without compromising individual liberty, argued that the main issue for modern democracy was not just "who votes" but "where" they can vote.[6] Yet this issue has become ever more difficult. The idea of a "where" where one votes depends on there being readily identifiable and coherent constituencies of interest. But modern societies do not make it easy to enhance democracy by adding a supplementary franchise to existing non-political institutions; divisions of labour and institutional patterns are complex and rapidly changing. This has also undermined the conventional supplements to liberal democratic representation: corporatist interest group representation, and industrial democracy – giving the "workers" a say in firms through workers' councils or seats on the board. Corporatism is threatened by the decomposition of relatively homogeneous interest groups and workers' representation in companies – both by changing employment patterns that reduce the number of long-service and full-time workers, and the recognition that it is no longer credible to claim that producer interests could stand for those of all other currently excluded stakeholders.

7.4 Institutional freedoms and particular liberties

Classical liberals have feared any crossing of the boundary between the state and civil society as leading to the inevitable authoritarian politicization of the private sphere. Thus they will resist any attempt to politicize civil society and pluralize political accountability within the public sector. The very idea of a "constitution" for civil society smacks of totalitarianism. In the past this concern was legitimate, since the main threats to the autonomy of civil society in this century have been totalitarian mass parties. Yet totalitarian political mobilization from above is hardly a serious threat now, rather the main danger to liberty is the piecemeal authoritarianism of unchecked managerial elites. Equally, the old liberal bugbear of the "tyranny of the majority" is hardly credible in demotic societies that lack coherent leadership and are fragmented into a plurality of minorities with different values.

The problem is that old fears are still powerful and that both left and right now define freedom overwhelmingly in terms of individual rights. Modern societies are demotic, if not adequately democratic. Thus they believe that citizens should be formally equal, and that all individuals should have the same liberties. But if institutions are to be adequately governed, and if their autonomy is to be preserved both against the central state and the market, then we also need *particular liberties*, both for institutions and for their participants. The idea of particular liberties, that is grants of distinctive powers and rights to specific institutions and their members, was easily understood in the medieval *Standestaat*. Cities, guilds, and religious corporations enjoyed privileges, and specific and differential grants of power.[7] Medieval constitutionalism was based on such powers, on rights linked to status and privilege. Modern liberalism sought to sweep such privileges away, to destroy status differences and to replace them with equal individual rights. It sought to solve the problem of liberty by making the state accountable through representative government and society free through equal access to contract and the market.

The competitive society that classical liberalism envisaged as the basis for freedom – one in which equal individual rights would suffice to protect the autonomy of social actors – was no sooner mooted than it was threatened as a political ideal by collectivism. Liberalism overcame absolutist government and a society of privilege. It was then challenged by socialism and meliorated by reformist collectivism. In a society in which the state could be seen as the dominant source of governance, in which people were satisfied with simple uniform collective services like basic social insurance and elementary schools, and in which large-scale standardized mass production could be nationalized or regulated by the state, then liberal collectivism and democratic socialism could be seen as effective means to overcome the limits of classical liberalism and to modify the economics of *laissez faire*.

The recent decline of liberal collectivism and social democracy as alternatives to classical liberalism and the free market is not just a matter of political fashion. It is due to three main reasons:

1. National states can no longer be seen as having a monopoly of public governance functions
2. Public services have become diverse and complex – no longer simply governed and locally replicable basic entitlements
3. Manufacturing and commercial services have diversified in ways that make uniform central control or standardized regulation less effective.

Much of this change is gain. But it also means that markets are more difficult to govern and services more diverse and thus less equally accessible. Moreover, even though states can less credibly claim a monopoly of governance, their powers of intervention in society and the scale and scope of their activities are formidable. Paradoxically, the contemporary state is seen as less effective and as less capable of solving problems, and yet typically it spends a higher proportion of GDP, regulates more extensively, and offers more public services than in the era when collectivism was seen as the solution to the major economic and social problems. The modern state is a power that regulates and intervenes whilst speaking the fashionable languages of the new *laissez faire.*

Herein lies its main danger to freedom and democracy. The language of political choice has been replaced by that of management. Politicians see themselves as managers of a state to be devolved to managers, using financial controls and supervisory auditing to control lesser officials and contractors. Further, they support the corporatization and contractualization of public services, running them like private businesses, and they use public power to support the private sector's "power to manage" in a market economy. This is no longer an "Anglo-Saxon" peculiarity, as other countries are beginning in follow the lead of the USA, UK and New Zealand.

In a highly centralized state like the UK, without the protection offered by a written constitution, such practices represent a serious threat to the autonomy of a wide variety of social institutions. The danger is that we are witnessing the creation of a bureaucratic monoculture spanning the public and private domains. This will proliferate unless there is both some countervailing power and coherent alternative ideas for the direction of institutions. A managerial stratum is being created, relatively homogeneous in attitudes, working methods and aspirations. Its members are able to move between the public and the private sectors, and as they do so the interests and expectations of this stratum begin to interlock.

Such a new elite is as threatening to liberty in its own way as were, for example, the centralizing royal officials of the absolutist monarchy in France to the particular liberties of the *anicen régime.* Tocqueville argued for the autonomy of secondary associations from the state precisely because he saw the consequences of the centralizing tendencies of those who had inherited and implemented the programme of the bureaucratic reformers under the monarchy, the officials of the Revolution and the Empire. Montesquieu had earlier also seen that liberty depended on the autonomy of social institutions from the central state. But he argued that such autonomy must be based on specific institutions enjoying constitutionally protected privileges and not just on individual rights or freedom from state interference.[8] Montesquieu was of course defending privileges – the rights and powers of nobles, lawyers, and office holders. His point, however, was that such particular liberties contributed to the defence of liberty in general. That was because they limited the power of the state, its capacity to redefine the powers of and remake other social institutions at will. We need to return to early modern theorists of liberty like Montesquieu, because political thought since then has been predominately a struggle between classical liberals seeking to restrict the scope of state power and collectivists seeking to extend it. The danger now is that the language of individual rights and equality between individuals can all too easily be turned against the defence of particular liberties of specific institutions, like the professions, or the BBC, that are necessary to wider freedoms.

7.5 The threat of a bureaucratic monoculture

Our problem is that the representatives of the new bureaucratic monoculture effortlessly speak the language of equality. Everyone is to be equally subject to common styles of managerial control, and resistance is stigmatized as representing privileged producer interests, or as the elitist defence of professional prerogatives, or as the attempt to avoid accountability and transparency. Indeed, in an egalitarian and demotic culture (although not one that cares much about equality of income and wealth) it is easy to mount such charges and difficult to resist them. The common people are enlisted by the new managers against claims to exceptional rights or powers.

This difficulty to resisting managerial centralization is further compounded by the fact that we find it difficult to think of preserving the *autonomy* of institutions, that freedom for individuals depends in considerable measure on giving institutions constitutionally protected powers and the members of those institutions specific forms of political voice. The idea of a society consisting of constitutionally ordered self-governing civil associations is ill-developed, not least because state socialism, the main form of opposition to liberal individualism, saw democracy as being enhanced by the control of collectivist bureaucracies imposing the goals of the people. Liberals saw the danger of socialist and collectivist centralization, of totalitarian control, but in the main they have been ineffective in opposing corporate and managerial power. The problem is that threats to liberty come in many forms and not just ideologically motivated state dictatorship or totalitarian mass movements imposing their will by the club and the jackboot.

Freedom is not threatened just by gross oppression; some of the most serious threats are insidious and almost invisible and thus difficult to resist. The most dangerous is the redefinition of freedom and liberty, away from the spheres of the political and governance. The danger is that citizens cease to identify with politics and come to see "freedom" as what they do outside of formal organizations, in the spheres of private life and leisure. Freedom at work and in relation to social and public services comes to appear as cranky, uninteresting and irrelevant. Better leave it to the professionals – to managers – to run things. This is just what the growing bureaucratic monoculture thrives on and is an attitude it seeks to cultivate. The managerial stratum has been remarkably successful at redefining accountability from a political category to an accounting one and of redefining legitimate authority in terms of the prerogatives of management. Both of these redefinitions are glossed over by the apologetics of "efficiency" – the claim that this is the most effective and least expensive way to do things. To tax-averse electorates who are distrustful of politicians such appeals are not entirely unattractive. To politicians who can lessen their unpopularity by redefining politics in managerial terms and, indeed, ceding most of the day-to-day responsibility for services (and therefore blame) to managers, this is not unattractive too. The fact is that it represents a very real threat to liberty and needs to be resisted by an articulate language of political ideas.

7.5 Bridging state and civil society

Accept for the purposes of argument the notion that we can arrive at a "social constitution" – a definition of those institutions that require a definite sphere of guaranteed autonomy and the forms of democratic self-governance they should enjoy. Indeed, accept that such a constitution is essential, since neither top-down collectivism nor managerial control has the legitimacy to impose the public will in an increasingly complex, differentiated and divided society. We shall need specific institutions to perform many of the governance functions that those who have favoured more than *laissez faire* in social arrangements have hitherto assigned to the state. This pluralization and constitutionalization of social governance has become ever more necessary, not least because the advocacy of *laissez faire* has now become the defence of corporate privilege and the power to manage. We need to develop a complex division of labour in democratic governance, bridging state and civil society, in order to cope with the complexity of an organizational society that tends to blur the two spheres.

We need to create a new balance between authority and accountability, decentralizing governance within the state and increasing the political responsiveness of private institutions to those who work in them or are affected by them. A complex public service state and an organizational society have placed the central law-making and supervisory functions of representative government under ever greater strain. Unless democratic governance is redistributed and extended in something like the ways suggested above, then the formal institutions of representative government will be undermined because they will be too overstretched adequately to superintend social affairs or to protect citizens from harms.

Throughout the western world our democratic institutions remain those devised by classical liberalism for small government and a *laissez faire* society. Modern democracy has added universal suffrage to these institutions – the rule of law, parliamentary supervision of government, and governmental regulation of social affairs. Previous critics of liberal democracy have sought to sweep it away, to replace it with another and allegedly superior form of democracy, such as direct democracy. This is no part of the case being made here: the institutions of representative government remain necessary, but they are inadequate if they remain trapped within the existing liberal conception of the relation of state and civil society. An extended and devolved system of democratic governance crossing the two spheres will need existing state democratic institutions in order to ensure ultimate legal accountability, to provide legitimacy for fiscal settlements, and to act as final arbitrator when conflicts arise in and between self-governing social institutions. Thus the institutions of liberal democracy will not be destroyed or replaced, rather they will be enhanced and preserved by being supplemented by other democratic practices within and between social institutions.

Many analysts and political reformers recognize some of the limitations of our existing democratic institutions, but few of them are willing to accept that these limitations are structural, a product of the increasingly problematic division between the public and private spheres. Communitarians, like Amitai Etzioni, seek to restore ailing institutions by changing people's values, and thus their attitudes and behaviour, thereby rendering major structural reforms less necessary.[9] Other critics see the problem as a democratic deficit, as too little influence by the majority or representative citizens over public decisions. Thus greater use of referenda, electronic democracy, citizens' juries, deliberative forums, and so on, will bring the people back into politics. There is nothing wrong with many of these ideas as such. The question is whether they are adequate responses to the crisis of modern democracy. Decisions are only half of the problem; the other part is the institutions that implement or administer those decisions. Even if the scale and scope of popular decision-making were extended it would still be necessary to change the ways in which rules are enforced and services delivered, for these too affect the liberty of the citizen.

One cannot feed democratic decisions into the top of authoritarian structures and expect to get democratic outcomes. One must radically circumscribe the "power to manage", that is the whole point of trying to create a social constitution. Democratizing both public and private governments, state and civil society, requires a double protection of autonomy that can only be achieved by major institutional reforms. First, the constituencies that organizations serve need to have their interests protected by being given an appropriate voice within the governing councils of such bodies, and they also need, where possible, to have the option of exit, that is, some choice between alternative providers of service in question. As far as is practicable, both public and private services need to be voluntarily subscribed to by their consumers, rather than being compulsory or unavoidable. Secondly, the organizations themselves need to be guaranteed a definite degree of autonomy, a freedom from interference which is consistent with their members having the power to make democratic decisions within their own sphere of operation. Thus organizations need to have their autonomy protected not just against central state encroachment, but also against the kinds of top-down management by external funding agencies and internal bureaucratic elites that enable those bodies' purposes and working methods to be redefined virtually without check. This latter requirement should be evident in the UK, where we have become accustomed to the closure of 800-year-old hospitals and long-established schools by the *fiat* of ministers and bureaucrats.

The key problem is how to define, assert and ensure such specific liberties for and within institutions. To advance the case for radical reform we need to combat the fact that politics has been defined into such a narrow sphere. Democracy throughout the western world has been so reduced in form and meaning that it has become little more than a plebiscite; thus elections empower and legitimate rulers who govern in essentially undemocratic (top-down) ways. Even in those countries where there are relatively decentralized forms of government, where politicians do make serious attempts to consult the people about major decisions, and where they do not have the degree of exclusive control of power and of contempt for the electorate they have in the UK, democracy still remains restricted in scope to periodic elections for national and subsidiary governments, to choosing the top personnel at each level. Those personnel, even when they are democrats by inclination, have at best a restricted capacity to control and superintend the mass of decisions and administrative actions made by governmental organs, let alone to check the big organizations that actually control "civil" society. In a classical liberal society those weaknesses inherent in plebiscitarian democracy would matter less, since the scale and scope of government would be limited. However, viewed from a strictly classical liberal standpoint, we are now living in a "postliberal" society.

7.6 Liberty and freedom in a postliberal society

A postliberal society needs new kinds of defences for liberty and freedom. We cannot hope to return to a nightwatchman state or a society in which private individuals could sustain production and exchange. That *is* utopian; the now illiberal dream of a strand of the New Right. At the heart of such new defences must be the recognition that the institutions that deliver services, whether public or private, are not just neutral administrative machines but are forms of governance. Therefore, we must be concerned not just with *what* services are provided and at what cost, but *how* they are provided and how much control recipients have over the provision. Hence the issue of governance needs to be at the heart of the debate on the pattern of public and commercial services we receive, how they should be regulated, and what kind and what scale of institutions should deliver them.

This is a debate that the Conservatives, and indeed most members of the political class and the policy elite have avoided. The sole issue in the UK today is how to deliver a bare minimum of public services as cheaply and efficiently as possible. Governance is either a complete non-issue or it is equated with the power to manage. Thus political decisions have been made as if they were technical matters, questions of administrative efficiency of concern to a small circle of experts and managers. Under the regime of a political party formally committed to liberalism, a practice of social organization and service provision has developed that pushes us even further in a "postliberal" direction. Far-ranging political changes have taken place whilst leaving the apparent dominance of classical liberal theory unchallenged. The result is a vast transfer of political power and an effective denial that this power is political.

Thus what amounts to a political revolution has taken place in the UK, and unlike most such changes it has been accomplished without an explicit political theory.[10] Conservative governments have permitted a widespread practice of the administration of services to develop that destroys the very idea that the providing organizations could be matters of public concern, let alone that they might and should be constitutionally ordered civil associations. Authority has been redefined as "management" – a generic skill and a domain of technical competence. Efficiency has been defined in a way that puts it apparently beyond political debate and choice. Management is not the proper concern of citizens; they should be satisfied in their capacity as consumers, by the services provided for them. Producers have no properly political place at all within the organizations in which they work; their task is

to be directed to their duties and monitored from above in their performance of them. Thus the Conservatives, often unwittingly – for some are
genuine libertarians – have allowed a new postcollectivist and postliberal
model of the public services to develop.

This new redefinition of the nature and role of the public service state is
the key point at which a much wider struggle for freedom in a postliberal
society must begin to be fought. The capacity to resist encroachments in the
public sphere, to define alternative and more democratic forms of service
provision, will decide whether an ongoing struggle for greater democratization can be sustained. Until public services can be rescued from the
managerial model, there is little hope that managerial prerogatives in the
private sector can be publicly challenged and new more accountable forms
of corporate governance made widespread. Certainly, there is little scope
for radical state legislation.

This does not mean that the job of rebuilding firms as more democratic
organizations is impossible, merely that it is very difficult. However, the
need for greater openness and accountability is real, and perhaps more
credible in a world where the spectre of "workers control" can no longer be
used to terrify publics into indifference to issues of corporate reform.
Actually firms not merely need reform, many would actively benefit from it.
Quality manufactured goods and marketed services depend not only on
highly committed and skilled workers, they are bought by increasingly knowledgeable and sophisticated consumers. Many of these firms are multinational, but this does not mean that they are beyond governance or
control, or that they will profit from an absence of political superintendence
of the company. Careless companies that make short-term narrowly
"commercial" decisions may suffer the wrath of consumers. Thus an oil
company that wrecks an environmentally sensitive area on the other side of
the globe may find that articulate consumers in, say, Germany, are
boycotting its products.

Companies can act to remedy the deficiencies of nationally based and
shareholder-oriented governance. Imagine that the company in question
had created a corporate senate, a body of honourable persons representing
a wide range of views and affected interests, and deliberative and advisory in
its powers.[11] Then perhaps it would have been saved much grief if it honestly
put the project in question to such a senate and accepted its majority veto.
Obviously, deliberately distorted data presented to stooge senators will
reduce the whole thing to a PR exercise. The company must mean it.
Companies, if they are responsible and have far-sighted leaders, rather than
just managers, can begin to build their own governance. If they need a push
to start, then the churches, NGOs, and the trustees of major shareholding
pensions funds can help them to see the costs of pretending that top-down
decisions from the boardroom are infallible.

Such changes will be slow in the company sector, but in the case of public services most of their "consumers" have no such power of boycott, and changes rely on explicit political decisions. The probable outcome is that until public services are reformed most citizens will be unable to affect them by the power of exit, by saying "I quit". Many public services are compulsory: some rightly so – one would not be happy if shops could choose their own environmental health officer; others less happily so, as when contributors to basic state pensions find the real value of the asset being devalued by government policy. Other services are discretionary, but are given to those in need or who make a case at the discretion of public officials. In other cases services are available as of right and optional in form, but for the majority of their consumers they might as well be compulsory. Thus having paid their taxes, parents do not in the main have the option of foregoing state education and paying for a private school on top and most parents find it difficult to do more than send their kids to the local school or accept the one that is assigned to them.

7.7 A new welfare state

The dissatisfaction of consumers with the compulsory nature of many public services and the desire for choice has been used as an argument against public provision, and in favour of marketization and privatization. That is not the point being made here. In some cases only large-scale public provision and collective consumption will suffice, for example, where needs and risks are pooled in social insurance schemes against unemployment, old age, and illness. Private provision will never suffice for the majority of the population in such areas. But it does not follow that compulsory consumption through one monopoly supplier, the state, is the only way to realize these advantages of the large-scale sharing of risks. Public and state are not identical; it is possible to have publicly funded services that give consumers a large measure of choice and control. Services can be organized so as to reap the benefits of collective funding and yet allow citizens choice over the particular fund or service provider, and, having made a choice, the option of a measure of active voice in the control of its affairs.

Compulsory collective consumption organized from above is what has given public services a bad reputation. This failure has legitimated the marketization and fragmentation of provision and entitlements, thereby destroying one of the supposed key advantages of public provision – common rights to a certain standard of service. The privatization of services, in combination with chronic underfunding of those that remain public, has not given consumers a better deal or greater control – in fact bureaucrats remain firmly in charge. This reinforces tax-aversion; people feel they are getting less from the public realm and must try where possible to meet the higher costs of private provision of pensions, schooling and health for themselves and their families.

The problem then is to break the link between collective consumption and compulsion. Who would want to suffer that mixture of neglect and administrative interference that local authority housing departments inflicted on council tenants in the past? The gratitude for basic services – the dole, a council house, payment of the doctor's bill – is long since gone and those services are no longer perceived as minimally adequate by the moderately successful. People want to craft their own services – to have possession of their own home, to have definite pension rights, to have the choice to send their children to university. What were once "middle-class" expectations have become normal. The problem is that we have not found satisfactory ways of providing them for the bulk of the population. Private provision will exclude the majority from adequate cover across the whole range of services, and tailoring public provision to cater for the poor and unsuccessful – targeting resources – will alienate the majority from services they pay for but increasingly decline to consume if they have another option. Collective consumption remains essential for the majority; most people will not earn enough to meet all their needs from private markets and private insurance. The requirement is, however, to enable consumers to craft such collective services to their own needs, to have the benefits of common participation without the disadvantages of compulsion and sub-jection to administrative discretion.

Once we begin to think of collective services shaped by choice and voice then we can begin to bridge the divide between the public and private spheres. Public pensions give too much discretion to the state in the UK, but the private insurance and pensions markets offer variations in terms and benefits that are a scandal. Consumers need more protection in both spheres. If public services and private providers were both answerable in diverse ways to their consumers, then the stark divide between the two realms would be reduced. In particular more choice and control over public offerings and facilities would reveal to people how little control they have over private welfare services, how much they are at the mercy of companies, and how little pressure markets alone enable them to assert over areas like pensions, and life and health insurance. Once consumers could craft public services to suit them and had the means to exercise some political control over currently "private" services, then the difference between the two areas would tend to decline, and with it much of the current obsession with the "cost" of public services.

If the sphere of "publicity" were to be extended, creating a broad range of self-governing institutions with consumer representation, spanning the currently separate categories of state and civil society, then much of the current concern among economic liberals with lessening the role of the state would appear less relevant. It only makes sense at present on the assumption that public provision is inherently inefficient, and that it is a net cost to successful taxpayers who do not want the services provided. It also only makes sense if we treat the private sector as based on the disciplines of market forces and competition that promote true efficiency, and that we ignore bureaucracy and hierarchy in the corporate sector. Whereas, of course, most firms are large organizations that plan and administer much as states do. It is only on the basis of such assumptions that an intelligent liberal like Robert Skidelsky can be so concerned to get state spending back to around 30 per cent of GDP.[12] But, if we are less starry-eyed about the virtue of markets and also convinced that we can improve the performance of both public and private organizations, then this begins to look like a fixation with certain conventions of national income accounting. Outside of the belief that the state inevitably and inescapably wastes money in providing services, it begins to look like a preference for giving our money to one set of managers rather than another.

Crudely put, populations need to spend so much on welfare and services, in which sectors they do so is secondary to the overall level of consumption. Thus if the total of public and private spending on health, education and welfare is aggregated – state and private pensions, spending on public and private education – then most advanced industrial countries tend to converge in their overall levels of spending. In aggregate the society spends so much on a given class of services, and the mix between public and private is secondary to that total spend. Whether it is the state or an insurance company that provides your pension, you cannot spend the premiums on other things. The balance of the sectors can only be the primary concern if public services must offer less value *per se.*

That proposition can hardly be sustained. It would be difficult to claim that the predominantely public Swedish health system delivers less care, lower life expectancy, and higher infant mortality rates than does the mixed US system dominated by private producer interests, or that it does so at a higher per capita cost. Compulsory state services may be less attractive, but they are not the only option for publicly funded services. The target of doctrinaire economic liberals is *all* forms of collective and public welfare consumption.

In a postliberal society this rigid thinking in terms of categories of national expenditure and rigidly differentiated social sectors, in which all spending on public goods has to be justified, and private expenditure is inherently preferable, no longer makes much sense. We can then no longer oppose the rigid state to the free market. If civil society is organized rather than spontaneous, then it too is a domain of government and some of its private powers are bigger than many states. One cannot, therefore, contrast "government" to "society", and treat either sector as if they had distinct and homogeneous attributes – as if being "private" could be inherently beneficial. The economic liberals can sustain their case only by pretending we live in another kind of society from the one we do. Even sophisticated thinkers like Skidelsky are using a classical liberal architecture to describe a postliberal society.

If that is the case and if modern societies spend on aggregate a great deal on welfare, then we need to start another argument, one about how welfare is to be provided *across* society, in both state and non-state but publicly governed institutions. Such a set of social arrangements would not only be postliberal, but also postsocialist. In such a publicity-governed mixed order the very notions of nationalization and privatization would lose much of their meaning. Questions of provision would turn on the precise mix of collective and private consumption, but the majority of organizations that provided services would resemble political societies, in that they would be answerable to the interests they affected.[13] Such a system would tend to evolve in a non-profit direction, consumers with voice would tend to constrain the revenue that managers of services could draw from their operations. Pension funds and insurance companies would be pressured towards lower levels of profit-taking and many firms would change into mutual institutions.

7.8 Principles of associative democracy

It will be obvious that it is impossible in the compass of a chapter even to outline how consumers could participate in the governance of services and how public provision can be combined with consumer choice. I have sketched out what such institutions might look like elsewhere.[14] Reform of this kind faces serious practical difficulties. The point is that people have first to see that there is a problem, that the present state of affairs should be of concern to democrats. Then they may be willing to explore seriously the question of alternatives to bureaucratic control and the ways in which public services may be reinvigorated by active consumer choice, thereby encouraging citizens to support their costs.

Of course it is difficult to find ways of representing some of the interests affected by organizations, and of course it is a fact that many consumers will be reluctant to become citizens in relation to services – actively to take up the option of voice. A society in which the majority are active democratic participants is highly unlikely. That should give us enough cynicism to face the problem of devising a democracy for the moderately lazy, but not too much as to believe it to be insoluble. To have real powers over organizations people do not have to attend frequent meetings. Given the option to craft services for themselves by choosing between providers (funds following the customer), most people will try to make well-informed choices. If they find a service is actually grossly unsatisfactory, or is evolving in a direction they dislike, then they can exercise their right of exit and move to another competing provider. It is also probably the case that enough consumers will be willing to vote for the activists willing to serve on governing bodies to give these representatives sufficient legitimacy in relation to the permanent officials. Choice, competition, and formal democratic accountability to consumers can be built into publicly funded collective services. The question is whether we care enough to want to have greater freedom in relation to the organizations that constrain and control us whilst purporting to serve us.

The concept of a pluralized state and a democratized society hinted at here is not novel. It was advanced long before the social changes that might now make it possible by such thinkers as P.-J. Proudhon, G.D.H. Cole and H.J. Laski, between the 1840s and the 1920s.[15] This doctrine, called associationalism, enjoyed some popularity because it appeared to offer a third way between capitalism and socialism. It was marginalized by the great wars and intense social conflicts of the middle decades of this century, that reinforced the powers of central authority in the nation state. Yet as we have seen, the threat of such wars and class conflicts has declined dramatically in the advanced countries, and the nation state has lost some of its monopoly hold on governance. We now have an economic and social system that has clearly outgrown the remedies of classical liberalism, but to which the ideas of nationalized ownership and compulsory state services no longer offer an attractive or credible alternative.

We also live in a world that has become, rightly and unsurprisingly, tired of utopias. Change needs to be effective, but also piecemeal and supplemental in form if it is to get started. People are tired of social and institutional turbulence, not least of that caused by the grandiose and failed promises of the New Right. People may recognize the defects of traditional forms of democracy and be convinced that conventional state authority is less effective at solving problems, but they need to be convinced that changes will be for the better. The great advantage of attempts to democratize organizations is that they can proceed piecemeal, institution by institution and sector by sector. Indeed, it would be almost impossible to introduce such changes in a "big bang" reform, since it would involve forcing consumers to choose – in effect compelling them to enter into voluntary associations. A radical alternative in the relation between state and civil society will only be accepted if it makes sense locally, in relation to particular strategies of institutional reform.

The danger at present is that the political and managerial elites are becoming so homogeneous that citizens have almost no choice within the existing system, and no alternative options. Political power then tends to become illegitimate. The plebs having no choice, elections signify little and fail to strengthen those who win office even if they have large paper majorities. The implicit and anti-political but very compelling doctrine of government and management we outlined above has bitten deep into the political class. In New Zealand, for example, both major parties accepted this managerialist view of the role of the state, and the public found itself with no choice at all. There is some danger that this might happen in the UK – that the Labour Party may become the vehicle for the younger more sophisticated sections of the managerialist elite. In the end hierarchy becomes compelling for those who find themselves at or close to the top of the pile, whether in government, public services or firms. Labour seems to have conceded to the corporate sector that it will do little to disturb the power to manage. It may also see its task as running public services more efficiently, offering a slightly more open style of postcollectivist public management.

In part Labour's caution is well justified: ill-considered radicalism could lead to electoral defeat. Competent government by a party that is not actively hostile to public services would be a distinct benefit. But this caution is also because Labour has lost the capacity to imagine that there are effective alternative ideas. It has embraced managerialist conceptions of government because it sees them as competence and practicality. It is encouraged in this by many of its members who are themselves managers. The battle for the soul of Labour is no longer that between socialists and pragmatists, but that between those who are managerialists and those who believe we can provide better services through greater democracy.

Notes

1. Of course, some variants of corporatism saw representative government as inadequate and sought to replace it by chambers based on corporate groups. The democratic variety presented itself as a supplement to representative institutions, as a pragmatic means to link state and civil society in order to achieve economic co-ordination by promoting the co-operation of the major organized interests. See Cawson (1986).
2. This is not the same as "globalization", a process that is supposed by many commentators to have dissolved distinct national economies, placed all societies at the mercy of international market forces, and undermined any possibility of effective public governance in the world system. For a critique see Hirst and Thompson (1996).
3. See Cohen and Arato (1992).
4. See Hayek (1944), and the perceptive comments of Gamble (1996). For Habermas see (1984/1987), especially Vol. 2.
5. Rousseau (1763/1913), p. 3. The passage in question is "Man is born free; and everywhere he is in chains".

6. Bobbio (1987), p. 56.
7. See Black (1984), especially Chs 1–7.
8. Actually, despite its Marxist *parti pris*, Althusser (1972), brings out Montesquieu's role as an aristocratic opponent of absolutism and a defender of particular liberties very well.
9. See Etzioni (1995).
10. See Weir (1996).
11. See Turnbull (1991).
12. See Skidelsky (1995) and (1996).
13. I am grateful to Luke Martell for emphasizing the importance of involving *affected* interests and not just those within the organization.
14. See Hirst (1994).
15. See Nicholls (1995) (2nd edn).

8

Can the Conservatives reinvent civil society?

Review of Green, *Reinventing the Civil Society*

David Green is one of a number of conservative intellectuals, like John Gray and Ferdinand Mount, who have come to recognize that something has gone very wrong with the project of the New Right. He argues that the Conservative governments of the 1980s concentrated too much on the market as a means to the satisfaction of self-interested actors' material wants. They regarded people simply as individual rational utility maximizers and failed to give due attention to the moral and institutional dimensions of a sustainable capitalist order as understood by Adam Smith and Hayek. Moreover, these allegedly market-oriented governments were in fact still wedded to state action, committed to the centralization of power, and more concerned with getting bureaucratic efficiency and "value for money" out of the welfare state than they were with changing its basic purposes and structures.

In consequence, the author strongly condemns a great deal of the recent Conservative reforms in education and health. He regards the National Curriculum as overcentralized and too *dirigiste*. The NHS internal market is more concerned with the bureaucratic rationing of resources than with giving market power to consumers, that is, patients. David Green is both a libertarian and a traditional moralist. He believes that the state has become too powerful, but that civil society needs to be organized around stable traditional families. Only such families can provide the foundation for the values necessary to freedom and individual responsibility – the precondition for true social independence in a market society.

In place of the nihilism of Chicago-style *laissez faire*, Green advocates "civic capitalism". In such a system economic action is firmly rooted in a social and moral order that governs and sustains it. The foundation of such a civic capitalism is an independent body of laws. The rule of law provides a stable set of norms to govern social life, above party and policy. Modern governments have captured the law-making function and have turned it into an instrument of executive power. The state has "politicized" areas of activity that should belong to civil society and has brought party interest into the regulation of the market; whereas such regulation can only effectively be done consensually by and for the whole community. The state, in substituting its bureaucratic provision for voluntary action in civil society, undermines the freedom and independence of individuals. This is particularly true when it has a virtual monopoly on the provision of a service.

Green's answer to this encroachment by the state is to advocate a return to the provision of welfare and other services through "civil society". His models for doing this are the friendly societies, representing the best of the British tradition of voluntarism in welfare. The bulk of the book is a study of the rise and fall of the friendly societies as welfare providers for ordinary citizens, with particular emphasis on medical insurance and medical care. It is interesting to see an enthusiast for the free market turn to such bodies rather than commercial insurance companies as examples of the sturdy independence of civil society in welfare provision. In contrast, recent Conservative governments have seen privatization of pensions and other welfare benefits as being provided only by the big insurance companies and other profit-making financial institutions. Modern Toryism has found no place for mutual and non-profit-making voluntary associations like the friendly societies. Where it has used the voluntary sector, for example, the housing associations, it has sought to centralize and managerialize voluntary bodies in the government's own image. Green's advocacy is to be welcomed, therefore, in encouraging both mutualism and participation. So committed is he to the virtues of the friendly societies that he makes the commercial insurance sector – organized into the "Combine" to lobby for a role in the Liberals' 1911 social insurance legislation – into one of the major villains in the demise of voluntarism in welfare.

David Green is so enthusiastic about the virtues of the friendly societies that he could almost be mistaken for an anarchist or associational socialist advocate of mutual aid and working-class self-action. Because he is an anti-collectivist he has limited options in his case for devolving welfare functions from the state to civil society. It would hardly be convincing to offer the big corporation as a genuine representative of voluntary action, since it is neither an example of a democratic organization nor one compatible with his belief in the efficiency of perfect competition in a free market. He pays far too little attention to *how* we might foster genuinely self-governing voluntary associations in welfare, in part because he fails to face the fact that both economy and society are increasingly dominated by the large bureaucracies of the state *and* the private corporations. Truly voluntary action in "civil society" is being pushed to the margins. Public and private governments are overwhelmingly top-down and managerialist.

Green also tends to evade the extent to which the friendly societies were, while not socialist organizations, part of a wider workers' movement. They were but one part of the working people's construction of their own civil society. This provided the means whereby workers and their families were protected by their own social institutions from the vicissitudes of a hostile market system. The friendly societies, along with trade unions, the co-operative movement, sports and social clubs, and non-conformist churches, were part of a great burst of creative energy on the part of the workers in the new industrial towns of the nineteenth century. Populations that had been uprooted and often brutalized by the harsh living and working conditions of early industrialization were able to fight back and to create the means to civilize their existence. The working conditions of early industrial capitalism were hardly propitious to stable family lives. Workers had to fight for and to create the values and social conditions Green and Hayek assume to be necessary for a stable market society, and to do so against their employers in the main.

If the new wave of uprooting and brutalization that began in the 1970s, with mass unemployment, homelessness and poverty, is to be resisted and reversed, it will also require a new popular creativity. Social and moral decline will not be halted by the state doing things "to" people, least of all preaching morality at them. Rather it will be by the people who have suffered most being helped with resources and public support to reconstruct blighted inner-city areas and revitalize local economies ravaged by deindustrialization. If Green has a positive lesson it is the value of voluntarism and it is one that the left should prevent being wholly appropriated by the right. And the left has a lot to relearn – so much so that it cannot afford to be snooty when the IEA reminds it of some of its lost and forgotten roots.

In the first four decades of this century, state socialism gradually but steadily gained ascendancy in the Labour Movement. As it did so, it robbed British socialism of the capacity to cherish and sustain the achievements of the people's civil society. Yet the final victory of collectivism came late. Into the 1940s there were strong voices for pluralism and decentralization in social insurance, for municipal services, and for retaining voluntarism in welfare generally. In 1945 these voices were ignored. Labour nationalized and centralized welfare, just as it handed the nationalized industries over to bureaucratic management. In retrospect we can see this turn to collectivism and state centralism as a fatal error. The NHS created a state health system funded out of general taxation, in which patients had no specific entitlements and precious few rights. National Insurance killed off the friendly societies and also any prospect of consumer rights or voice in respect of pensions and unemployment benefits. All this was done with the best of motives, in the belief that the large-scale and centralized management by public officials made for efficiency. But these reforms made the people's health, education and welfare provision subject to the whims of central government policy – and that in a state without a written constitution and in which the executive dominates the legislature. Since 1951 the Conservatives have been in power for three-quarters of the time and have been able to shape the welfare state in their own interests because it has been a monopoly of the central government. Citizens have had neither rights in welfare nor secure entitlements based on insurance contributions. Benefits and services have been at the discretion of the state. Consumers have been virtually powerless. Thus the NHS has shifted from doctors rationing medical resources to managers in trust hospitals and health authorities doing so.

The Labour Party was in part the cause and part the victim of the erosion of a working-class civil society. As against the political party and the unions, the other elements of Labour Movement voluntarism and activism slowly died. Labour politicians and intellectuals were convinced of the virtues of large-scale, planned and public provision; it would be more efficient and offer better and more uniformly delivered services. In making social provision dependent on the state, the Labour Party contributed to destroying many of the sources of its own support. The party gradually lost the energy and commitment that stemmed from contact with an organized substratum of voluntary action that went far beyond the unions. As the organizations of working-class civil society withered, so too did the active social base of the Labour Party. Labour's concern about its declining membership is a belated recognition of several decades of indifference to the wider social base of the Labour Movement. By failing to develop self-organization and self-provision in welfare and social insurance, Labour lost many of the affluent and enterprising among the workers. In 1979 many of them rallied to Thatcher because among other things they wanted more than state benefits and a life regulated by local bureaucrats if they were council tenants.

Imagine that in 1945 Labour had sought to combine redistribution and enhanced public spending with voluntarism and citizen control of services; that it had created insurance and pension funds in which contributing members had a say and from which they had definite minimum entitlements; that it had accepted decentralized municipal and voluntary control of health, education and welfare services. Consumers would have had a measure of control, both because they had definite entitlements, and because they could choose the service provider that most suited them. In effect Labour would have chosen to make what were then middle-class privileges available to all: the right to choose one's doctor, one's children's school, to have a pension fund, to control one's dwelling, and so on. Instead it chose to "nationalize" the working class, giving them services where choices were made for them by bureaucrats.

The loss of voluntarism and mutualism as real options in the provision of public welfare has enabled the Tories since 1979 to promote the "private" as the only superior option to rigidly delivered and underfunded public services. "Private" has invariably meant corporately controlled and profit making. Thus the scandal that has followed allowing people to contract out of SERPS (State Earnings Related Pension Scheme) shows the private sector at its worst, with greedy and far from impartial financial advisers and profit-hungry financial institutions rooking consumers who were driven toward them by the state. The option of building a healthy, mutual and non-profit-making sector for pensions was considered neither by Crossman nor by the Tories. Labour has stuck with state collectivism and the Tories with corporate capitalism.

The problem is that both sides of the political spectrum have virtually ignored co-operation, mutualism and voluntary association as methods of social organization. Green exemplifies this in his consistent equation of socialism with state collectivism. After 1945 this became more and more the case. Yet the UK had into the twentieth century one of the strongest associational socialist traditions and an experience of working-class voluntary action almost unrivalled in Europe. The Labour Party largely threw away these assets, abandoning voluntarism for bureaucratic "modernity". The problem now is that the tradition represented by the friendly societies or the co-operative movement is more or less dead.

This is a major problem with Green's book in that he lauds institutions that were by the 1900s in the process of marginalization. He can see their decline as caused only by the will-to-power of hostile agents: doctors, insurance companies and state officials. The problem here is that mutualism and voluntarism in welfare could only have revived both with public support and with the injection of public money to supplement private contributions. In examining the societies' decline, Green does not adequately assess one of its sources in the scale of benefits offered, when measured against need. Nor is he effective in challenging the need for state insurance by down-playing the problem of those not covered by their own voluntary contributions. To argue as he does that many of the poorest "chose" to pay doctors' bills as they occurred is to present desperation as if it were an acceptable option. The poorest could not afford to contribute to voluntary schemes and so lived in fear of illness.

A decentralized system of social insurance could only have survived on the basis of voluntary organizations if the benefits it offered were boosted by public cash. This would enable the majority of the employed to supplement their voluntary contributions with public entitlements, ensuring a level of benefits that met need, and it would allow the poorest to contribute to a voluntary scheme that provided at least a bare minimum of provision. That would only be possible if public entitlements were underwritten by a measure of redistributive taxation. This combination of guaranteed public entitlements and partial state funding, with voluntarism and local provision of services, was by no means impossible and had many advantages. The author, as a true disciple of Hayek, is wholly opposed to income redistribution through taxation. In a society with a distribution of income and wealth as unequal as it was in 1910, there could have been no hope of decent services for the majority unless their ability to contribute was bolstered by taxing the well-to-do. We are returning to an Edwardian scale of inequality today, as the Commission on Social Justice's report *The Justice Gap* shows. Welfare without direct state control of services is one thing, "welfare without politics" – that is without the rich paying for the poor through taxation, is moonshine.

David Green presents a civic capitalism in which the free market will ensure allocative efficiency and in which it is underpinned by institutions that produce honest, industrious and independent citizens who deal fairly with others and avoid becoming a burden on the state. The traditional family and a conservative social order are for him essential foundations for a sustainable market system. These views are sincerely held and a response to current social decay. Clearly it would be silly to respond by advocating criminality, idleness and benefit scrounging. The problem with Green's view is that it is both backward-looking and utopian. Modern mores are inescapably pluralistic, and many honest and honourable people will actively reject both the traditional family and traditional morality. Single parents are no threat to social stability or to the sustainability of welfare spending; mass unemployment and large-scale poverty are.

David Green cannot accept that markets need much more active co-ordination and regulation if they are to produce the outcomes for welfare on a national scale that most people desire. Markets do not behave like first-year economics textbooks say and public policy cannot make them do so. An economic system cannot therefore be co-ordinated by sales and purchases alone, supplemented by a little morality. Mass unemployment and poverty are the effects of a badly regulated economic system, one in which macro-economic adventurism by governments .and the neglect of promoting co-operation by the major social interests go hand in hand. Markets *do* need morality, especially honesty and fair dealing. But they also need to be embedded in a context of regulating social institutions that sustain effective economic performance. Such institutional arrangements are diverse and correspond to no simple model, but typically they operate to attain the following outcomes: to balance co-operation and competition between firms – enough co-operation to ensure the public goods vital to an industry and enough competition to ensure industrial efficiency; a partnership with public agencies and private industry to provide effective collective services; and co-operation between unions and employers' organizations. Such social embeddedness is very different from either state *dirigisme* or *laissez faire*, it is neither collectivist nor individualist but depends on co-operation, voluntary co-ordination and dialogue. These are practices and virtues that have analogies with those of the institutions of voluntarism and mutualism in welfare. It is a pity that Green did not broaden his remit and look at the organization of industrial "civil society". He might then have found much in the associationalist doctrines of the past and the practices of many firms, regions and societies in the present to deepen and enrich his concept of the modern market economy and its governance. This is a valuable book both in pointing us to the strengths of the voluntarist tradition in welfare and because it provokes those on the left who favour decentralization and mutualism the better to define their own views.

9

Sidestepping the state

The 1970s ended throughout the "Anglo-Saxon" world with a determined intellectual and political assault on state bureaucracy, collectivism and the welfare state. In the UK, USA, Australia and New Zealand, more or less sustained efforts were made to curb the growth in public spending on welfare and to rationalize provision along the lines of economic liberal doctrines. Tight budgetary controls, cuts in direct taxation, the privatization of services and tax subsidies for market provision were intended to promote the primacy of private over public provision in welfare and to reduce state collective provision to a minimal safety net that only the poorest would use through dire necessity. By now it is clear that such economic liberal solutions to welfare problems are in ruins. They have not improved service delivery or quality; they have not tackled the perceived problem of an "underclass" trapped in a "dependency culture"; and they have not contributed to increasing the rate of economic growth by reducing the overall tax burden on the mass of income earners.

The economic liberal agenda has lost its intellectual legitimacy, but the mass attitudes that provided political legitimacy for free-market quick-fix solutions are still there. In the UK the Labour Party went to the polls in the April 1992 election with a determined effort to present itself as the party of welfare, to claim that the people had "seen through" economic liberalism, and to suggest that higher income earners would accept proposed tax rises as fair. It failed. None of the presidential candidates in the USA proposes seriously to tackle the problems of poverty and urban decay, despite the spur of the Los Angeles riots.

J.K. Galbraith's *A culture of contentment* has provided a straightforward and widely accepted explanation for the failure of redistributionist and welfare politics. According to Galbraith, the postwar mixture of sustained economic growth and welfare spending provided the means for the majority to escape into relatively comfortable and "middle-class" conditions. The consequence of this was that collectivist solutions began to seem to them steadily less necessary. In this account the new mass "middle class" is reluctant to make major sacrifices for that socially containable and politically ineffectual minority which has not benefited in the same way. Welfare states are thus the victims of their own past successes. There is an element of truth in this thesis, but it overstates the extent to which people are simply tax resistant, and it underplays the fact that they also have other good reasons not to support simply spending more on existing forms of bureacratic state welfare. The real problem is that supporters of the extension of state welfare services have been unable to come up with a clear new strategy that encompasses reforms to both funding and service delivery. Rather they have sought to break down public resistance to "more of the same" – with moralizing and with the patronage of possessing superior principles. Yet resistance of the expansion of state welfare will only be overcome by new ideas that inspire people, and not by school-teacherly social democratic exhortation to be altruistic and pay up.

There are three main problems which limit public willingness to be taxed for welfare provision:

1. Throughout the "Anglo-Saxon" world we find the deadly combination of low economic growth and high expectations of private consumption on the part of the mass of the employed. The result is resistance to taxation – even though survey evidence also shows that a substantial majority would prefer high standards of welfare services like education and health to be publicly provided at low direct cost to the consumer.
2. People are widely resistant to the bureaucratic deformations of mass welfare services (administrative discretion, low public accountability and the absence of a "consumer" culture in the provision of services). People do not want to be supplicants, to have to wait and to be treated rudely in squalid circumstances.
3. The alleged benefits of national public services – fairness and equal treatment – are by no means apparent to consumers or available in fact. "National" services are by no means uniform: there is considerable variability in the way services are delivered between regions and house-holds in most countries. Nor are "universal" benefits equally distributed or specific services and benefits effectively targeted at those most in need.

The problem that most supporters of a social democratic mass welfare ethic fail to accept is that bureaucracies do not empower citizens. The vast majority of citizens expect to be treated as articulate, sensible individuals in charge of their own affairs and not as objects of tutelage. Yet state welfare bureaucracies habitually patronize and at worst demean a high proportion of recipients of their services. In the UK, for example, post-1945 local authority housing involved many absurd and humiliating restrictions on tenants. One could not even paint one's front door the colour one pleased.

In the UK John Major has tried to exploit this dissatisfaction with "Citizen's Charters" which are supposed to specify the minimum service standards the public has a right to expect, and the mechanisms for obtaining relief if they are not met. Likewise, his administration has sought to improve the accountability of public servants. Yet measures such as these make little sense in conditions where service failure is largely determined by government underfunding, and where accountability is a "top-down" process that reduces the autonomy of welfare personnel in relation to their senior managers but does not directly empower the public. John Major has tried to demoticize economic liberalism but, in the absence of major new ideas from his government about how to improve the funding and delivery of services, he is hardly likely to do more than marginally improve welfare provision.

The position is therefore one of stalemate. Social democrats have no new ideas and the public will not trust them to spend more on the old services. Economic liberals have failed to revitalize or transform those stagnant welfare states which survive, albeit in an underfunded and ineffective state. Indeed, mostly those welfare states subsist merely in the absence of anything better, and are run by right-wing rulers who have little sympathy for them. How can the deadlock be broken? The answer, I believe, can be summed up in two sentences. First, the provision of public welfare and other services should be devolved to self-governing voluntary associations. Secondly, such associations should be enabled to obtain public funds to provide such services for their members. The principle of social governance involved here is called "associationalism". Its fundamental objective is to renew modern societies by transforming the private–public division; making the "private" a sphere of social co-operation and collective governance, making the "public" as far as possible nothing more than the mechanism for providing rules and funds that enable self-governing "private" institutions to work.

Associationalism is a form of social organization that can deliver all the political benefits economic liberals claim to seek from the market without the same scale of economic costs and injustices that unregulated markets impose. Associationalism simultaneously proposes solutions to the problems of funding, service delivery and citizens' involvement. It is attractive to citizens seeking greater autonomy; it is easy to understand in principle; and it explodes the terms of the conflict between economic liberalism and welfare collectivism.

Associationalism offers, first of all *extended governance without big government*. Economic liberalism fostered the delusion that the answer to overextended and unaccountable government was deregulation. The result has been the unwanted and unintended consequences of "free" markets. Governance is essential; modern industrial societies need extensive "policing" to ensure that acceptable standards are set and complied with.

This is true even in straightforward commercial transactions where consumers have to be able to trust the honesty of the vendor and be aware that they can obtain relief through public agencies if that trust proves to be unfounded. The problem is government not governance: government becomes too big, too multiform and too bureaucratic in struggling to cope with those diverse tasks that complex modern societies of necessity impose.

The advantage of self-governing voluntary agencies rather than state bureacracies is threefold. First, personnel will be more committed to an agency with whose principles they are in agreement and which is chosen by them as a place of work for that reason. Secondly, self-governing voluntary associations will be internally accountable to their members; this ensures a first-line form of policing of service delivery by members, and reduces the load on the state. And thirdly, the delivery of welfare services through voluntary agencies effects a separation between the service provider and the state as the "governor of governors". In contrast at present the state is in the contradictory position of providing services through its bureaucratic agencies and also acting as the guarantor of the standard of those services.

In the second place associationalism offers *thick welfare with thin collectivism*. Bureaucratic collectivist delivery of welfare typically entails high administrative discretion on the part of providers and low consumer choice. For that reason it is less and less attractive even to the moderately successful. However, market-based insurance schemes can hardly serve as the general answer to this problem. They can assure a high and uniform level of welfare provision only in a society of mass affluence – one that does not have a substantial pool of long-term unemployed or a significant underclass. Even then, market-based systems entail serious distortions in provision due to strong financial incentives for suppliers to overdeliver services.

Associationalism, by contrast, both promotes consumer choice and – because of the joint producer–consumer self-governance of associations – also provides a mutual check on the tendencies to overconsume and overproduce that are inherent in any form of decentralized welfare provision. In such a system individuals can craft the package of services they need. This is because of the high level of choice in the type and mode of services on offer, due to the fact that service providers are voluntary organizations in competition, and their provision is mainly demand led. Consumers have a large element of choice in the services they receive, but also considerable discretion in determining the overall level of funding for them. Thus when it comes to paying for services, individuals will tend to behave differently from the way they do now. Employed consumers with a substantial disposable income will have high discretion in controlling what they get; therefore they will be willing to adjust expenditure to meet their own perceived needs. The poor will get minimum entitlements, but still will be able to choose which agencies should fulfil them. The system will not be inherently egalitarian, but it will tend to promote higher welfare spending and incline individuals toward meeting their needs through collective consumption. Welfare expenditures will tend to rise to the extent that consumers see *they* can control services and that they benefit from consuming collectively. Associationalist welfare systems thus have the potential to unblock the tax constraint on welfare spending. Because they take the responsibility for making spending decisions from the state and place it in the hands of consumers, they promote real consumer choice in many ways markets do not, and they ensure accountability to consumers in a way markets do not.

Associationalism is a well-established idea and its principles are easy to understand. Why then has it not already gained widespread acceptance as the new basis for welfare systems? The answer: it is not a technical quick-fix solution. It requires fundamental changes in the forms of authority predominant in both state and civil society. Social democrats, for example, tend to be hostile to associationalism on the grounds that it lessens the power of the state. They remain committed to their perception that only the state can offer true welfare, because it is supposed to be able to deliver universal and uniform benefits. Yet this is an illusion; no system of welfare can reliably and over the long run ensure equality and uniformity in the way desired by classic social democracy.

An associationalist welfare system involves a quite different political principle: it offers greater empowerment, rather than equality of outcomes, as its means to the goal of social justice. It recognizes that such empowerment cannot come from state centralism and the inevitable bureaucracy that accompanies it, but only from decentralization and a degree of popular control. Associationalism is based on the principle of federation – that is the principle that activities should be administered and controlled at the lowest level feasible, and that "higher" authorities should be limited to their specific functions and unable to appropriate those of the agencies and authorities "below" them. Associationalism is thus decentralizing and pluralistic, and looks messy to statists because of the inherent weakness of top-down control in such a federative system.

The federalist and associationalist position is no longer the irrelevancy it appeared to be when the militaristic Keynesian welfare state was a going concern. The period of prolonged industralized wars and cold wars between the great powers required the complete social mobilization of populations. Then the welfare state had a clear rationale – as the locus of a pact with organized labour and as the orchestrator of the welfare measures necessary to "social efficiency". Yet the rationale no longer holds. The problem for social democrats is that the nation state has lost its centrality as the principal economic and social regulator and yet it is essential to their project. It has lost the capacity to determine the level of economic activity with the demise of "Keynesian" strategies of national economic management.

Regional economic regulation and the regionalization of economic activity have grown apace. The divisions in the levels of prosperity *within* nations are as substantial as those between them. Nation states are at once losing salience upwards, to economic blocs like the European Community, and downwards, to regionalist practices of economic regulation and regional sources of citizen identity. This suggests that in Europe at least the old project of a "uniform" national welfare state is probably doomed. Italy and Germany offer clear examples of such regionalist rejection of national redistribution. The regional autonomist Northern Leagues, for example, protest that the south of Italy produces 25 per cent of GDP and consumers 49 per cent of it. German working-class voters in the western *Länder* are unwilling to carry the main tax burden of integration of the east. The only possible long-term answer to this crisis of national states in Europe is a "federalist" solution in which EC, national and regional governments accept specific and partial functions in welfare. The EC would set minimum framework standards for social regulation and social welfare, and then ensure the supranational redistribution between rich and poor regions to meet them. This project is itself problematic, since national governments are unwilling to concede such powers, and such common standards are currently quite low. Regions would then be free to determine welfare policies consistent with their explicit political objectives and their underlying economic performance.

Such a regionalized and federal system can in theory work either with associations or markets playing the main role in welfare. The real problem for economic liberals in accepting associationalism is not their addiction to the "free" market. The real stumbling block is their commitment to a strong central state that protects market freedoms (and which in particular ensures that there is no political or social obstruction of the market from local government or voluntary associations like labour unions) as well as their commitment to corporate dominance of economic and social provision. In fact, contrary to economic liberal ideology, centralized state power and top-down corporate management go together. Decentralization and the principle of self-governing voluntary associations are threats to economic "liberals" (with a few honourable and genuinely libertarian exceptions), because the freedoms they really value are those for corporations to act in weakly regulated markets. Modern economic liberalism is passionately addicted to "management", and convinced that top-down authority and hierarchy are the only routes to social efficiency.

Associationalism would be a radical change from this managerial mentality. It would break up the current ossified private hierarchies that ensure that most of "civil society" is a domain of authority and not of freedom. The citizen, at work and in purchasing private welfare (insurance), is

148

at the mercy of largely unaccountable corporations. Associationalism, by beginning to restore citizen power, would threaten the corporate dominance of "civil society". The chief reason associationalism has not been seized upon as a solution to welfare problems is because it is radical. It is at once too decentralist for social democratic conservatives wedded to the nation state, and too democratic for corporate apologists in the guise of economic liberals. It might, therefore, appear to be marginal – except that existing doctrines of social organization are bankrupt, the problems of welfare provision are very real, and it is implausible that sophisticated and individuated publics in industrialized societies will continue to accept passively the existing patterns of authority forever.

Moreover associationalism can appeal to and unite diverse social forces, break down the old opposition between left and right, and can profit from a variety of reform strategies. Indeed, one could argue that the one thing holding back the crystallization of a variety of groups around an associationalist strategy has been the absence of a common concept that would allow such diverse entities to communicate and to recognize one another as having shared interests. Thus the task of developing the concept is urgent, and the core of that development must be a credible model of social organization.

That said, it is impossible to present in any depth the possible models of an associationalist welfare state within the compass of a short essay. We have suffered enough from the relentless organizational monism of economic liberalism, where there is no alternative and only one simple, comprehensive "Year Zero" solution. Associationalism has the advantage that it can be added slowly and experimentally to existing welfare states as a principle of renewal and reform. It is not just another slick idea to attract funding, since it offers both recipients and providers of welfare a say in its governance and delivery. It is also compatible with a variety of methods of funding, and it can co-exist with those elements of collectivism and bureaucracy that are inevitable and inescapable in a complex contemporary society.

The easiest way to present a picture of such a welfare state is to state some basic principles:

- Provision is by voluntary self-governing organizations that are partnerships between the recipients and the providers of the service: such associations will be at least formally democratic and recipients will have an annual right of exit.
- Such organizations are funded predominantly from public sources (possible methods are outlined below) and are subject to public inspection and standard-setting.
- Any voluntary organization – church, trade union, charitable trust – may establish as wide or narrow a range of services as its members choose

(for example, a Muslim charitable foundation may wish to establish schools, hospitals, old people's homes and so on). It is assumed therefore, that (at least in urban areas) there will be a range of competing services with which citizens may choose to register.

- All such organizations must meet conditions of registration to receive public funds. Among these would be compliance with public standards, acceptance of exit rights and recipient choice (for example, to register with a Catholic school but with a "neutral" trust hospital), and participation in the public/associational governance of the whole system. It is assumed here that the setting of standards, allocation of funding and inspection would be "consociational" – that is, as far as possible governance would be by representatives of associations acting either by service (such as education or health) or regionally.

Such a fully developed associationalist welfare state would be "confederal" in that the core organization of provision would be the region, at which level public funds (including interregional transfers) would be distributed. Associations would co-operate with one another in the public governance of the distinct services and of the whole system, sending representatives to public bodies which would perform the central regulative and distributory functions. Voluntary associations would thus enter into public governance in a decentralized state; the associationalist principle would not only renew welfare provision, but also the state and governance itself.

In this confederal welfare state the associations would be democratically self-governing internally and would also contribute to a system of federated indirect democracy in the governance of the regional state. Representative democratic bodies would remain at central and regional level, and would be the standard-setters of last resort. Citizens would have several "votes", as well as the crucial power of exit from direct service providers. The state would retain major reserve powers over welfare provision – for example, power to curb excessive growth in aggregate spending and to challenge standards of provision – but it would not have the unilateral powers available to politicians and officials in bureaucratic collectivist systems. Welfare professionals would be subject to strong public pressure and yet have far more say in how their own unit and the service of which it is a part is run.

How might such a welfare state be funded? The answer is that it could use for different purposes and in different combinations all or any of the present methods: general taxation, public or private insurance, markets and private purchases, charitable donations and so on. A citizen's entitlements would depend on the precise nature of this mix. I will assume for simplicity's sake that all welfare spending is funded from general taxation. Another important element in funding such a welfare state would be a Guaranteed Minimum Income (GMI) scheme, in which every citizen has a (low) basic income assured by the state. This GMI would be exempt from taxation, so that it could be supplemented, for example, from part-time or casual earnings without loss of benefit. The minimum level might be pitched at, say, £300 per adult per month. Assuming current levels of unemployment (11 per cent) this would still be economically sustainable. It would give citizens just sufficient income to pursue private activities the market does not value but which may be socially useful, or to undertake voluntary service. A GMI scheme would thus increase the potential personnel of the "welfare state" at low cost. In an ageing society such a GMI scheme may become not only economically viable but essential. It may be more rational than collectivist welfare, if households/families are to be given the resources to care for elderly partners/relatives.

More specific entitlements would depend on needs and status (a school-age child, a disabled person) and would relate to specific provision areas like health or education. The assumption here is that each citizen would be entitled to register annually with a service provider for each relevant service and receive a publicly specified quantity and quality of the service. Funding to associations would thus follow the election of citizens to use a particular service. I assume that the vast majority of citizens would reregister with the same service provider and that the annual public costs of turnover from one provider to another would be small. Inevitably, certain public services like policing, social work supervision of childrearing or compulsory psychiatry would not be at the citizen's discretion and would be similar in form to bureaucratic collectivist welfare today – except that the service providers might be voluntary associations fulfilling public contracts (such as a co-operative of social workers or a private psychiatric hospital).

If the desire is to build in strong components of citizens' choice in funding and to keep state discretion to a minimum, then the following methods might be used. Each service would develop (through the consociational machinery) a formula for funds per citizen election (dependent on age and status). Voluntary associations would thus receive annually funds proportionate to their previous years' registered (and publicly audited) membership for a given service. This might make up the bulk of the welfare budget available to associations (say 70 per cent). A number of objections need to be dealt with at this point. It might be argued, for instance, that associations would merely compete and not co-operate, that they would encourage inefficient duplication of expensive capital equipment, and that professionals would have little *esprit de corps* but be fragmented in specific associations. To meet these objections, two additional sources of citizens' election or voluntary initiative might be available. First, taxpayers might be enabled to allocate a portion of their annual tax payments (amounting to, say, 5 per cent of the total budget for associations) to a limited number of publicly registered associations of their choice (say five). This would allow citizens to target issues of public concern through choosing what to spend a portion of their taxes on.

Again, about 25 per cent of the budget for associations could be assigned to be spent through the consociational machinery on major new projects, on bids for extra funds or on co-operative ventures. This would give the consociational machinery real teeth, encourage associations to participate actively in it and provide professionals in a particular service with the means to co-operate across associations. It would both provide for major new capital spending and encourage associations to manage a particular service in a region as co-operatively as possible, developing common facilities where it was necessary and efficient to do so.

The many other complexities and difficulties of such an associationalist system cannot be explored here. One in particular does need to be dealt with, however. The associative model may appear to favour the well-educated middle classes with a "consumer" mentality and the skill to "work" the self-governing component of the system – defeating the poor and unskilled by the complexity of choices required. Actually, by giving the power of "exit" the system would empower the poor to a considerable degree. They could walk away from bad schools for example – something that is difficult to do in a collectivist-bureaucratic system. And because it does not require them to participate extensively in the democratic machinery of an association, it avoids the tendency for well-educated articulate citizens to dominate, which bedevils, for instance, school committees. Likewise, because the system could easily be made open to campaigning associations, it would enable those groups actively concerned to improve the position of the poor to obtain public funds by persuading poor people to make elections on their behalf. It would also enable alternative groups and non-establishment groups to set their own welfare agendas in ways that current bureaucratic welfare states do not permit (for example, providing proper medical services for "travellers"). For these reasons it has a strong potential to attract radicals as well as those who favour consumer choice.

Associationalism could contribute to resolving the current impasse of both policy ideas and public attitudes in the area of welfare. It would, as we have seen, promote greater citizens' choice and give citizens the initiative in funding rather than bureaucrats. It thus provides citizens with a rationale for spending more on welfare. Associationalism also offers a model that could be extended to other public and private services and their governance. Indeed, it offers a new model of *governance*: publicizing the "private" sphere of voluntary associations, and decentralizing and democratizing the public domain through self-governing associations.

Associationalism also has the immense advantage that it is tied to neither right nor left; likewise well-to-do and poor alike can exploit its possibilities.

As such, it is the one social doctrine that spans the major divisions of our current politics and enables diverse groups, political and apolitical, to co-operate while pursuing their own several projects. It is neither utopian nor dependent on a single social "carrier". Of all the current major doctrines of social organization, it is the one that has not failed. Unlike the socialism of the traditional left and the corporate apologists of the right in that it gives the power of choice to the people, associationalism has a chance of becoming truly popular.

Note

1. "Welfare" is understood here in the broader sense (current in America) of that changing bundle of public services that the state determines is necessary for its citizens to lead a satisfactory life as members of the political community. This includes sectors such as health and education, as well as "welfare" in the narrower British–Australian sense of the word.

Part III

Global pressures and
democratic governance

10

The state, civil society and the collapse of Soviet communism

The dissolution of Soviet rule in eastern Europe and the collapse of the Communist Party's monopoly of power in the Soviet Union has opened up the necessity to think about the political and constitutional future of those countries. This necessity is no less real in the west than in the east. At the same time we have no ready-made answers to guide that thinking. Marxism offers no guide, it has spurned concrete political and constitutional debate in an obsession with building a socialist society. It treated both liberal-democratic states and actually existing socialism as unstable halfway houses to be superseded by a social condition in which the state and law would "wither away". The dominant western concept for analyzing actually existing socialism – "totalitarianism" – is now obsolete, as the political structures which it attempted to capture have dissolved. Western liberal-democratic theory cannot analyze the complex processes of transition to new political regimes, as it offers a political ideal that is nowhere accomplished in eastern Europe and which is, at best, the goal of some of the reformers in those countries. The political thinking developed by the democratic oppositions in the satellite states of eastern Europe may appear to be more of a guide. Yet, as I shall try to show, it too is obsolete; shaped by the experience of resistance, it offers no adequate political model once the states dependent on Soviet power have collapsed.

This theoretical vacuum is matched by the ambiguity and uncertainty of political conditions in eastern Europe. The Soviet Union in particular is threatened by dissolution and political chaos. This is an exceptional situation without historical precedent and which leads to complex and con-tradictory political responses. The Soviet leadership, for example, is trying to move in two apparently contradictory directions at the same time. It is attempting to turn the Union into a real federation of self-governing republics based on a new treaty. It has also created an executive presidency that it hopes will prevent the secession of republics and contain conflict by ruling by emergency decree. In neither the Soviet Union nor in the ex-satellite republics is it clear that "democratization" will solve the political problems they face. Indeed, in the Soviet Union greater democracy may simply create the political mechanisms for intense social conflict and national fragmentation.

This is a difficult situation for the western left to comprehend. In retreat from fundamentalist socialism, it has staked its political future on the advocacy of the democratization of both state and civil society in the west. It has hailed the revolutions of 1989 in eastern Europe as offering the hope of democratic renewal and removing the antagonistic structures of the Cold War that inhibited radical reform in the west. The euphoria of the revolutions is already over, and new and harsh political realities confront the reformers in the east. The western left has quickly to comprehend these realities if it is not to be seduced by its own naivity and its own illusions. The Cold War is at an end, but this does not mean we are on the verge of a new era of peace and international harmony. Developments in eastern Europe could well result in an altogether more complex and threatening situation.

The arguments in this essay fall into two main parts. On the one hand I shall examine some salient examples of the political theory developed by the oppositions in eastern Europe. I shall argue that it offers no guide to the rebuilding of these states and that in particular the idea that they can be renewed on the basis of a "civil society" forged in opposition to the communist regimes is fallacious. On the other hand, I shall argue that the Soviet system collapsed for reasons that had little to do with opposition in eastern Europe or with the growing dissidence in the Soviet Union. *Perestroika* began as an attempt to *renew* Soviet power. I shall also argue that the collapse of the regime has left no pre-existing basis of unity, that the Soviet state is faced with fragmentation because nationality and religion were sources of opposition to the regime, and that if fragmentation were carried to its logical conclusion the result would be uncontainable conflict and untold suffering. In this context a new rationale emerges for a federal state, once it has separated itself from the rule of the party, and that is the most basic and primitive legitimation any state can have – the guarantor of public peace.

10.1 The anti-politics of Václav Havel

Marxism, as developed as a political theory by Lenin, is dominated by a secularized eschatology of the end of politics. Leninism combined an intense political pragmatism and realism in the current situation with the goal of creating a postpolitical world in which all need for domination and political conflict would be overcome in a society with a single material interest, without social divisions and in which abundance would remove conflicts over resources. Such a society, present in Marx's writings, is raised to the level of an immediate political goal. Lenin's libertarian illusions in

The state and revolution (1917) reinforced the authoritarianism of Lenin's immediate political practice, that is, the monopolization of power by hierarchical party. Authority must be concentrated to strike down all opposition to the building of a new society. Leninism creates an all-powerful state, a party dictatorship, in the service of creating a postpolitical society. The dictatorship of the proletariat was to be a transitional phenomenon, one that used dictatorial power to destroy the old society and create a new condition of real freedom beyond the formal and illusory structure of bourgeois legality. But this dictatorship foundered on the contradiction that its utopian and unattainable objectives could only reinforce an authoritarian form of power that must persist in the absence of a route to their realization. A.J. Polan's *Lenin and the end of politics* (1984) is a brilliant exposition of these contradictions in the doctrine and shows why Leninism continued to provide the core ideology of the Soviet state up to the advent of the radical reformers of the later 1980s.

Many socialists will reject this view of Lenin. It is true that Lenin was not a thug, that he believed in an emancipatory socialism and that he never envisaged the Soviet system would evolve into the Stalinist terror. At the end of his life he advocated a pact with the peasantry whereby the socialization of urban industry would develop *pari passu* with the gradual conversion of the market-based rural economy into a system of genuine peasant co-operatives. However, for all his last-minute conversion to a "liberal" course of socialist accumulation after the horrors of war communism, he could never concede the need for liberal political structures that would sustain his economic programme. The Lenin–Bukharin economic programme was vitiated by its failure to allow a significant measure of political pluralism. They clung to the Bolshevik Party's monopoly of power, to the system of secret police control, and to the inherently authoritarian practice of democratic centralism. They imagined that spontaneous mass action by the "toilers" could make this authoritarian set of institutions a "democracy". Leninism, as a political doctrine, was thus wide open to the Stalinist seizure of power within the party.[1]

The post-Stalinist system in the USSR and eastern Europe continued to be founded on Leninist political doctrine and legitimations. The end of the terror could not create the conditions for radical reform whilst the communist project and the party's monopoly of power remained the political cement of the system. Soviet rule remained predicated on the assumption that contradictions had no place within the socialist project, the conflict and opposition could only come from anti-socialist forces that opposed the construction of a new society and that would be superseded by its development. Politics could, therefore, only be official and socialist politics. All opposition remained a political crime for Brezhnev, Husák or Honecker as much as for Stalin, even if the methods of its repression became less brutal.

All true citizens subscribed to the project and to official ideology.

It is in this context that we must understand the anti-political thrust of Václav Havel's essay "The power of the powerless" (1987). Havel's essay is given prominence here because it is widely regarded in both eastern Europe and the west as one of the best and most thoroughgoing examples of an indigenous attempt to construct a political theory of the post-Stalinist Soviet satellite state in eastern Europe, and of the possibilities of internal resistance to it on the part of active citizens. Havel recognizes the Soviet system as an authoritarian anti-political regime, one which denies conflict, which negates any social goal but its own, and lives through ideology. Hence the centrality of resistance to the demands of ideology in Havel's text. For Havel, as for Czesław Miłosz in *The Captive Mind* (1953), the Soviet system relies on making ideology reality, imposing communism as the only possible historical course and making its citizens conform to this reality. However much the Soviet project may be rejected by the mass of the people as a genuine goal, they must be made to live in and through the forms of socialist ideology that were made real by power. Havel sees this as the enforced living of a lie, making the absurd real and, therefore, rational and inescapable.

There can be no conventional political response to an authoritarian anti-political state – which denies opposition and contrariety. Orthodox politics is powerless before a regime that excludes its possibility. Reform communism – making the system substantively rather than ideologically real – is negated both by the official denial of its legitimacy and by the fact that no genuine life can be breathed into Soviet institutions. Reform either implies dissolution of the Leninist project or another, and ultimately fatal, attempt to renew it. Havel's answer is "living within the truth", refusing to legitimate the lie by one's own conformity with the system, resisting its imperatives and creating parallel structures and initiatives based on the "independent life of society".

Given the centrality of ideology, given the dependence of power relations on making ideology real, truth is subversive and corrosive. Havel thus inverts Marx's analysis of ideology. Ideology is supremely characteristic of Soviet not capitalist societies. In actually-existing socialism it is ideology itself which rules rather than any social group or political clique, which cloaks its rule in ideological justifications. The "post-totalitarian" society is not a dictatorship in what Havel calls the "classical" sense – that is, the rule of a small group who hold power through force and are distinguished from those they govern. Because ideology is all-pervasive the "rulers" are subject to it too; rule is not based on a social group but on all-pervasive power relations stemming from ideology. This diffuse and omnipresent system of control cannot be opposed as if it were a dictatorship based on force with a definite social location; one that can be opposed by force with another social location.

Havel claims:

> This inevitably leads, of course, to a paradoxical result: rather than theory, or rather ideology serving power, power begins to serve ideology. It is as though ideology had appropriated power from power, as though it had become the dictator itself. It then appears that theory itself, ritual itself, ideology itself, makes decisions that affect people, and not the other way around. (1987: 47)

Havel's account mirrors Marx's view of the alienation inherent in idealism, in which hypostatized essences and conceptual entities are conceived as engendering the real. Soviet rule is a form of political fetishism, except that ideology, far from masking real relations, attempts to constitute them. Soviet systems are a practical idealism, they make ideology real.

Hence the need to expose the inversion, to deny the reality of ideology through resistance and "living in truth". Havel thus derives his anti-politics from the anti-political realization of the imaginary which is the inbuilt aim of the system. The problem here, as with the western concept of "totalitarianism", is to see the system as resting upon an enforced homogeneity, upon a denial of politics that makes political mobilization toward the anti-political goals of the system real and effective. However, if Leninism is an anti-politics, it is difficult to see how, in the long run, it could be an effective politics; how without a monopoly of force and a measure of economic prosperity it could succeed. How can it succeed if its goals are utopian? It must in fact rest on real powers and real inducements if it is to make good its claims, yet its ideological aims undermine its capacity to deliver.

Havel recognizes this when he claims that "the post-totalitarian system has been built on foundations laid by the historical encounter between dictatorship and the consumer society" (1987: 54) and when he sees the "automatism" of the system converting power into "ritual". But then, the system needs consumer satisfactions to survive and cannot create enough of them, and power can only be ritualized if it possesses enough force – enough military force – to secure it against external enemies, and enough police to ensure the internal political demobilization of the opposition. "Post-totalitarian" power needs economic success. It also needs sufficient resources to maintain its means of repression. If power becomes ritual, then its servants lack inner conviction. Failure to produce enough goods is fatal – the system cannot then sustain enough motivation in its servants in order for them to fight politically, rather than to act as mere technicians of repression. Soviet power ebbed, as I shall show, for straightforwardly economic and political reasons in both the USSR and eastern Europe – not because its citizens undermined it by "living in truth". Havel, like Marcuse's analysis of capitalism in *One dimensional man* (1964), gives too much emphasis to the realization of alienation.

Havel's anti-politics is not thereby justified as a response to a system whose goals are anti-political. The two forms of refusal of politics as conflict and struggle, Leninism and the resistance to it advocated by Havel, do not match up – the forms of resistance he advocates do not recognize or mesh the actual sources of failure of the Soviet-Leninist project. Havel's anti-politics is also "anti-political" in a broader sense established by Carl Schmitt, for Havel refuses to conceive politics as defined by struggle, as the conflict of friend and enemy.[2] For Havel the system cannot be opposed by organized groups but only by a conflict within each citizen, a personal refusal based on living in truth.

A project of resistance to power based on truth is no innovation in western political thought. Havel repeats a classical theme of Enlightenment thought – the opposition of absolute power and the truth located in the free conscience of the citizen and "civil society". My argument is derived from Reinhart Koselleck's *Critique and crisis – Enlightenment and the pathogenesis of modern society* (1988). Koselleck argues that absolutism emerges from the conflict of the religious civil wars in Europe in the sixteenth and seventeenth centuries. Confronted with a society and state riven by struggles between religious/social factions who each regarded the other as an enemy, absolutist thinkers like Jean Bodin and Thomas Hobbes sought to justify a public power that would be above "society", that would reserve to itself the right to determine all matters affecting its citizens (including the legitimate forms of religious belief) and which could ensure public peace. For the absolutist political philosopher this public power appeared to be "innocent", above and uncontaminated by the conflicts of a social order steeped in the guilt of religious prejudice and conflict. The doctrine of the state as a pure technology of power, of *raison d'état* concerned purely with the needs of political order, of a neutral power which annulled conflict, could appear as a positive value.

Once established, the absolutist state abrogates politics to itself. Politics becomes an *arcanum* enclosed within the realm of interstate conflict and the maintenance of internal "order". It thereby becomes associated with force *per se*, with repression, and with an immoral *raison d'état*. The state which could appear innocent to Hobbes *because* it was embroiled in no morality other than that of security, could thus come to appear to Enlightenment thinkers as immoral, as purely political and as unaccountable. "Civil society" by contrast could come to emerge as a positive concept. "Civil society" is the source of wealth, of truth, and of men living together in concord. It is subjected to the demands of a state which stands above it and pursues an immoral *realpolitik* which masks the truth. Civil society now becomes the truth of the polity, the source of criticism and the source of renewal. The state must be answerable to civil society and subordinate to its purposes. Once this is attained then the harmony which characterizes civil society can transform the state – the guilty secrets of *raison d'état* can be replaced by the public and innocent needs and aspirations of civil society made manifest in government.

Civil society is anti-political because it is harmonious. The state can be de-politicized if it becomes no more than an expression of the will of civil society. Religion becomes a matter of private conviction; wealth a matter of the free pursuit of interest in the market. International relations become pacified as the harmony of civil society in each state reduces the matter for war. These are the illusions of the Enlightenment – of a conflictless economy, of representative government, free trade and perpetual peace. Civil society is innocent and the truth of its innocence will remove the guilt inherent in the naked and immoral pursuit of power. These illusions of the Enlightenment were dangerous in both domestic and international affairs. Conflict could be removed neither from the struggles within new representative polities nor from their relations one with another. The anti-political illusions of the Enlightenment led to terror in the service of the creation of a harmonious republic of virtuous citizens and to war against despots and reactionaries in the case of the French revolution.

How close this account seems to much opposition writing in eastern Europe, and to Havel in particular. The Soviet state is a pure negation, founded on lies; in this case *raison d'état* in the service of utopian ideology. Civil society, the "independent life of society", is a source of truth, of critique of the guilty state, and of harmony. Citizens "living in truth" are united against the alienated and arcane rituals of power. "Civil society" is the source of all true opposition and the basis for renewal. "Civil society", opposed to the anti-political utopianism of the state concretized in an automatist *realpolitik* without genuine conviction on the part of its servants, is united and seeks a common goal, the needs of "life". Once freed from the chains of Soviet ritual, "life" can develop freely and spontaneously – citizens united without parties or conflicts in new democratic initiatives.

In Havel's writing and in much of Solidarity's ideology, "civil society" becomes a purely positive pole, outside of and uncontaminated by the state – the source of a new order.[3] Absolutism and Soviet power are not exact analogues, but the eastern European dissident endorsement of "civil society" as the basis for critique of and opposition to the state comes remarkably close to the structures of thought in the Enlightenment critique of absolutism. On pp. 169–75 below we will consider how far this stance of critique can be sustained after the fall of the Soviet *ancien régime*. Can one "live in truth" without being confronted by a regime that seeks to impose ideology as reality? Can "civil society" remain harmonious when not faced with a state-as-enemy?

I do not wish to be unfair to Havel. His opposition was heroic and involved great suffering and sacrifice. But political theories are no more sustained by the virtue of their proponents than they are invalidated by the political errors of their advocates. Havel's account of the "post-totalitarian system" is inadequate because it relies so much on the critique of ideology through truth. If his account of the Soviet regime is bedevilled by Enlightenment illusions, is there any prospect that his conception of politics after Soviet power has collapsed will be any more effective?

If Havel's critique bears all the marks of the most problematic aspects of the Enlightenment, his positive stance is even more flawed, for it draws on a source critical of Enlightenment reason and lacking in its positive features of scepticism and irony – Martin Heidegger's concept of "authenticity". Havel supports an "existential revolution" against the modern world. Traditional politics are bankrupt, east *and* west, because they rely on the inauthentic and alienating illusions of technical progress:

Technology – that child of modern science, which is in turn a child of metaphysics – is out of humanity's control, has ceased to serve us, has enslaved us and compelled us to participate in the preparation of our own destruction. And humanity can find no way out: we have no idea and no faith, and even less do we have a political conception to help us bring things back under human control. (Havel 1987: 114)

But "humanity" is not a political agent, it is part of Enlightenment metaphysics. Havel rejects dictatorship, but also the consumer society – unlike the vast mass of his countrymen, who have never seen enough of it.

Havel rejects not only Soviet dictatorship but also western democracy.

This planetary challenge to the position of human beings in the world is, of course, also taking place in the Western world ... Heidegger refers expressly to a crisis of democracy. There is no real evidence that Western democracy, that is, to a democracy of a traditional parliamentary type, can offer solutions that are any more profound. (1987: 115)

Parliamentary democracies "can offer no fundamental opposition to the automatism of technological civilization and the industrial-consumer society" (1987: 116). Quite so – parliamentary democracy can only survive on the basis of a successful consumer economy. Such a society imposes its own forms of "depoliticization", that is, it reduces politics to interest-group bargaining and prevents it turning into a decisive struggle of friend and enemy. Material prosperity demobilizes the conflict of social groups and confines political contestations within the limits that can be sustained by political pluralism and liberal norms of the conduct of political life.[4] Havel is rejecting our only known means of social peace and political stability in the service of nebulous goals expressed in the jargon of "authenticity".

Western democracies, for Havel, impose another form of alienating automatism. He has another vision: "I see a renewed focus of politics on real people as something far more profound than merely returning to the everyday mechanisms of Western (or if you like bourgeois) democracy" (1987: 117). The source of this political transcendence is an "existential revolution" which would "provide hope of a moral reconstitution of society" (*ibid.*) in a "post-democratic system" (1987: 119) based on fluid structures of "social self-organisation" (*ibid.*). A communalist "polis" based on the "independent life of society" is suspiciously like the Leninist illusion of a substantive popular direct democracy without the formal structures of the bourgeois state. Havel imagines this in quite another spirit, but Lenin was a utopian idealist too.

Such a system cannot be had. We cannot create a conflictless *polis* without formal structures of state and law. We cannot solve our problems without technology, nor can we ignore the common people's desire for material comfort. This synthesis of Enlightenment illusions and Heideggerian mystical anti-metaphysics is the worst kind of "political romanticism".[5] Havel is a political romantic because he wishes to transcend the real choices in politics, the real decisions, the real conflicts in an imaginary alternative. The *real* choice – western parliamentary democracy and the rule of law – is refused. East and west are both denied as inauthentic and alienating automatisms in favour of an imaginary resolution in a postdemocratic polis in which "humanity" returns to its authentic roots; Havel's essay has been widely admired in the west – its enemy being our enemy we have ignored its dangerous positive message. It has also been admired in the east, where much political thinking – *sans Heidegger* – has also sought a "third way" – until the fall of the *ancien régime*.

10.2 The reasons for Soviet collapse

When Mikhail Gorbachev came to power in 1985 the west was still involved in the second Cold War that began with the invasion of Afghanistan in 1978. No serious western observer imagined that in five years the monopoly of the Communist Party over Soviet politics would be for all practical purposes broken, that there would be intractable conflicts between democratically elected governments in the constituent republics of the USSR and Moscow, and that the full extent of Soviet economic failure would be publicly accepted by the Party. In 1988 no serious western observer could have predicted the revolutions of 1989, which destroyed the Soviet empire in eastern Europe. The same is true of even the most acute members of the east European opposition.

Some western thinkers had long indulged in the hope of Soviet collapse, many had portrayed the Soviet Union as an inefficient and ramshackle command economy but the Communist Party's iron grip on political power remained an inescapable fact. In practice the west *had* to deal with the Soviet system as a going concern – to attempt openly to subvert Soviet power was to court the edge of the nuclear abyss. In 1956, in 1968, and even after Afghanistan, western governments were forced to practice *realpolitik*. So in a different way were the oppositions in eastern Europe. They were forced after 1968 to treat Soviet domination as a fact, to work within the constraints and contradictions of Soviet rule. As Adam Michnik pointed out in 1976, it was in nobody's interest in Poland to provoke a Soviet invasion – the people would suffer, the local communist regime would lose all autonomy, and the Soviet Union would suffer crushing political defeat that would wreck any prospect of *détente* (Michnik 1985: 143–4). Until the very last gasp of Soviet power the opposition was forced to accept that Yalta was irreversible, but, given that, they sought to exploit Soviet weakness. The opposition began to act "as if" Poland, for example, was a free country, thereby attempting to undermine state power up to but not beyond the point where it would provoke a fatal crisis of the regime.

How did the Party's grip loosen? From the 1920s until the 1980s official Soviet writers presented the construction of Socialism in the USSR as a story of uninterrupted economic and social progress. That progress was accepted by Soviet commentators to have been diverted by political events, by Stalin's terror and by the German invasion, but these events could be presented as external constraints on a system whose basic economic development was healthy. Indeed, Soviet socialism did "succeed", in the sense that it built a modern urban industrial society in what had been in 1914 a rapidly developing but still backward and overwhelmingly rural peasant country. In 1970 some 55 per cent of the Soviet population lived in cities of 100,000 people or above, whereas in 1910 at least 80 per cent of the population lived in the countryside (Kerblay 1983: 55, 59). Into the 1970s the Soviet system notched up impressive rates of growth. Soviet socialism built an industrial society by brutal ruthless methods, but it brought the USSR to the brink of modernity, where comparisons with and expectations of competing with the west became appropriate. At this point its failure became apparent and inescapable: a system created by "primary socialist accumulation" and the continuous expansion of heavy and defence industry reached inherent limits of organization that imposed declining returns. Soviet industry expanded by the extensive exploitation of natural resources and labour reserves, growth by ever more lavish squandering of inputs. By the 1970s the limits of such extensive accumulation had been reached.

The Soviet administration of the economy – a complex, cumbersome, and inefficient structure of overlapping "ministries" – could not switch to

intensive accumulation: to the extended production of manufactured consumer goods, to the enhancement of labour productivity in manufacturing
industry, and to the development of a modern system of distribution and
services. Soviet propaganda had under Khrushchev and Brezhnev created
the expectation of modern mass consumer society, that the Soviet economy
would match and supersede that of the west. This it was incapable of doing,
even if the Soviet economy had not been burdened with accelerating
military expenditure and an ever growing demand by military for scarce
resources of R&D, high-tech production and skilled labour.

However, despite the inefficiency of the Soviet economy there was no
reason why the Soviet leadership should have accepted either the reality of
failure or the need for reform. The Brezhnev era survived on the presen-
tation of failure as success, official pronouncements reaching new levels of
cant, lies and absurdities that would not have disgraced Stalin and his
henchmen. The USSR entered on an arms race with the west, expanding
military expenditure and force levels and seeking to match western weapons
systems. The USSR could have embarked on a course of continued
confrontation with the west and an aggressive foreign policy, imposing
sacrifices on its citizens in the course of containing enemies without.

Why did it not continue to do so? Soviet ideology has always been two
sided. On the one hand, Soviet leaders since Lenin have preached the
utopian goals of abundance and material success, calling for sacrifices now
to build a better future. The Soviets have shared with western capitalist
nations the goal of material prosperity, whilst claiming that a planned
command economy is a better and more efficient means of attaining it. This
may be called the Saint-Simonian pacific and "industrial" side of Soviet
ideology – legitimating Soviet power by the reality and the hope of material
progress. On the other hand, Soviet ideology has also been a militant
revolutionary faith, claiming to struggle against class enemies within and
without. This may be called the Jacobin side of Soviet ideology – stressing
struggle and sacrifice. Legitimating Soviet rule through quasi-military
metaphors and rituals. However cautious Soviet policy may have been,
however little the genuine commitment to real revolutionaries abroad,
however much the advocacy of "peace" and the claim Soviet military power
was defensive in intent, the ruling Party had maintained the rituals and
rhetoric of a revolutionary sect. The myths of containment by the capitalist
west and of imperialist aggression could have sustained a militant policy.
This would have legitimated Soviet rule by the need to resist foreign
enemies, strengthening authoritarianism by creating crises and confron-
tations with the west and imposing ruthless discipline on the population
through the Party.

What prevented this neo-Stalinist policy emerging is a matter for con-
jecture. There can be no doubt that even many of the top Party leadership

were sick of the insecurity and fear created by Stalin's terror, of which they too were victims. But faced with internal failure other states have sought release in foreign confrontation. The answer is that by the mid-1950s nuclear deterrence had removed the option of a policy of wholesale rather than piecemeal and proxy confrontation with the west. Soviet military expansion was in large part the attempt to match the west in the numbers and sophistication of nuclear weapons. This brought no advantage, only a stalemate. A reckless policy of confrontation was checked by the fear of a nuclear exchange should a crisis get out of hand. The Cuban missile crisis simultaneously forced upon the Soviet leadership the reality of nuclear confrontation, the covert recognition of the reality of deterrence that has only now come to be accepted in Soviet military doctrine, and the need for accelerated spending on nuclear arms to achieve parity with the USA.

The effects of this militarization in the Brezhnev years was to reinforce economic retrogression. Given the inefficiency of the Soviet economy, military expansion forced an ever greater burden on the civilian economy – consuming between 25 and 30 per cent of GDP. The drive for parity brought with it a resolute western response, an arms race whose costs the western economies could bear far more easily (the USA spending in recent years on average about 6 per cent of GDP on the military, most other western powers 3 per cent or less). Soviet leaders therefore faced an inescapable crisis by the mid-1980s – accelerating military expenditure that neither brought "security" nor the means of diversion from domestic ills through foreign confrontation. Stalemate was purchased at an ever higher price. Western leaders like President Reagan and Mrs Thatcher were clearly prepared to sustain the arms race to levels where the USSR could not compete.

The west "won" the Cold War, but only because the Soviet leadership possessed the rationality to give way. At first this surrender to the needs of internal reform and external peace was cautious and conducted through Leninist rhetoric. Mikhail Gorbachev came to power as a reformer committed to renewing the Soviet system so that it could become more efficient and preserve its grip on power. The aim was threefold: to lessen international tension, reduce the burden of arms spending, and to make Soviet institutions work efficiently but without relinquishing the Party's monopoly on power. *Glasnost* was to permit the flow of information and discussion in order to breathe life into official policy-making, undoing the illusions and lies that passed for official thought in the Brezhnev era. *Perestroika* was to restore legality, to recreate inner Party democracy, and to combat corruption and incompetence in the bureaucracy. But, as Gorbachev's own book *Perestroika* (1987) shows, not to abandon Leninism (at least formally). Gorbachev still relied on the illusion that the Leninist state could be renewed, that a "true" efficient communism was possible. As a senior official of the KGB he had intimate knowledge of Soviet corruption and failure, but in the first stages of reform he was far from abandoning the leading role of the Communist Party or the basic structures of the command economy; on the contrary, these were to be rebuilt by honest communists who could both speak freely and act within the law.

Slowly, but inexorably the agenda of reform was shifted in response to both the realities of the Soviet crisis and the effects of freer public debate. Gorbachev may have secretly harboured more radical aims when he began, although this is unlikely. His regime has been driven to radicalism because it permitted a measure of objectivity to enter into the debate about the true nature and future of Soviet society. Only a hermetic Brezhnevite world of official absurdity could have continued to contain this. Gorbachev was driven toward a more radical foreign policy by the desperate need for accommodation with the west. A lasting peace was impossible while the Soviets retained the option of containing reform in eastern Europe through force. Any move like 1968 in Czechoslovakia would have renewed the iciest depths of the Cold War. The Soviet Union thus at first left its satellite governments in eastern Europe to their own devices, leaving them to make what accommodations with their peoples that they could – a process that led to what Timothy Garton Ash called "refolution", evident in Hungary and Poland, absent in the DDR and Czechoslovakia where the existing elites staged a last ditch defence.[6] "Refolution" became revolution once the Soviet Government made clear it would not back militant repression by force and when the KGB began to work against rather than with the client communist regimes. Collapse followed swiftly, because fear of military force vanished once Moscow refused to play the role of gendarme Russia had exercised in eastern Europe since the nineteenth century. The revolutions occurred, not because the opposition could seize power through an internal dynamic – it was weak in the DDR and in Czechoslovakia, and on the verge of failure in Poland – but because Moscow abandoned the satellite parties and left them neither the means nor the will to resist.

Is the USSR too passing from reform into "refolution" and, finally, in the not too distant future into dissolution? It has passed to "refolution" certainly. It has become evident even to cautious reformers that an adequate programme of economic change cannot be achieved without radical political change. The economic renewal of the Soviet Union requires the decentralization of economic decision-making, the autonomy of enterprises, the creation of markets, new incentives for labour to enhance productivity, and the creation of alternative sources of investment. This involves the dissolution of the economic control of the "Ministries", autonomy for the republics, privatization, the creation of a "hard" currency, the ending of the state monopoly of foreign trade, and the creation of capital markets. This is simply incompatible with the Party's monopoly of power and it requires the separation of Party and State. Once this is accomplished the Party cannot refuse genuinely free elections, multiparty competition, and the sovereign autonomy of the republics. The Soviet system is at the edge of what can be attained by "refolution" and is currently hesitating. Reform has come too late to be an orderly process, and was never possible within the existing constitution once the national aspirations and antagonisms, so long suppressed by the centre, could be given expression.

However, the possibility and the success of the necessary economic changes remains in doubt. If Soviet political institutions are inexorably transformed and yet the economy fails to be transformed and fails to begin to deliver some measure of prosperity, then the prospects for a relatively stable transition to a new social system are bleak. The Soviet system cannot cope with an open conflict between the centre and the republics, with conflicting agendas for reform, with defections from the Union, *and* with mass unemployment and poverty. We shall return to this crisis and how it may be resolved.

10.3 Can "civil society" sustain the post-Soviet democratic state in Eastern Europe?

Czechoslovakia, Hungary and Poland are in the process of constructing western-style parliamentary democratic states and market economies. The new leaderships recruited from the democratic and anticommunist opposition see this dual process as an essential precondition for removing the objective foundation of the postwar Soviet system. Political pluralism and the winding up of the command economy are *politically* essential if the sources of the monopoly of power by the Party are to be eliminated, even if they bring in train conflict and economic dislocation. Reform has a political legitimacy which can sustain it against elements of the old regime even in the face of short-term unemployment and a fall in living standards, even if marketization fails to provide an immediate "economic miracle". The population of all three countries (and of the DDR before unification) showed its understanding of this political necessity by giving the majority of votes to those parties and electoral groupings most committed to dismantling the system, spurning reform communists even where they had taken the lead in promoting "refolution" – as in Hungary.

Nevertheless, some elements of the new political elite in both Czechoslovakia and Poland continue to cling to a source of legitimacy that had force in opposition as a basis for avoiding conflict in the new transitional period, that is, the reliance on "civil society" and the idea of a unified "citizens" movement standing above traditional party-political divisions. Elements in both Civic Forum/Public Against Violence in Czechoslovakia and Solidarity in Poland have until as recently as the early summer of 1990 clung to the hope that these movements can remain majority coalitions, sustained by popular citizens' initiative at the base.

The majority of the new elites are clear there is no "third way" between the Soviet and the western *social* systems. The idea of a third way enjoyed some currency in the 1960s and beyond among reforming communists in the east and social democrats in the west, who hoped that a new system could be created that was neither communist nor capitalist, but took features from both in a humane democratic socialism. That idea is now dead. The consensus in eastern Europe is that the communist social and political system must be dissolved, that there are no positive features of the old regime that can be conserved. This consensus does not mean that all members of the new elites favour orthodox westernization at any price. Argument centres on the price of dissolution of the old regime and the need for measures of social support and welfare to cushion the costs of transition. Hayekian liberals in eastern Europe, who do not follow the thesis of "civil society" favour rapid conversion to the "free market". The problem is that Hayekian liberalism cannot address the *political* crisis in eastern Europe, it presupposes a political stability that has to be built. Hayekian economic reforms will exacerbate this crisis by imposing intense social strains consequent on economic dislocation. Elements of the old opposition forces who are not dogmatic economic liberals are forced in addressing this crisis to turn back to the forms of solidarity that sustained them under Soviet rule in order to create a new basis of political stability.

Elements emerging from the old "civic" opposition in Czechoslovakia and Poland favour clinging to the concept of a politically united "civil society" to cushion the antagonisms created by the introduction of market mechanisms. This view is in effect tantamount to the idea of a *political* rather than a social "third way", different from both communism and western party systems. The idea is that the dissolution of communism can be managed by a single dominant political coalition that preserves the vast majority of the old opposition and citizen voters within a single grouping looser than a conventional political party and built upon the experience of solidarity against the divisive pressures of the old regime whilst in opposition.

One should remember that this experience of opposition was entirely novel and that the advocates of resistance through "civil society" were responsible for a remarkable innovation in political strategy. Havel, Michnik and others preached non-violent resistance and Solidarity was able to practice it on a social scale in Poland after 1980. By not contesting political power, by building parallel structures, by mixing dialogue and resistance, the opposition in the Polish case was able to build a base of power beyond the reach of state repression. Martial law in Poland could suppress opposition and drive it underground, but not eliminate it. As a strategy for resistance, for creating opposition to communist attempts to pulverize political alternatives, it worked – up to a point. Where that strategy could be practised it prevented the terrifying political vacuum after the communist defeat one sees in Rumania, for example. This experience was formative of the new political elites, as resisters. It in no way equipped them for power.

"Civil society" made sense in the context of the communist regime's attempts to monopolize all social life and culture. It drew on sources of autonomy the regimes could not crush except at the price of wrecking their own compromises essential to the survival of their power – like the concordat with the church in Poland or, less effectively, their formal sub-scription to the Helsinki accords. However, therein lies the great weakness of the appeal to "civil society". Once social life is not monopolized, once independent political, cultural, educational and other institutions have the space in which to emerge, then the basis for the homogeneity of the forces united in opposition to the illegitimate state dissolves. Civil society, in another sense, opens up a field of potential conflict and competition between the forces hitherto brought together by a repressive state, hitherto possessing a common interest in helping each other to survive.

Martial law initially demobilized and repressed Solidarity. It had relied on acting "as if" Poland were a free country. Once it became a military dictatorship the space for non-violent and open opposition disappeared. Martial law failed because, whilst it could suppress the opposition, it had no means to make either the economy or the society work. That demanded co-operation with Solidarity, but such collaboration undermined the forces of repression. Jaruzelski's government was condemned under martial law to immobility in the face of socio-economic crisis. Yet the new Polish govern-ment has inherited the self-same crisis raised to a new power. ROAD (Civic Movement-Democratic Action) and the Centre-Alliance, the two main wings of Solidarity, are divided as to how to resolve it. The social and political forces loosely grouped around each camp are a fundamental line of cleavage in a once homogeneous "civil society".

"Civil society" has been seen as a means of avoiding fundamental conflict by those who fear such a cleavage in Poland and by those who fear the consequences of Slovak nationalism and a move to ruthless economic liberalism in Czechoslovakia. The economic modernizers, Leszek Balcerowicz and Václav Klaus, are pursuing reform strategies that will test their respective economies close to the point of destruction, however "inevitable" they may be. They are pushing economic programmes on a technocratic basis, without reference to the political conditions on which they can be sustained. This is where the voices from the old opposition come in and why their adherence to the solidarity of "civil society" against or as a supplement to the strategies of the modernizers may appear rational. "Civil society" is the locus for an attempt to avoid the "political" – in Carl

Schmitt's sense – preventing conflicts from developing to the point of irreconcilable antagonism on the basis of ideological parties in the new representative democratic system. As we have seen such a hope is explicable on the basis of the experience of opposition to an apparently monolithic regime. Many people of goodwill are dismayed that unity and civility shown in opposition to a brutal state cannot be preserved once freedom has been gained. The confusion is understandable, but it is naive to hope that unity can exist without a common "enemy", a regime whose crass authoritarianism could provide a common basis of opposition for all who were not careerist servants of the state.

Goodwill, trust and co-operation would have to be recreated on a new basis. Yet a *new* solidarity cannot emerge without the institutions for some new form of political co-operation. Appealing to the *old* solidarity, to the *old* unity of "civil society" is trying to recreate a political experience whose conditions are past. The appeal is credible to those who voice it because political parties are as yet prototypical, and social interests are still incoherent and not yet institutionally defined. Yet, the process of political definition of the opposing groups cannot long be avoided if new sources of stability are to be introduced into the system. These sources will not spring from the old "civil society" and they cannot recreate the old "solidarity". The new societies of eastern Europe will not quickly create the civil society of western Europe. But they must quickly create the forms of political stability characteristic of western Europe – parties that define clear political alternatives and act as a political check one upon the other. Without such explicit expression *and* containment of political conflicts, the antagonisms that are emerging cannot be deflected by normal political processes of opposition, bargaining and compromise. These antagonisms are powerful – national and regional differences, the divergent interests of city and countryside, and of workers in large and inefficient socialist enterprises versus the economic modernizers.

"Civil society" is not homogeneous, and clinging to the political myth of its homogeneity fostered by the experience of opposition will probably do the opposite of what is intended, that is, accelerate the conflict between certain interest groups and the state. Only the creation of a party system and the building-up of a political culture that accepts competition within democratic norms can secure the transition to western representative democracy in any meaningful sense. This will be difficult if economic success and consumer prosperity do not come relatively quickly. If they do not, and that is the most likely outcome, then political stability may be threatened. Social interests may become increasingly antagonistic and political forces increasingly polarized. Antagonistic pluralism is a real threat if the previous constraints of the authoritarian regime cannot be quickly replaced by a system of institutionalized pluralist conflict and a stable party system. In this context constitutional questions are of the utmost importance. The state must be strengthened both as a means of protecting citizens' rights through constitutional guarantees and an independent judiciary, and as a means of preserving political order through the constitutional defence of the power to govern. In central Europe this balancing act may just prove possible. To look on the positive side, neither Poland nor Czechoslovakia has the kind of intense political divisions stemming from nationality and religion that characterize the USSR or Yugoslavia. Poland has a remarkable degree of ethnic and religious homogeneity, despite strong potential sources of social conflict. Czechoslovakia has a strong democratic tradition and a federal structure that may just prove capable of guaranteeing sufficient autonomy to check Slovak nationalism.

The advocates of "civil society" and an overarching "citizens' movement" are seeking to delay this process of formation of a party system in the interests of short-term political harmony. As we have seen they are continuing an anti-politics shaped in opposition to the communist state into the post-Soviet era. They are seeking a democratic depoliticization through a unified majoritarian rule of a citizens' bloc over and against the aim of political containment through a western-style party system. The theory of "civil society" developed on the liberal left. It has found western advocates on the left, seeking the renewal of western democracy through citizens' and social movements, like John Keane.[7] The advocates of "civil society" like Václav Havel and Adam Michnik were non-violent anti-authoritarian radicals. Yet the idea of a majoritarian bloc, building a mass base of support and containing the parties, could well develop in an altogether less libertarian direction. The question is who builds such a bloc? Solidarity is no longer unified, and divisions are developing in Civil Forum.

A democracy which contains political competition, utilizing the idea of a common citizens' interest, may develop in the direction of a national popular regime. Such a regime is easier to imagine than a liberally inclined citizens' coalition led by radicals. It is difficult to see how such a bloc can function without a degree of authoritarianism. By internalizing conflicts within an overarching and yet incoherent political entity a liberal-left regime would make the internal politics of government explosive, by marginalizing the losers in the process of transition, and by forcing opposition to operate outside the regime but without the means of influencing policy. "Civil society" as a homogeneous *political* force is an idea at variance with modern pluralist mass democracy, which relies on the *divisions* of civil society expressed in political competition contained within the party system to ensure social and political order. Homogeneity can only be preserved if interests are not radically divergent. If they are, then a majoritarian regime can only work through a degree of authoritarianism which contains and suppresses other interests, which marginalizes political competition. This cannot be liberal. Such a regime is more likely to be of the centre-right.

It is more than possible that the political divisions in at least one of the eastern European countries will not be contained in stabilized political competition, that such divisions will lead to a conflict in which one party prevails. In that context, however, the new majoritarian-monopolistic regime may draw on at least some aspects of the ideology of civil society and appropriate the experience of opposition as the basis for a new legitimacy. Regimes in decolonized countries in the third world, like Indonesia or Ghana in the immediate postindependence period, used the myth of national homogeneity and the unity forged in the liberation struggle to justify "guided democracy" or one-party rule.[8] It would be sad but not impossible if such an analogous regime were to emerge in eastern Europe.

To speculate – something that is most dangerous as the results of the Polish presidential elections will long precede the publications of this essay – one could imagine a Wałesa presidency evolving into a hybrid between the regimes of Pilsudski and De Gaulle. This would not be a brutal dictatorship: it would marginalize rather than crush the opposition. It would, however, merge nationalism, workerism, a Catholic confessional conception of Polish society, with the claim to inherit the true conditions of Solidarity. It would be opportunistic, claiming support from worker resistance to change, claiming the peasantry for its own, and building a hybrid economy that was a mixture of free markets and concessionary subsidies. It would claim to unite "civil society", meaning the union of Church and People, peasants and workers. This, of course, is to imagine a possible regime, and nothing more. The purpose of such speculation is not idle; however, the aim is not to guess the future but by means of a rather hasty thought experiment to show how the idea of political homogeneity at the root of the oppositional idea of "civil society" could be turned into a legitimation of a regime far removed from those ideals of the resisters of the communist autocracy. My aim here is not to sully the experience of opposition, rather it is to show that the experience cannot be translated to the postcommunist regime. Political ideas can undergo strange mutations, let us hope this one does not. Let us hope also that the explicit commitment of Václav Havel and the more ambiguous promises of Lech Wałesa to construct a western-type pluralist democracy are what happens, and that these countries find stability through a modern party system.

In the long run, eastern Europe can only create a modern western-style "civil society" and the party system based on it, if it ensures a satisfactory level of economic prosperity. Without such prosperity, democracy will be both a source of instability and a means of pursuing social conflict. An eastern Europe plunged in poverty and unemployment may repeat the political experience of this area between the wars, where dictatorship was the norm rather than the exception. Western Europe has a powerful interest in ensuring stability in such countries as Czechoslovakia, Hungary and Poland by providing them with the aid, investment and technical assistance necessary to prosperity. This is in our immediate political interest, and, in practice, gives a priority to western aid over and above even the pressing need for greater social and economic justice in the third world. They have become *our* satellites now, not the Soviets'.

The collapse of Soviet rule in eastern Europe has in effect restored the "cordon sanitaire" the western states created against the USSR in the 1920s. That zone of economically and militarily weak states, governed predominantly by fragile dictatorships, constituted a source of weakness rather than strength. With the renaissance of German power under Hitler they became a zone of contestation between the Nazi and Soviet imperiums. The precise conditions of the 1930s are unlikely to be repeated, but a zone of weak states on the border of an unstable and dissolving Soviet regime, outside the western security system, offers multiple sources of conflict. Even the most encouraging scenario is fraught with problems. The successful incorporation of the eastern states into the western economic, military and political order will inevitably push the "West" towards the Soviet border. It would then face the Soviet world on a new frontier and one which gives both the USA and the EC a real interest in the political future of the area which was the core of the Soviet Empire. A USSR that achieved the transition to democracy and economic renewal would pose no great threat. An unstable and dissolving USSR is a real menace to the west, if the west has to think of a frontier that begins in Poland. For that reason, the west has an immediate interest not only in the states of Eastern Europe, but in the political future of the USSR. Will the Union survive? And how? – are questions not only for Moscow but for Brussels and Washington.

10.4 Democracy, nationality and the Union – the basis for legitimacy of Moscow's power after communism?

The break up of the Soviet Empire exceeds the wildest dreams of the most hardened Cold Warriors. Not only have the satellite states collapsed, but Soviet rule in the USSR seems on the verge of dissolution. Suddenly the dream has gone sour. The USSR is still a superpower with a massive nuclear arsenal and the question arises, who in the case of a dissolution of the power centre will control the missiles? The joint pressure of the superpowers has helped to contain nuclear proliferation, Soviet foreign policy has both used third-world states as a means of contestation with the west, and yet has been able to impose limits on the conflict, forcing its clients to accept a subordinate role for fear that regional conflicts would escalate into a nuclear confrontation between the superpowers. Soviet rule may be wholly unjustified in the Baltic Republics and in Moldavia, but how should the west view the ending of Moscow's control over the southern, predominantly Islamic, republics of the USSR or over the Ukraine and Belarus?

US policy-makers and analysts have discovered an interest in the survival of something resembling Moscow's control of the Eurasian land mass. Some, indeed, fear that we shall come to look on the era between Yalta and 1989 as a period of stability and certainty in international affairs broadly favourable to the west. The west, of course, cannot ensure the fate of Mr Gorbachev. Even the greatest successes in disarmament and the reduction of regional conflicts can no longer ensure the future of a regime whose primary sources of conflict and instability are internal. Soviet politics are shifting from international settlements firmly under the control of Moscow, to the issues of relations between the republics and economic recon-struction where the agendas are set by the radicals and the independence movements.

The destruction of the Party's monopoly of power has brought to the surface all the conflicts suppressed by centralized authoritarian rule. Unity in the Soviet system was identified with the Party. To present this as Russian domination is too simple, the Party had pan-national sources of support and created a system based on the suppression of nationality – including purely Russian nationalism. Because of this, the sources of opposition to Soviet rule and oppositional identity were located in nationality and religion. The break up of the Party's monopoly of power and ending of the fusion of party and state have left no coherent basis of legitimacy for the Union. If "socialism" unified the Union, its collapse leaves an ideological vacuum. Into that vacuum have stepped the national movements, national churches and national cultural forces (stressing local languages and cultural traditions) that have no common ground and often have bitter antagonisms stretching back into the Tsarist era. In eastern Europe Soviet rule tended to unify the opposition against the state, nationalism and religious and cultural identity were cohesive forces. In the USSR the opposite is true; national, religious and cultural identities threaten a supranational state which inherited the rule of the Tsarist imperium over lesser nations.

Thus the advent of "politics", of the possibility of opposition and debate, has opened the space for conflicts the existing system has no hope of containing. Far from giving the space for the expression of a homogeneous "civil society" which would be the foundation for a new representative democratic order, the dissolution of Soviet power has created the space for heterogeneous and antagonistic forces to compete against one another and the centre for power. It is not easy to see how a united "civil society" based on ideological differences and social interests could be created over and above the conflicting national interests of and within the republics. The option, possible – if difficult – in eastern Europe, of building a western-style party system seems remote in the USSR. Democracy cannot, therefore, be sustained by organized political competition alone, rather, the more "democratic" the system becomes the more it offers the means of conflict to political forces that find it hard to achieve a common interest. This is as true *within* certain of the republics as it is between them. In Lithuania or Azerbaijan, for example, Russian or Armenian minorities are in conflict with relatively homogeneous and dominant nationalist groupings.

Economic reforms cannot remove these contradictions. Republics like the Baltics and the RSFSR (Russian Soviet Federal Socialist Republic) have radically different agendas for reform from that of Moscow. It is unlikely that either the radical or the cautious reform programmes will bring rapid increases in prosperity. The radical programme, if it does take place, will lead to unemployment and dislocation. It will also weaken the powers of the centre over the economy and accelerate the divorce of Party and State. Cautious reform is unlikely to increase output and will also bring unemployment and dislocation on a lesser scale.

The Communist Party is likely to fragment, and is already being "balkanized" as its leaderships in the republics struggle to assert their autonomy to bolster their power as the leaders rather than becoming the victims of nationalist dissent. If Party and State are separated, if a new Union treaty creates rights for the republics, including secession, on the model of Sakharov's proposed constitution, then the centre will become increasingly an inheritor of a supranational state, but without a clear national social or party base. Gorbachev is feared in radical circles as a new "dictator". Radicals fear the President's capacity to rule by emergency decree and believe that he will become the focus for conservative forces.

It is important to note what kind of dictatorship this would be. Gorbachev would not be a new Stalin, as some radicals claim. Stalin's dictatorship was in Carl Schmitt's terms a "sovereign" dictatorship, committed to revolutionizing society and sustained by a Party cadre loyal to him, with strong powers of political mobilization of the masses. Gorbachev will not have a political base, fashioned out of the fusion of Party and State. His authoritarian rule will be in form at least closer to that of a "commissarial" dictator in Carl Schmitt's terms, a defender of the constitution and the established order.[9] However, this will not be a constitutional office as in western democracies forced to rule through emergency powers, because the Soviet constitution is vestigial and unstable. Gorbachev cannot seek to restore the *status quo ante*, because it is in ruins. He has been given exceptional powers, but to contain conflict so that a new legal-constitutional order can be created.[10] He will have to rely on the Supreme Soviet for the legitimacy of his rule by decree and upon the forces of the state – principally the troops of the Interior Ministry – to enforce it. Such a quasi-commissarial dictatorship can only hope to "manage" the worst strains and symptoms of change; preventing intercommunal violence and dealing with clashes between republics, taking emergency action to deal with specific economic crises, widespread strikes, and so on. It presupposes a broader political will to sustain at least the core of the Union. If such a will cannot be created and expressed in the Supreme Soviet, Gorbachev's constitutional position will become impossible, and a move to such a dictatorship futile.

Gorbachev's exceptional powers, far from raising the spectre of Stalin, are strictly limited and are probably inadequate as the basis for even a commissarial dictatorship. They can only work, within their present limits, if they serve to contain the strains in creating a new relationship between the republics and a new basis of authority within them. The state cannot hold the Union together, it cannot stifle the multiple antagonisms or prevent them becoming fully "political" in Schmitt's sense, by pure political will or by military force. A commissarial dictatorship in a limited and legal sense can only arrest such a process if it can rally forces outside itself. The Union may survive the orderly, phased and negotiated secession of the Baltic States and Moldavia. It could not survive the secession of the Ukraine, or the republics in the Caucasus and Central Asia. In that case both the federal Soviet state and Gorbachev's function as President would cease to have any function.

The danger of a wholesale secession is real and from a western perspective worrying. This is not because the Ukraine and the RSFSR would not be viable states – both contain large populations and the bulk of the natural resources and industrial production of the Union. Rather the danger is the political situation created by large-scale secession, and here the Ukraine will be the crucial factor. The threat is of a Great Russian backlash, that faced with collapse, with bitter struggles between pro-Russian and ultranationalist factions in the Ukraine, the existing and fragile political balance of forces may be broken. The military, conservative element in the Party, Gorbachev himself, or even Yeltsin – an accomplished opportunist who may yet play the Russian national-populist card – may react to this situation by trying, and perhaps succeeding, to restore Russian hegemony on a new basis. The new basis would be an authoritarian state ruled by a postcommunist conservative elite, using Great Russian nationalism as its basis for legitimacy. Such a regime would rest on force, not law. Such a regime would find it difficult to continue the current rapprochement with the west, and the western powers would find it difficult to tolerate its repressive measures against the nationalities, although it could do little to check them.

This danger is possible. After 1917, when the Tsarist empire dissolved, the communist rulers in Moscow fought back in a bitter civil war, not only against the Whites, but against Nestor Makhno in the Ukraine, against the Georgian Menshevik Republic and against the independent Poles, in order to recreate a Great Russian state in a new form. Independence movements and emergent states were suppressed by military force, despite popular support. This battle was legitimated by the claims of revolutionary socialism not imperialism, presenting Soviet rule, falsely, as the restoration of workers' and peasants' power in free republics linked in a genuine Union. The Soviet bid for hegemony in eastern Europe was stopped by the Poles before Warsaw in 1920 but this did not prevent the Bolsheviks from recreating Moscow's rule throughout most of the old Tsarist empire.

In this context, the survival rather than the break up of the Soviet Union may appear the more attractive option. The forces for conservatism in the Union do not come from communist reactionaries alone. Russian populations in the non-Russian republics have much to fear from majority nationalisms. Republics like Armenia have a great deal to fear from their neighbours. Those who favour a liberal religious policy, a secular state and secular education, and the emancipation of women have much to fear from political fundamentalist Islam in the Central Asian republics. Economically, many of the lesser Republics are unviable unless they are able to export to the Union and have access to Russian raw materials at something other than prevailing world prices paid in hard currency. This is far from providing a politically coherent base for a policy of maintaining the Union as a federation of free states, but it does provide the centre with some room for manoeuvre and some contingent support.

For the foreseeable future the Soviet Union cannot hope to move to a western-style liberal parliamentary system. No such system has ever survived the kind of centripetal forces and social strains faced by the Union. At the same time the rule of the Party must be dissolved and political competition will take its place. An executive presidency answerable to the Supreme Soviet is, paradoxically, essential if democracy is to be developed without destroying the political system in the process. Rights for the republics and for all Union citizens are also essential, but they will be ineffective unless they are backed by executive power in the last instance. The Union was built on injustice and violence, but its dissolution could lead to comparable injustice and violence. Without central authority able to intervene in intercommunal violence, deportations and the wholesale displacement of persons could quickly become the bitter reality underlying the assertion of freedom by the republics.

We have returned to one of the most basic legitimations of political power – that it ensures order and public peace. Sustainable political power has one ultimate legitimation, that it offers order. To offer *order*, not authoritarian chaos through state power, as in Hitler's or Stalin's rule, political authority must be based on the combination of a commitment to the rule of law and the possession of the force necessary to uphold it. This is the lesson Bodin drew from religious civil wars in sixteenth-century France – the message of the *politiques*, that civilization first of all demands order rather than the fulfilment of ideological goals. Against the amorphous and yet powerful ideologies of the emergent nationalism, it is a message that needs to be heeded in the USSR. Democratization alone cannot guarantee the political order that is necessary to ensure its own survival. Whether order can be maintained in the USSR is anyone's guess, but to welcome the dissolution of the Union is to court chaos. To do so, to brand efforts at stabilization as "dictatorship" in the interests of an abstract principle of democracy or national self-determination, is dangerous in the extreme. The west may in fact suffer few real losses from a Soviet break-up, but the peoples of that imperfect Union will suffer from social antagonisms and intercommunal violence.

Postscript

It is inevitable that an essay like this will be overtaken by events in the course of publication. It was written in September 1990 before the military crackdown in Latvia and Lithuania and before the resignation of Edvard Shevardnadze. The paper argues that democratization alone cannot solve the problems of the USSR, because greater democracy provides the means for social tensions and national conflicts to be expressed but does not provide the means to contain them. It goes on to argue that a central authority with exceptional powers is necessary if such conflict is to be checked, so that a transition to a postcommunist system can continue. Such an authority must attempt to use exceptional powers only to uphold law and order and must itself be legitimated by the grant of these powers from representative bodies. Such limited exceptional powers are contrasted with the likely regime that would follow a conservative backlash and an authoritarian *coup d'état*. Indeed, the main justification of such powers is that they may contain conflict and thereby forestall the conditions for such a *coup*. Now, however, recent events call into question the possibility of the Gorbachev regime acting as a "defender of the constitution". Is the central government able to control conservative forces in the military and the Party? Is it capable of enforcing or respecting the rule of law? Is Gorbachev exploiting his emergency powers as part of a rapidly accelerating conservative seizure of power? At present these questions are not resolved. The USSR could never have moved directly from dictatorship to democracy. The real question was whether central authority using emergency powers could hold the ring while reform took root or whether the strains and costs of the process would lead once again to naked dictatorship. The odds on the latter seem to have increased.

(7 February 1991)

Notes

1. See, for example, Grossman (1986), a challenging assessment of the positive and negative sides of Lenin and Lenin's role in building the authoritarian regime, where a released political prisoner muses on the past.

2. Many of the concepts used in this essay are derived from the work of the German political and legal theorist Carl Schmitt: that is politics as "friend–enemy relations", anti-politics, depoliticization, political romanticism, the state of exception, and the distinction between commissarial and sovereign dictatorships. For a valuable introduction to Schmitt's thought see Schwab (1989); see also Schmitt (1976) and Hirst (1987).

3. See, for example, Michnik (1985), especially "The New Evolutionism"; see also Pelczynski (1988) and Ash (1984).

4. Schmitt argued that liberal parliamentary democracy could only exist on the basis of certain fundamental "depoliticizations" in the nineteenth century, most notably religion and the economy. These could not be sustained in the face of intense social conflict, and, therefore, democracy and liberalism were incompatible when groups were polarized within the political system and sought to use the majoritarian power of decision in democracy to make their position prevail over that of others – see Schmitt (1926/1985). Schmitt wrote in the Weimar Republic with its economic crises, its mass unemployment and the absolute antagonism of Communists and Nazis. He did not foresee new depoliticizations conditional on mass prosperity, which have breathed new life into liberal parliamentarism in Germany.

5. For Schmitt's concept of political romanticism see Schmitt (1986) and for an interpretation see Hirst (1988).

6. See his essay "Reform or Revolution" in *The Uses of Adversity* (1989).

7. See Keane (1988).

8. It is embarrassing now to recall western political theorists' rationalizations of such practices, see for example, Macpherson (1966).

9. For the distinction between a sovereign and a commissarial dictatorship see Schwab (1970), Pt I, Ch. I. "Commissarial" here means a legal "commission" to perform the role of defender of the constitution – not the rule of commissars!

10. On lawful dictatorship in constitutional regimes in situations of war and emergency see Rossiter (1948).

11

Security challenges in postcommunist Europe

The security situation in Europe has obviously changed out of all recognition since the collapse of Communism that began in 1989. The principal change is that economic issues have taken precedence over military ones. Up until 1989 the key issue remained the division of the continent into east and west. As the second Cold War thawed, policy shifted from the need to contain the USSR to the aim of reducing the military confrontation between the two armed blocs of NATO and the Warsaw Pact. Now the most advanced postcommunist states – the Czech Republic, Hungary, Poland and Slovenia – are predominantly concerned with economic reconstruction and with seeking support from and eventual membership of the EU. Neutral states like Austria, Finland and Sweden face a fundamental reappraisal with the demise of the blocs, the development of major domestic economic problems, and the objective of EU membership in the near future. Thus the future of European security can best be considered by concentrating on the policy of the EU as it defines its relations with the rest of Europe. These relations are predominantly economic, and it is the pace of the Union's own political and economic integration that will define the security situation in the next two decades.

The EU will not become a superstate and it is unlikely to possess its own supranational military forces for the foreseeable future. It has, however, become the primary focus for member nations in approaching their relations with the rest of the continent and the wider world. In this respect, and because of the primacy of economic issues in external policy, the EU is far more important than any of the possible frameworks for the regularization of the military aspects of security, such as NATO or the WEU. The EU's member nations have overwhelming military and economic superiority over their immediate neighbours. The major external powers, who once structured the affairs of the continent, are now either gravely weakened and removed from direct presence in central Europe, as is the case with Russia, or in the process of military disengagement and in potential economic conflict with the Union, as is the case with the USA. Western Europe enjoys a degree of security without parallel in this century; it is threatened neither by external enemies nor by the possibility of internal interstate armed conflicts. However, it faces a complex variety of economic, social and low-level security threats that are serious and which if not addressed, could present significant problems for the EU. The danger is that they will not be effectively addressed because they do not have the compelling necessity of an overriding external threat. Western European nations may exploit their immunity from military threat to evade their responsibilities and the absence of a unifying external threat may slow the pace of European integration, leading to an intensification of conflicts between national policies and to an inability for coherent action in relation to the economic and social problems of the countries on the periphery of the Union.

The collapse of communism is clearly an immense benefit to the whole of Europe. The ex-Soviet world offers the western European nations investment opportunities and potential markets that could, if decisively exploited, launch it and its neighbours into a period of sustained boom like that from 1945–73. The collapse also poses a very real challenge because it has removed the vital impetus to unity and integration provided by the Soviet threat. The Union has lost an enemy that provided it with much of its political identity and rationale, and it is now faced with the problem of finding an effective source for identification with and legitimation of the European project. Severe recession has compounded this problem. It is forcing the member nations of the Union to compete economically and is revealing divergent interests. It has shown the fallacy of the technocratic conception of European unity, in which economic development and integration would inevitably create the conditions for political integration. Now it is clear that the strengthening of central political institutions and the building of legitimacy for them is a condition for effective economic policies that restore prosperity, and that the Union's economic progress is closely tied up with the success of its neighbours in eastern and central Europe in reconstructing their economies.

It would be foolish to ignore the extent to which the EU was a product of the Cold War, and that the ending of that conflict poses problems for it as well as advantages. The European Community was never co-terminous with NATO – it included neutrals like Ireland and military independents like France – but it has been inescapably structured by the division of the continent that began at Yalta. It is worth beginning our discussion by characterizing the fundamental features of the period 1945–89, and then trying to assess those of the subsequent state of affairs.

It is an obvious fact that after 1945 the position of western Europe was defined above all by the Cold War. It is easy now to forget how rigidly and radically the continent was divided. The Western powers, hitherto enemies, became allies – united by a common and overwhelming threat. The societies of central and eastern Europe became members of an enemy bloc, and virtually passed out of normal political and economic contact for decades. These societies hardly had an independent existence, and were primarily appendages of Soviet policy. Western Europe's security was defined by a single major threat – the possibility of a war with the Soviet Union along a common land frontier. Europeans recognized that their fate in this respect would be determined externally, as a function of a crisis between the USSR and the USA. Europe's armed forces were organized to fight a war in Germany. It was a war that most politicians knew to be a remote contingency, but that threatened to devastate the continent should it occur. The very scale of the threat and its consequences ensured that it was more apparent than real. The risk of mutual extinction, understood in a primitive way on both sides, paralysed both of the superpowers from too active and too direct a confrontation. Europe was lucky that the leaders of its external hegemonic powers were possessed of at least minimal rationality, that the various superpower crises resolved themselves, and that the need for dialogue and *rapprochement* constantly reasserted itself.

Thus in fact the western European countries gained in many ways from the Cold War, despite the threat of disaster should it turn hot. Above all they enjoyed a unity imposed on them by an enemy who was too serious to be ignored but who it was unlikely they would ever actually have to fight. The threat of the USSR and of domestic communist takeovers in the immediate post-1945 period led to large-scale US economic aid to western Europe as part of a strategy of political containment. Marshall Aid may not have been decisive in European recovery, but it certainly contributed to it. Throughout the Cold War the USA provided a significant portion of the forces and much of the military infrastructure for Europe's defence. This allowed most European states to spend a relatively low percentage of GDP on the military, and undoubtedly contributed to domestic economic growth in consequence. The massive threat just across the border undoubtedly hastened and deepened the Franco-German reconciliation that was the core of the European Community. The Soviet threat and American leadership of the Atlantic Alliance made it easier for European states to see what they had in common and facilitated the process of the surrender of their national sovereignties in the course of the integration of the Community and the growth of its powers. Union was possible without "blood and iron" – something virtually unique in the construction of larger political entities. From having been for centuries a hotbed of conflict, western Europe became one of the most stable and peaceful regions in the world. In this Cold War regime most European states became accustomed to peace and accepted US military hegemony. They either ceased to have experience of fighting or were constitutionally prevented from acting except in self-defence, as was the case with West Germany. During the Cold War there could be no question of military intervention elsewhere in Europe, short of starting

World War Three. Western Europeans may in retrospect see this period nostalgically as one in which politics were simplified and the concord of their national states assured by a common external threat.

From the signing of the Treaty of Rome until the collapse of communism, the Community enjoyed two other fundamental characteristics that ensured its political stability and coherence. The first was prosperity. Most member states of the EU have enjoyed relatively rapid growth in national wealth since the 1950s, with brief recessions, and have been able to return to growth despite severe external shocks like the oil price hikes of 1973 and 1979. Some, like Italy and Spain, have gone from relative industrial backwardness to advanced nation status as a result of Community membership. The second, closely connected with the first, is political homogeneity. Politics has been dominated by centrist parties since the 1950s, with the extremes of left and right being politically contained and excluded from government. This homogeneity of the main political actors, most being either Christian Democrats or Social Democrats, committed to pragmatism, a market economy, and social welfare, facilitated the intergovernmental accommodations that were central in creating and developing the Community. Politicians enjoyed high autonomy from their national publics in Community policy-making because prosperity allowed social conflicts to be contained or bought-off, even if at immense cost (as with the CAP). Western Europe's homogeneity was historical and contingent; it depended on the utter discrediting and defeat of fascism and on the identification of communism with an external threat. It was, however, real – unlike the false uniformity imposed in the Soviet satellite states by political repression and ideological indoctrination.

Each of these fundamental features has changed since 1989. The continent is no longer divided militarily and there is no hegemonic power in the east. Russia is penned-up, immured in the east behind Belarus and the Ukraine. Neither of the latter states, nor Poland, nor any lesser power could credibly threaten eastern Europe. The military strength of the Union's states is unassailable in Europe. There is now no need for US forces to be stationed in western Europe for the purpose of its defence. However, if the military division of Europe has vanished, the continent remains as divided as ever. A GDP-per-capita curtain has replaced the old frontier. The gulf in wealth and living standards between the core states of the Union and the ex-Soviet world is vast. For example, Poland's GDP per capita is less than a tenth of that of Germany's. The economic conditions in most ex-Soviet states are intolerable, not least because they have highly educated populations accustomed to living in industrialized and urbanized societies. These populations have been sustained by the hope that the destruction of the command economy would lead to a rapid increase in prosperity. With the possible exceptions of the Czech Republic and Slovenia, they are likely to be substantially disappointed. The ex-satellite and postcommunist states of eastern and central Europe have few options but to struggle on trying to convert to market economies. This seems to be the case even when excommunist-based parties return to power, as in Poland. The immediate neighbours of the Union – the Czech Republic, Hungary, Poland and Slovenia – are all desperate to develop trade with it and ultimately to join it. In these countries, the consequences of slow economic adaptations are likely to be domestic political and social conflict, rather than interstate violence requiring western military intervention.

The other postcommunist and ex-Soviet states pose no direct threat to the EU and are unlikely to lead it to large-scale military intervention in local interstate conflicts and internal crises.

Some advocates of military intervention by the western powers in the former Yugoslavia have argued that inaction is short-sighted and contrary to the longer term interests of those powers. The claim is that the existing Balkan conflicts carelessly neglected may lead on to wider wars. This is to see current events in the light of the situation leading up to 1914. But the analogy is far from apt. Then both Austria-Hungary and Russia had what they perceived to be vital and conflicting interests in the region. Now the states of western Europe have no fundamental interests in the region. Despite the horrors of the war in Croatia and Bosnia, and deplorable as the west's failure to protect human rights may be, the fact remains that the dismemberment of Bosnia and the rise of a Greater Serbia poses no serious threat to any of the western European states. The Balkans have no vital economic significance to the Union and are, after the end of the Cold War, of no great strategic consequence. The same is true of Russia's interests in the Balkans, Slavophile posturing by elements of the Opposition aside. There is little likelihood that the major powers in eastern and western Europe will take sides and clash over the Balkans.

Greece is the one member of the EU with a direct interest in the region. Even then, its concerns are more symbolic than economic and strategic. Greece has experienced the rise of the ugliest and most intransigent ultra-nationalism over the Macedonian question, and this position is common across the political spectrum. Greek interests in this matter are divergent from those of the rest of the Union. The most dangerous possible outcome would be a serious conflict between Greece and Turkey over the Balkan crisis, inflamed by long-standing differences over the Aegean and Cyprus. Both are members of NATO, Greece is a member and Turkey a potential member of the EU. Undoubtedly the EU and the USA would put intense pressure on both states to prevent an open clash, both having a great deal to lose economically if they were to refuse mediation. Greece, moreover, would almost certainly be defeated if it came to war. But, in the extremely unlikely event that war were to happen, the major powers would not actively intervene. Britain did nothing during the Turkish invasion of Cyprus, and that is likely to be the model for the response of the western powers to further Balkan wars.

In the case of conflicts on the periphery of Russia, western interests are even less salient than in the Balkans. The EU and the USA have little option but to concede Russia's primacy of interest in its "Near Abroad". The Western powers might as well accept Russia's version of the Munroe Doctrine in this area. Neither the EU or the USA will challenge Russia over conflicts in Central Asia, especially when ethnic Russians are under threat. The loss of Russian goodwill would be too great a price. Russia, although in economic crisis, remains a formidable military power. It can also obstruct western policy elsewhere in the world were it to use its Security Council veto. In the case of a serious clash between Russia and the Ukraine, the west would presumably offer mediation and press the threat of such economic sanctions as it could apply. Should it go beyond sparring to armed conflict, the western powers would remain horrified spectators. Giving military guarantees to Belarus, the Ukraine, the Baltics, Georgia, or any other state on Russia's periphery would be an act of utter folly. As would building a greater Europe in the east by letting the Czechs, Hungarians, and Poles join NATO. This would threaten the Russians and make them insecure, pushing them toward hostility through fear of encirclement. Better to assist and appease Russia, cajoling it into being a better neighbour rather than deterring it as an enemy. At best, therefore, western troops may be required for peacekeeping missions in the former Soviet world and only with Russian agreement.

Thus, the odds against the EU states intervening militarily and on a large scale in any local conflict in the excommunist countries are very great indeed. Had Bosnia's integrity been of vital interest to enough of the Union's states then the odds are that the Serbs would have been intimidated by a massive show of force early on. The conflict in the former Yugoslavia has exposed the very real divisions between the member states of the Union on foreign policy issues. The collapse of communism has exacerbated those divisions by lessening the risks of independent national policies, and yet the illusion of common action has made no state truly responsible for the outcome of the Union's initiatives. Thus Germany played a decisive role in pushing the recognition of Slovenia, Croatia and Bosnia and yet is constitutionally incapable of guaranteeing their sovereignty. A truly common foreign and security policy is a long way off. Even then, the likelihood of a majority of member states for active intervention in a purely local conflict is small, such conflicts will seldom directly impinge on more than one member.

The Bosnian Muslims have suffered, as do most of the conflict zones in the third world, from the fact that the advanced countries are more and more absorbed in their own affairs. They no longer have to fear communist advances and to contain hostile revolutionary forces in conflicts by proxy. Western, and particularly US, intervention has in the past helped to create many of the worst of those conflicts, from supporting UNITA in Angola to funding Pol Pot after his expulsion by the Vietnamese. They are now mostly just messy conflicts without sponsors and have degenerated to being just bad news on the TV for most western citizens. The interests of the advanced world's states are overridingly economic and the bulk of world trade is conducted between these states themselves, overwhelmingly within the triad of the EU, Japan and the USA. Oil is the only exception to this self-absorption. The massive western intervention in the Gulf was not unconnected with the need to secure the oilfields of Kuwait and Saudi Arabia against Saddam Hussain. Slobodan Milosovic poses no comparable threat and a greater Serbia is a power in a region of minimal economic interest to the western powers. I am not making this point in opposition to the Gulf War or because I am indifferent to the fate of the Bosnian population that does not want to be part of a greater Serbia. The point is that one is obliged to consider how the advanced states do and will behave, not how in conscience one would wish them to act.

It is naive to imagine that western states will commit vast resources and face the death of many of their soldiers when neither their territorial integrity nor their vital external economic interests are at stake. Western states are above all concerned with economic issues, since material prosperity is the dominant concern of the bulk of their populations. Moreover, as they are democracies their leaders have to justify large-scale military intervention to the voters. The threat of large numbers of sons and daughters dying in foreign countries the existence of which most citizens are hardly aware does not appeal to elected politicians.

To many western citizens with an altruistic and justified concern for human rights, basing foreign policy upon economic interests appears nothing less than sordid. But such interests are a necessary core of external policy in states whose citizens' primary concerns are economic, and they can be perfectly legitimate, provided they involve no unjustified seizure of the resources of others. Economic interests have one great advantage, they limit the causes of wars and large-scale military interventions to circumstances where such interests or assets are actually threatened and thus impose a degree of rationality on the use of force. It is by no means inherently immoral or unreasonable for states to go to war in defence of legitimate economic interests. States have the right, for example, to defend the world free trading order against authoritarian regional powers annexing wealth by force. In doing so they will use the traditional grounds of international law, the defence of the sovereignty and integrity of states and the preservation of international agreements. But they will do so only in cases of violations of those principles central to their own interests. War for oil sounded obscene to the opponents of the Gulf War in the west. Yet the defence of economic interests is a legitimate *casus belli*, particularly when compared with the main causes of war in the modern world – the aim of ethnic homogeneity, religious fanaticism or dictatorial ambition. Economically motivated war is limited in its aims and governed by a calculus of the proportionality of costs to benefits. For this reason, such interests must be vital before liberal states with democratically accountable governments will commit themselves to war on economic grounds.

On the other hand, going to war to defend human rights – while apparently easier to justify in moral terms – is by no means unproblematic. Western publics as a whole are not yet ready to impose the new international law of human rights, and they will only support giving sanction to the old international law of the sovereignty and territorial integrity of states when some other major national interest compels them to do so. Of course, it would be better if the international community could act to prevent horrors like Pol Pot's seizure of power in Cambodia or the rape of East Timor. One doubts, however, that a western crusade to secure and defend human rights in the rest of the world would not founder on the inevitable ambiguities of military intervention. The unsettling experience of Somalia is all-too-likely to be the norm in such a new world order.

To say this is not to abandon all hope of the protection of human rights. To begin with western states can best do it by *not* intervening to arm factions and give political forces the capacity to prolong civil wars. The disasters of Angola and Afghanistan are all-too-evident arguments for doing nothing, not actively intervening in local conflicts and civil wars in the future. Secondly, western states can achieve more by judicious economic aid and economic sanctions than they can by armed force in most cases. Western direct economic aid is well below the levels deemed the barest minimum by the UN.

The second fundamental feature of the period from 1945–89 – economic prosperity – may also be changing. Europe's growth and prosperity are by no means assured. This is not just for conjunctural reasons connected with the current depression. Europe's long-term growth rates and capacities for technical innovation are slowing. The political settlements that have underpinned the national production systems of key areas like western Germany and northern and central Italy are failing and are threatening to undermine those systems themselves. The Community's policy-makers staked a great deal on the boost to growth provided by the creation of the Single European Market and the processes of economic and political union that were its essential accompaniments. It looks like calculations of the benefits of the single market were profoundly wrong and that a more activist economic policy than monetary union is required to create both a coherent economic zone and acceptable rates of growth and employment. The difficulties in ratifying the Maastricht Treaty, the improbability of its provisions for monetary union in the current economic crisis, and the virtual collapse of the ERM show that integration in economic policy is if anything going backwards. National states are edging toward competitive macroeconomic policies, such as competitive devaluations and the poaching of inward direct investment.

Most excommunist states would be glad to enjoy the Union's problems. It remains a fact that none of those states (with the possible exception of the Czechs) will be able to join the Union for the foreseeable future – their GDP per capita simply will not let them conform to common EU standards. Greece, Portugal and Spain entered when the European Community was a much less integrated entity; they enjoyed substantial regional development funds, and they benefited from a period of western European economic growth. The excommunist states are standing at the door at a time of severe recession. Further, if the "neutrals" (Austria, Finland and Sweden) were to join in the near future they would dilute the political mechanisms of the EU at the very moment when they are faltering. Those political forces most opposed to European integration, Mrs Thatcher and a sizeable chunk of the Conservative Party being chief among them, wish to admit the central and east European states as fast as possible, in effect diluting the Union into a free-trade area. This is by no means in the long-term interests of the excommunist states, unless they wish to remain low-wage appendages of the richer states.

The third fundamental feature of the period up to 1989, political homo-geneity, is also under severe threat. This threat is principally from the far right and it is the more serious because these political forces are aided by two objective features of the current situation. The collapse of communism and demographic pressure in Africa threaten the advanced states with the steady pressure of migrants driven by political turbulence and economic hardship. The ageing and economically stagnating societies of the EU are increasingly unwilling to admit large numbers of migrants. Migration is particularly explosive given the very large numbers of unemployed in the EU and the fear that migrants will accept jobs at wages western Europeans are unwilling to consider. That migrants might be a source of economic growth is generally discounted. The right is willing to exploit the issue of migration and put pressure on immigrant communities within the Union. It is unlikely to take political power, but its main effect is to drive the parties of the centre right, that do have power, to compete with it in cracking down on migrants. The right is also able to define economic policy in nationalist terms, promoting competition with other member states and favouring protection against non-EU competitors. Faced with large quantities of cheap food from eastern Europe and highly competitive manufactured goods from the Pacific Rim, the farmers and industrial workers of western Europe may see protection as a salvation. That this is a retreat from effective competition into subsidies and tariffs will seem a less than convincing argument if Europe is failing to compete and to grow. In this sense the right has real issues that it can exploit and which the centrist political forces have found few means of addressing in terms other than those the right proposes.

The only way to tackle these issues of migration and protectionism that the right can exploit so well is to find policies that restore full employment and promote competitive performance. The EU is missing a golden opportunity to restore prosperity. Whereas none of the member states is a large enough economic entity to follow an expansionary policy, the EU has the resources and the scale to pursue a quasi-Keynesian strategy of internal reflation linked to external aid. This would work only if it did not simply boost domestic consumer demand and public spending, which would rapidly lead to budgetary and trade deficits of the kind spawned by Reaganomics. A large-scale programme of aid and specifically long-term trade credits and capital grants for the renewal of capital goods and infrastructure targeted at central and eastern Europe would have the combined effect of boosting effective demand in the postcommunist countries and exports and employment in the Union. Falling unemployment in the Union would reduce social costs and budgetary deficits, promoting domestic consumption.

Both halves of the continent would benefit from such a "Euro-Keynesian" policy. Eastern Europe is a vast reservoir of frustrated demand, which (if it could be converted into effective demand) would offer vast markets to European producers. Western Europe has significant levels of over-capacity in a wide range of industries, particularly in heavy capital goods and motor vehicles. A means of linking eastern frustrated demand to western excess supply could well inaugurate a new long boom. Eastern Europe generally has a serious capital shortage that prevents the formation of new enterprises, or the restructuring of old ones. It is unlikely that private capital will invest on the scale required to turn such societies around – the risks and uncertainties are too great. Eastern Europe generally has a chronic foreign exchange shortage that prevents the acquisition of foreign machinery and other capital goods. Targeted trade credits would ensure that such boosting of effective demand was sourced in western Europe.

By boosting employment and output in the west, trade credits would also facilitate exports from the east. In a period of stagnant demand and high unemployment, there is great resistance to imports from the east in the EU. Promoting effective demand in this way would do a great deal to reduce social conflicts in eastern Europe and to facilitate the more rapid integration of these countries into the EU. A new trading system of this Euro-Keynesian kind would undercut pressures for protection, since it would promote domestic output and it would mitigate pressures for migration, providing the peoples of eastern Europe with hope that they can prosper

191

and find work in their own homes. One cannot be sure that such a large-scale programme would work in the absence of appropriate structural transformation in the domestic economies of eastern European countries. In all likelihood it would make a material difference in the Czech Republic, Hungary and Poland. In Russia the question of whether aid can facilitate structural transformation is open, but to do nothing will make the situation worse. Moreover the immediate benefits of such aid to the west would be real. Even if much of the aid to Russia were "wasted" it would have the same effect as Keynes' only half ironic advocacy of burying money and have the unemployed dig it up.

Jacques Delors wanted to launch a modest version of such a programme. He was refused the expansion of the EU's central budget that was necessary to facilitate it. Only if the EU makes rapid progress in political integration could it devise a coherent economic policy of this kind and have the legitimacy to implement it. That it would benefit EU citizens is irrelevant; the member states could not agree upon and co-ordinate such an ambitious programme in the absence of stronger central structures in the EU and a far greater common budget under central control. The EU is unlikely to make such political progress in the near future. It is faced, if anything, with greater fragmentation and competition between the national states. The problem, moreover, of the wider political sources of support for such a programme seems almost insuperable. In many states (Italy being the most glaring example), the electorate has lost confidence in the traditional political parties and what they can accomplish. Nationalist, localist and single-issue organizations are growing in political strength throughout the Union. The Northern League, for example, is unlikely to support an ambitious programme of aid for eastern Europe if it is unwilling to subsidize Southern Italy.

Eastern Europe is not the only peripheral region of the EU that raises security issues. The southern Mediterranean littoral must also give serious cause for concern. Syria, Egypt and Algeria are all threatened by rapid population growth, a failure of economic development to keep pace with this growth and large-scale unemployment. Coupled with this is the rise of political Islam in Egypt and Algeria in particular, feeding off popular discontent and the perception that integration into western markets has led to nothing but poverty and gross inequality. The consequences of rapidly growing populations, where the majority are under twenty, are combined pressures to migration and to religious fanaticism. In no case can the regimes be regarded as strong enough to contain the political pressures or competent enough to address the economic problems. The threat to secular regimes and open societies in this region is too serious to ignore. It cannot be coped with by military means and is potentially far more serious than any of the problems posed by the postcommunist world for Europe. Add to it large numbers of migrants and residents from North Africa in western Europe, and particularly France, and one has the makings of an explosive situation. This will be particularly so if conservative governments are restricting migration and discriminating against current residents. Europe will pay dearly if it neglects this issue, if it follows an illiberal course with migrant communities, and if it fails to make every effort to sustain secular regimes and open societies by greater economic aid.

The EU is faced with a historic opportunity by the collapse of communism. It has two basic courses of action open to it. To carry on as at present, that is, to do very little to address the problems of its own political unity, to neglect eastern Europe, and to ignore the southern littoral. The odds are that political and economic union will stall until at least the end of the century. There is likely to be no more than a moderate recovery from the slump, growth rates will remain low and levels of spending high. The EU will remain profoundly cautious in its external policy. The alternative is to follow the combined policy of deepening of political and economic integration and large-scale economic aid both to eastern Europe and to the southern Mediterranean littoral. The result of promoting full employment through a "Euro-Keynesian" policy would be to reduce social and intercountry strains within the EU and to promote economic development and prosperity in its neighbours, thus reducing their own internal conflicts and any tendency toward external conflict with the Union. The promotion of prosperity remains the best security policy. Such a policy would enable the EU to weld the greater part of Europe into one co-ordinated trade bloc, larger than NAFTA. This would strengthen its hand in dealing with the other two major blocs.

Such a radical policy departure is no more than a remote possibility.[1] Lack of credible political forces to sponsor it dooms it to irrelevance. It has value, however, in showing that Europe is not inevitably trapped into its present impasse. Doing nothing about the economic and social condition of its neighbours is simply not an option. A European Union that is surrounded by failing economies, that can do nothing to counter its own tendency toward stagnation, that has an ageing population and low birth rates but refuses to accept migrants from surrounding countries, that will find it difficult to maintain its current international competitiveness in a world free-trade system, and that has no hope to offer its neighbours, cannot be secure in the long run. The EU will be encircled by poverty and political failure, whilst offering no lead and little material help. Western Europe would remain able to bomb its opponents into the stone age, but it will not be threatened by invading armies. Security has many other dimensions than military force or war. Multiple economic, political and low-level security problems will breed a self-defeating "fortress Europe" mentality.

The one great exception to this analysis is the future of Russia. It is evident to all that the present situation is unsustainable. The Russian economy has not effected a transition to a viable market economy, output and living standards are still falling. The introduction of market relations has not favoured new investment or resulted in a more efficient allocation of resources, at best it has benefited merchants not manufacturers and at worst it enriches gangsters. The old problem of the relations between town and country is returning, with urban residents unable to buy enough food. This time, however, the terms of the exchange are reversed, for Russia is an overwhelmingly urban country. The Russian birth rate has fallen below replacement levels, and Russians are now paranoid about competition from minority peoples within the Russian Republic as well as the fast-growing populations of Muslim Central Asia. The political system lacks the capacity to administer in this crisis or to ensure legitimacy for the new order. A weak "civil society", that is, social fragmentation and the absence of strong independent secondary associations leads to weak, unstable and numerous political parties, and therefore, to no stable link between social forces and the regime. Russia, once the classic example of strongly authoritarian government – both Tsarist and communist – now has a "weak state" more typical of Latin American democracies. The state has neither a high degree of autonomy *vis à vis* society, as did the communist autocracy, nor is it a stable regime based upon powerful social forces. The state is faced, moreover, with serious peripheral conflicts and the difficult task of protecting minority Russian populations in the ex-Soviet republics.

No sensible person would predict what is going to happen. However, it is worth cautiously entertaining the worst scenario, short of complete anarchy and the falling of the Russian nuclear arsenal into the hands of the highest bidders, and assessing the consequences for European security. One possible outcome of the current crisis might be the fall of the democratic, market-oriented government and its replacement by a Great Russian nationalist regime.[2] Nationalism and economic conservatism might stem current discontents, directing anger outwards, and buy off the numerous losers in the new economic order with guaranteed prices and subsidies. This regime could best be called a "Red–White" coalition based upon conservatives in the army and the Church, upon ultranationalists and the remnants of the Communist Party. This neo-Slavophile regime would be the most unlikely to enter into direct confrontation with the west: it would be bankrupt, it would share no common land frontier, and it would have conflicts near enough at hand. It would squeeze the Baltics economically, although it would be unlikely to provoke a full-scale crisis with the west reannexing them. It would be a bad neighbour to its western neighbours Belarus and the Ukraine, constantly squabbling with them over economic issues and the rights of ethnic Russians. It might very well be further embroiled in shooting wars in central Asia than is the present government. It would not be like the old Soviet Union, but concerned above all with Eurasian rather than world affairs. In short it would be containable well short of large-scale rearmament in Europe and a return to the Cold War.

We should not assume that the Yeltsin regime will not be driven into some of these actions by necessity or to stave-off conservative political success. For example, it is possible that Russia might be forced to intervene should the Ukraine collapse into civil strife – the predominantly Russian populations of its eastern industrial zones revolting against economic failure. The west should do no more in these circumstances than act as an honest broker, seeking to prevent war and acting to support the populations of the western part of the Ukraine to retaining their independence.

Europe's security is best sought not through military intervention but through economic partnership with its neighbours to aid their social reconstruction. Europe would benefit from measures to restore its growth rate, employment levels, and, therefore, economic power, measures directly connected to aiding its neighbours. It would benefit greatly, given a reduction in unemployment and a restoration of growth, from allowing a steady flow of migrants into Europe and ensuring their security once there.

Military and security issues would remain, even if socio-economic policies aimed at reducing threats were successful. Even allowing for a substantial measure of migration the EU would still require strict frontier controls and the policing of immigration quotas. The supply of economic migrants fleeing wretched conditions throughout the world is inexhaustible. Italy and Spain are serious weak points for illegal entry. Even a liberal policy toward migrants would require Europe to put far greater resources into border security. The Union's states also need to create more mobile and professional military forces capable of external intervention if need be, and to switch away from conscript armies. Many of the conscript forces are little better than militias and are unfitted for demanding roles such as supporting the UN relief effort in Bosnia. Had the EU wanted to intervene effectively to keep the peace in Bosnia, rather than to engage in the gesture politics of bombing the Serbs, it would have been faced with a serious shortage of fully trained soldiers. A key point is that the EU continues to depend for a great deal of its extra-European security upon the USA – without which it could not, for example, have defeated Iraq or led the coalition against Saddam Hussein. European nations played at best a secondary role. The EU, like Japan, relies on the USA for the defence of the world free-trade order against regional powers that threaten vital western economic interests. It continues to rely on the USA for its nuclear deterrence. Europe's nuclear arsenals are either ultimately dependent on the USA, like Britain's, or still too weak credibly to confront a power like Russia, as with France's. Lastly, although Europe as a whole would benefit from a trade war with Japan (Japan having a vast positive trade balance), the same is not true of its relation to the USA and so the EU needs to be cautious in following protectionist policies. The EU may be without rival in Europe, but in world terms it needs to remain on good relations with the USA and cultivate the Atlantic Alliance, even though the Soviet threat that brought the alliance into being has disappeared.

The EU is quite unlike the states of the old pre-1945 Europe. The ensuing half-century of peace and prosperity has changed the outlook of western Europe's politicians and citizens alike. They have no interest in war or territorial expansion, and are reluctant to intervene militarily even for active peace-keeping. This is a positive change for which we should be grateful. Western Europe has no desire aggressively to exploit the situation created by the collapse of communism, pushing its military frontier eastwards at the expense of Russia. The problem is now the reverse of bellicosity – the passivity and economic self-absorbtion of the states of the EU. This has led to a failure actively to engage with the economic and social problems of eastern Europe on the scale that they require. If western Europe is to enjoy military security and social stability in the longer term it has to provide a measure of economic security and hope for its eastern neighbours now. This lesson needs to be learnt rapidly, that mutual prosperity is the key to security, and that economic action now will obviate the possibility of military action in the future.

Notes

1. For a developed outline of such a policy see Hirst and Thompson (1992).
2. This was written before the Russian elections of December 1993 and the success of Mr Zhirinovsky's Liberal Democrats.

12

Endism – Francis Fukuyama

It is surely remarkable that an essay by a state department official in the conservative quarterly *The National Interest* should provoke a storm of debate in the USA and be syndicated by papers throughout the world. The burden of Francis Fukuyama's argument is that we are witnessing the end of history. That end will not be as it has so often been imagined – either apocalypse or utopia. History, in the sense of fundamental ideological and political change, will cease with the worldwide triumph of western liberalism. Fukuyama is far too clever to play this theme without a certain irony. He knows how well-worn a trope "endism" is; standing as we do at the end of two millennia of Christian eschatology. The blunt political message that the Cold War is over and the west has won, is softened by suitably edifying references to high social theory. Much of his essay is taken up with a discussion of Hegel, and a kind of Hegelianism is central to the argument.

Essays of this kind do not attract massive media attention because they make the right up-market references, and Hegel is hardly a bestseller nowadays. Fukuyama has become news because he has caught a mood and because he has justified that mood by seizing upon a fundamental and novel fact.

The fact is that western liberal democracy is now secure against effective political competitors in a way that it has never been since 1914. Into the 1980s western liberals have feared the threat of powerful authoritarian regimes and political movements. That fact seems to me to be true, but we can explain and interpret it in other ways than Fukuyama's. He implies that liberalism's survival, its outlasting of its competitors, was because of its superiority as a political and economic system. Yet part of the power of the threat to liberalism was the weakness of liberals – especially in the 1930s. It is easy to forget how craven liberal regimes were when faced with the fascist threat, how much they relied on the illiberal Soviet regime in defeating Nazism, and how far they tended to overrate the Soviet threat once the Cold War had set in.

Liberalism was certainly threatened with extinction in the 1930s and yet the democracies did precious little to strengthen the cause of anti-authoritarian struggle. Appeasement of the fascist powers fatally weakened the democracies' military and, more importantly, moral strength. The enemies within, the fascist and Stalinist parties in western states, were therefore able with some rhetorical credence to portray "bourgeois liberalism" as part of a dying world; as unjust, corrupt and enfeebled. Fascism and Marxism-Leninism claimed to be superior doctrines of government to liberal democracy. They saw themselves as the inheritors; the future would belong either to the master race or to the proletariat.

In 1945 fascism ceased to have a future and by 1950 Stalinism had no hope of seizing power in the west. Fascism's credibility was destroyed by its failure in terms of its own values. It vaunted the military prowess of the master races of Germany and Japan and their capacity to conquer. The unconditional surrender of both regimes forced upon the inhabitants of those countries the recognition of utter failure of their leaders. The first newsreels of Belsen destroyed any possible moral appeal fascists might make out of the ruins of defeat: 1945 was not to be like 1918.

The USSR ended the war as a victorious superpower, but its ideology rapidly ceased to have the capacity to move beyond the range of Russian tanks. Marxism-Leninism was destroyed politically in the west by the great postwar boom and by the exposure of western publics to the truth about Stalin's purges and the Gulag. However cautious Soviet policy might be in practice it remained an external competitor. The USSR continued to harbour the illusion that it was a superior social system to the west and that it would eventually triumph over it. Even Nikita Khrushchev threatened "we will bury you", by peaceful means.

Soviet power ceased to be a threat in this sense only in the mid-1980s. By then the legacy of failure from the Brezhnev years had become inescapable and insupportable. Reform had become inevitable, but nothing guaranteed it would take the radical form inspired by Mikhail Gorbachev. *Glasnost* has liquidated a regime based on illusions and lies. Almost nobody in the eastern bloc now believes that Soviet-style socialism can compete with the west in terms of economic performance. Almost nobody actually believes that Marxism is a superior means of understanding and directing society. The USSR is far from becoming a liberal state, but it has ceased to be a challenge to liberalism. With a Solidarity government in Poland and the rapid progress toward multiparty democracy in Hungary, the triumph of liberalism appears credible. Even the horror of Tiananmen Square has done little to shake the new confidence of the west. The Chinese students died defending their status of liberty. The vengeful geriatrics who suppressed them can only rule by pretending to be in a time-warp.

The fact that western liberals have suddenly found themselves secure in the mid-1980s has generated an immense feeling of relief. Intense cold war between nuclear armed states was insupportable. We have all lived too long with the constant prospect of an immediate and horrible end to history. Even as bellicose and ultraconservative a leader as President Reagan could sense this mood and respond generously and appropriately to Soviet peace overtures. Fukuyama's essay gives expression to this mood and provides it with a coherent rationale. His use of a neo-Hegelian philosophy of history serves to rationalize the fact that liberalism has survived its putative grave-diggers and that we have escaped the perils of the Second Cold War.

Fukuyama's theme is also deeply congenial in the USA in that it both contradicts and yet follows swiftly upon the heels of another intellectual *cause célèbre*. The "endist" thesis assures the USA that it faces no serious threats to its military predominance and that it will remain the leading power in a world economy dominated by free markets and free-trade policies. How refreshing when Paul Kennedy's gloomy bestseller *The Rise and Fall of the Great Powers* dominated discussion in 1988. Kennedy's thesis was that the USA is losing the economic and military capacity to act as the hegemon of the liberal world order. American power must pass as surely as British and Spanish power did. Fukuyama answers a book based on empirical historical analogies with an argument grounded on the philosophy of history. Fukuyama chides Kennedy with economic determinism. The fate of states depends in Kennedy's book on blind and material processes. Fukuyama believes that history is not deterministic, rather historical outcomes are decided by the quality of the ideas that motivate human beings. Liberalism is an ideal that has triumphed, and it is central to the self-identity of America. Americans can, therefore, feel confident in the future whilst they hold to the ideals of democracy and the free market. No wonder "endism" has gone down so well; it has provided a sophisticated rationale for the commonplaces of American political life. But almost everything else in the essay is sheer *chutzpa*.

Consider first Fukuyama's use of the philosophy of history. It is staggering to see the author of the thesis that history ends in the dominance of liberalism seeking to derive support from Hegel, even in the guise of Kojève's interpretation. Hegel is notorious for his spirited critique of liberalism. Hegel saw representative democracy as a disaster; as giving political expression to the antagonistic interests in civil society but without overcoming these antagonisms. Freedom properly so called was more than mere individual will; it involved the transcendence of such immediate self-interest in a higher and more universal good. The pursuit of self-interest, which is so central to classical economic and political liberalism, is powerfully criticized by Hegel. The result of such pure individualism cannot be a society, it is merely a collection of petty private purposes. Hegel was perfectly serious in defending, as a politically superior alternative to liberalism, a monarchical state with a system of corporate representation and a "universal class" of civil servants to secure the good of the whole society. No attentive reader of

199

Hegel's *Philosophy of Right* could ever confuse the author with a liberal.

Hegel's political theory is the view of a Prussian conservative who felt that the reforms after the defeat at Jena in 1806 had gone quite far enough. Hegel's dialectic endows this politically timorous opinion with the force of world historical necessity: the Prussian monarchy is the highest current incarnation of the idea of freedom. Hegel's dialectic should not be lightly dismissed, however. The concept of dialectic is powerful and its content a celebration of freedom. The dialectic is not really compatible with the concept of history as a "process with a beginning, a middle and an end" (Fukuyama 1989: 4), as Fukuyama sees Hegel. But that is to diminish the dialectic to the level of vulgar historicism. In fact dialectic is most consistent when it is conceived as a potentially *infinite* development toward higher and higher levels of self-consciousness and freedom. What presumption can stay the dialectic and pronounce history at an end? How can we know that a given state of affairs represents the realization of the most complete freedom? Only by the philosopher making himself greater than the dialectic. Hegel's *Philosophy of History* comes close to such vulgarity, but the whole of his philosophy speaks against it.

As an infinite process dialectic makes some sense, but it is then divorced from any connection with concrete events. Once the dialectic has to be actualized in actual historical events it reveals its fundamental arbitrariness. How does one move from the idea to its incarnation? The answer is, of course, that the connection of the ideal and the actual is entirely at the mercy of the dialectician's prejudices. Marx was acutely aware of this, but he thought Hegel's failure lay in his idealism. Remove the idealism and the dialectic could be made the foundation of a historical process that was not arbitrary in its relation to events. Marx sought in his philosophy of history to retain the form of dialectical development, but to provide it with a new materialist "motor" that would drive its contradictions. Marx substituted a new "end" to history in the form of the victory of the proletariat as a universal class and the consequent abolition of all human exploitation and oppression.

Yet Marx ended up with a problem exactly analogous to Hegel's difficulty in relating the rationality of the dialectic and the realities in which it has to be embodied. How could the notion of a universal class be embodied in concrete social groups? Marx identified both historical necessity and freedom with the workers' movement and was thus a captive of every vicissitude of that movement. Marxism as a philosophy of history was damaged by Stalinism. Marx was still a prisoner of Hegel's logic, he assumed the real would be rational. He could no more imagine a party using his name led by a cruel and twisted dictator than he could imagine the long-run survival of capitalism.

Surely what we can learn from Hegel's dialectic and from the failures of the post-Hegelian philosophy of history is that the very notion of an "end" to history is pernicious. If we suppose that human freedom and individuation have developed in history to higher levels, then what gives us the right to assume that the given state of affairs today is unsurpassable? There can be no "end" to history in the most important sense Hegel gave to it – the striving for self-consciousness and freedom. If history is at an end, then so are we. It is at this point that Fukuyama makes use of Max Weber, and his deep historical pessimism. History is at an end in a radical disenchantment of human purposes.

Fukuyama has committed a similar error to Hegel's and Marx's. He has identified history with fundamental contradictions. History can only continue if there is the possibility of alternatives to liberal regimes:

> Have we in fact reached the end of history? Are there, in other words, any fundamental "contradictions" in human life that cannot be resolved in the context of modern liberalism, that would be resolvable by an alternative political-economic structure? (1989: 8).

But why should we assume that the continuation of history depends on the existence of alternatives to liberalism and the possibility that they can supplant it in some new stage of development? Are there not "contradictions" (in the sense of political issues) *within* liberalism capable of sustaining history (in the sense of large-scale tasks and changes) into the foreseeable future? Are liberal institutions capable of no development? Are there no major problems within liberal politics that are not capable of fuelling conflict and controversy worthy of being called history?

What is wrong with Fukuyama is his staggering complacency. History is over, because all problems can be settled by fully developed liberal institutions that give us all the freedom we are ever likely to get. This is frankly as plausible as Hegel's celebration of the Prussian state.

The record of liberalism after 1945 needs serious critical attention. Western Europe, the USA and Japan all offer ample evidence of the failings of liberal political institutions. Democracy may now be dominant, but it is also deeply compromised in its major heartlands. Our liberal-democratic polities offer low levels of accountability and citizen influence when measured against democratic ideals, rather than against ailing autocracies. Fascism and Stalinist communism made the bare minimum of democratic accountability worthwhile. The chance to vote out the government is an inestimable benefit if one is faced by dictatorship. Once that threat is removed, then the minimalist defence of democracy will no longer do. We need a new standard of democratic accountability, one that enhances the rights and capacities for political influence of the largest number of the citizens that is attainable. If the certainties of the Cold War have ended, then liberals have no right or excuse to be complacent.

The postwar governments of Italy and Japan have relied on systematic corruption as a tool for exercising and maintaining their power. Both countries have been virtual monopolies of the conservatives for decades. In the USA federal government can hardly be considered as more than minimally democratic. President Bush was elected on the votes of about 20 per cent of the electorate, with massive abstentions of registered voters and a large number of citizens failing to register. Political office is an option only for the relatively wealthy. The rich and large business corporations have vastly disproportionate influence. Democratic political life and con-testation in the USA has sunk to a level that only just removes it from the category of oligarchy. In the UK we have an unjust and inequitable voting system that has preserved an extremely partisan government in office on a minority of the votes cast. British government is highly centralized and highly closed and secretive. The UK lacks a written democratic constitution and the legal protection of citizen's rights by constitutional law.

Further democratization of political institutions is a vital and current issue in many western democracies. When representative democracy becomes little more than a choice of who shall govern – a plebiscite – and does little more than legitimate the powers of the governing party, then the ideal of democracy is compromised. Hence the growth of movements seeking to assure greater accountability and the defence of citizens' rights. The new movements for political reform, like Charter 88 in the UK, have been very successful precisely because of these failings. The issue of democratization is moving towards the centre of the political agenda. A large part of the success of Green politics in Europe is due to the dissatisfaction with remote and bureaucratic agencies making decisions without reference to their consequences for ordinary citizens and in obsequious deference to influential business interests. The growing credibility of the Socialist Party in Japan is mainly due to the feeling that the government is a closed and corrupt oligarchy directly in league with big business.

Many of these movements for political reform are radical, but they are not authoritarian. They aim at the diffusion and decentralization of power and influence. They are dissatisfied with the outcomes of the unhealthily close link between big government and big business. Radicalism cannot now be so easily contained by the fear of communism. The future of liberal democracy is likely to be one of conflict and change, not complacent celebration.

Fukuyama's view embodies the common sense of the US establishment, a conventional wisdom that assumes economic and political liberalism to be inextricably tied together. The victory of liberalism is held to be due in a large part to the economic success of the free market and the high standards of living and consumer durables it is able to deliver. The success of economic liberalism is taken for granted and is reinforced by the failures of the command economies of eastern Europe. Economic liberalism, however, is not the inevitable concomitant and bulwark of liberal democracy. Unrestrained economic liberalism poses a very real threat to political democracy, because it permits the growth of grossly unequal influence by privileged economic actors, the major business corporations. The unregulated free market does not guarantee economic equality; it does not empower the ordinary worker, small owner or trader as economic liberal apologetics claim it does. On the contrary, it permits uncontrolled concentration of economic activity in the hands of large firms and it leaves these firms in the hands of unaccountable -top management. A society cannot be democratic in which power over the most vital areas of life is beyond public control. Shareholders' control of corporations is largely a fiction and their employees and consumers have little or no direct say in the affairs of the companies.

Moreover, it is something of an illusion to suppose that free markets and unregulated corporations "deliver the goods". The two countries that have followed the economic liberals' prescriptions most closely in recent years, the UK and the USA, have suffered the greatest deindustrialization, have lower GDP per capita than other more successful manufacturing countries, and have growing problems with their balance of payments.

Only from the olympian detachment of the state department could one propose the following:

> But surely, the class issue has actually been successfully resolved in the West ... The egalitarianism of modern America represents the essential achievement of the classless society envisioned by Marx. This is not to say that there are not rich people and poor people in the United States, or that the gap between them has not grown in recent years. But the root causes of economic inequality do not have to do with the underlying structure of our society, which remains fundamentally egalitarian and mildly redistributionist ... (1989: 7)

This comes close to telling us we live in the best of all possible worlds. Candide should have waited some 200 years to find an appropriate tutor. Fukuyama thinks he can explain away the co-existence of wealth with poverty in the USA. I find his attempt at an explanation little more than a confession of moral bankruptcy. He has the gall to blame the poor: inequality and poverty are due to "the cultural and social characteristics of the groups that make it up, which are in turn the historical legacy of pre-modern conditions" (*ibid.*). Black poverty is due to slavery, a premodern and precapitalist institution. Slavery was, arguably, neither premodern nor preliberal but, either way, it cannot carry the burden of poverty in modern America. Are all the poor, the homeless, the prisoners of drug addiction, the descendants of slaves?

This kind of indifference in the face of misery and want has its price too. The USA, like the UK, has failed to adopt interventionist policies to develop the skills of the whole of its population. Creating an underclass may offer a pool of cheap labour, but it also imposes a burden of low aspirations and low productivity sectors corresponding to them. A democratic state cannot write-off a large part of its population as if they don't matter. A state that does this is willing to write-off many other things too, including the future. It is no wonder that the USA and the UK have not only failed to address inequality ignoring the benefits of a high-wage, high-skill, full-employment economy, they have also failed to address the need to sustain long-term investment in manufacturing. Ultimately one pays for such complacent "short-termism".

The day of reckoning is not some apocalyptic future, it is happening now. The most successful industrial economies in the modern world – Japan and West Germany, northern Italy and Sweden – have not favoured an economic free-for-all. They have in contrast pursued strategies of economic co-ordination, regional regulation and co-operation between industry, labour and the state. In Italy and Japan such strategies, particularly at the regional level, have helped to compensate for the failings of their national political systems. The UK and the USA have set their face against such strategies, failing to see the economic benefits of a more collaborative political culture and prizing above all the sovereignty of the market and the right of management to manage without check.

Fukuyama supposes the free market and the command economy to be polar opposites and ignores what may lie in between. In fact the economically successful western democracies have tended to pursue a middle way in which the market is regulated, in which co-ordination takes place but not by means of centralized planning, rather by the active consultation of the major organized social interests. The result is an economy far removed from a free-for-all and in which the enhancement of the influence of social groups through consultation offers a route to greater democratic accountability to counter the defects of the former electoral and governmental system.

Fukuyama's complacency is coupled with a diminished view of what liberalism can offer. Idealistic striving and ideological conflict "will be replaced by economic calculation, the endless solving of technical problems, environmental concerns, and the satisfaction of sophisticated consumer demands" (1989: 18). This is not only to assume liberalism is complete, it is to belittle the problems that face us in dealing with the world outside the sphere of affluent consumerism. Will the battle to save the environment require no struggle, no idealism, no danger? Tell that to Greenpeace. Will the hungry masses outside the liberal consumerist world have nothing more to hope from us than the crumbs of foreign aid?

Perhaps Mr Fukuyama, having half-digested Hegel, might complete his course in the German idealists and consider what is implied in Kant's principle that we should treat *all* other human beings as ends and not as means.

Fukuyama's Americo-centrism leads him to regard the European Community in derisive terms: "those flabby, prosperous, self-satisfied, inward-looking and weak-willed states" (1989: 5). In doing so he fails to recognize that the European Community is no longer an economic convenience, it is also a political ideal. The most enlightened politicians and social groups in the Community are not merely interested in a single market, but in the construction of a new "social" Europe, promising greater consultation and representation in economic and social affairs. While the best of our leaders are not satisfied with the bare minimum of liberal democracy there is room for hope. History is not at an end because there are major new ideals. A revitalized democratic Europe is one, the defence of our world environment is another, and, as an essential part of that cause, so is the challenge of creating a world in which all can enjoy a decent standard of life and have democratic self-government. If history is the struggle for freedom, then its end has been well and truly postponed.

13

The myth of globalization

The notion that an integrated global economy has developed in recent decades has become part of the new common sense. It is widely believed that nations, firms and individuals have no option but to adapt to the intensifying global competitive pressures or go under. Distinct national economies it is claimed have dissolved into the world system, and with them has gone the possibility of macroeconomic management by national governments. The new global system is driven by uncontrollable international market forces and is dominated by transnational companies that produce and sell wherever economic advantage dictates. States cannot govern world markets and they have to accept, if they are not to disadvantage their societies, that the only role remaining to them is to help make their territory attractive to internationally mobile capital.

Globalization is not just a trendy concept – belief in it by politicians, media commentators and academics is politically highly consequential. The question is whether globalization is the case – have world market forces in fact developed that are beyond all governance? In a moment we shall consider the evidence for and against the existence of a process of globalization. But first we need to spell out the social and political issues at stake, for if globalization is occurring then we face a very bleak future indeed. A truly global economy will make the expectations developed in the advanced world during the long boom after 1945 completely obsolete.

Some commentators see the process of globalization as an entirely positive development. The management guru Kenichi Ohmae in his influential book *The Borderless World* (1990) argues that globalization means that at last markets have developed on a scale where they can escape from the inefficient and interventionist grasp of governments. World free markets facilitate companies allocating resources to maximize benefits for the consumer.

Others, less convinced of the inherent wisdom of the market, like the bulk of the moderate left, nevertheless feel powerless before the logic of globalism. They can see no alternative policy to meeting the demands of international competition. At best public policy can strive to maintain national competitiveness by promoting training and investing in the public infrastructure that business requires. This broadly is the view of the US Secretary of Labour Robert Reich in *The Work of Nations* (1992). The left has become convinced that states can neither tax too heavily to do this nor can they sustain overextensive welfare states. If they do, they will become uncompetitive and global capital will move elsewhere. Thus even the left holds that many of the policies of post-1945 social democracy are now unsustainable in the face of globalization. It has become the victim of a widespread and pathological tendency to overdiminish expectations.

If the left feels thus constrained, then the free-market right regards globalization as a godsend. They are convinced that both between societies and within societies there will be no option but a brutal competitive struggle for existence. The civilizing of capitalism by public policy and state action, countering and regulating market forces at national level, will have to be abandoned. Globalization means a return to the savage capitalism of the nineteenth century and the social Darwinist belief in the supreme value of the survival of the fittest.

The dominance of global market forces would mean that market failures could now occur on a colossal scale and that because they are beyond the scope of national governments acting singly or in concert to control them they would be virtually uncorrectable. A global economy would in fact be fragile and highly vulnerable to the unintended effects of markets. For example, it would be vulnerable to a major slump brought on by the crash of volatile and interconnected financial markets, and vulnerable to irreversible environmental damage caused by extensive and unregulated industrial development in poorer countries fuelled by foreign direct investment seeking the advantage of lower wages.

In such an ungoverned and unstable economic system the lives of all but the super-rich would be extremely insecure. If states are unable to alter their macroeconomic environment, and their welfare spending is constrained by international competitive pressures, then public and collective forms of response to and protection against such uncertainty would be undermined. As states can do less, so individuals will expect less of them and desert weakening forms of common security. Individuals would thus increasingly seek to protect themselves, investing in their own competitiveness and privately insuring themselves against such risks as they could afford to cover. The need for self-protection will reinforce the tax-aversion of the successful and tend to make them hostile to welfare spending on others. Those who fail in the competitive struggle for existence will increasingly be judged inadequate rather than unfortunate – they failed to strive, to invest in their skills, and to make provision for contingencies.

In such a climate social solidarity would collapse, not only will the rich and the successful be motivated by self-interest but they will no longer be

207

part of a national community. Society would divide not only on the basis of wealth but of mobility, into an internationally mobile elite of managers and highly skilled professionals, whose first loyalty is to their transnational corporate employers or to their own careers, and a nationally bound mass whose skills are easily replicated. The constraints of competitiveness will ensure that the interests of the elite and of mobile capital will tend to prevail, and if they do not, then the country in question will become an impoverished backwater.

This conception of society is not pure speculation. It is what underlies the politics of radical Republicans like Newt Gingrich. In a globalized world atomized individualism and highly local loyalties make more sense to the successful than continued commitment to communities based on what appears to be increasingly powerless national states. The right believes it has economic logic on its side in preferring the market to the state and in seeking to limit the activities and the cost of government.

In a globalized economy, mainstream politics – political parties competing to control the policies of the nation state – would matter less and less. In this context, it would be exceedingly difficult for the moderate left to sustain mass interest in an alternative politics that amounts to public spending in order to make the country attractive to business. Necessary as this might be, it will seem like municipal politics – providing essential services in the same way as local authorities deliver street lighting and sewers. This would undoubtedly bore the talented and alienate the committed, who would desert professional politics for business, the media and issue-based activism. Thus the weakening of the capacities of the state brought about by global markets will become self-reinforcing; people will expect less of national politics.

At the international level too, politics will matter less and less in comparison to the power of the global markets. Economic activity will become independent of political power and military force will become secondary to the muscle of the markets. Of course, advanced states will still have the military means to render themselves invulnerable to direct threats and would find conflict one with another self-defeating. States that tried to threaten the interests of world business would be crushed by devastating, if unplanned, economic sanctions – collapsing exchange rates, capital flight or boycott, and plunging trade balances. The dream of free-market liberals like Cobden and Bright will at last be realized, free trade will triumph over political authority. Only authoritarian societies willing to pay the price of economic backwardness for religious or ethnic reasons will be outside this logic. The world as it became more integrated economically would become more polycentric politically, but politics would cease to have central importance in most people's lives.

Most of these consequences would certainly follow in a globalized economic system. But the question that needs to be posed is, *has* globalization taken place? For all the vigour with which the new conventional wisdom is being presented as fact, evidence and conceptual argument for it are in short supply. Most globalizers, rhetoric apart, are unclear what a truly global economic system would look like, and, therefore, have little idea what could count as decisive evidence for or against its existence. For example, it is clear that some important aspects of economic activity have further internationalized since the early 1970s, but is this sound evidence for globalization? Not necessarily so, since most of these trends neither prove that national economies are dissolving nor that the international economy is ungovernable. Most of the evidence is compatible with something very different, an open *inter-national* economy in which trade and investment take place between the distinct national economies of the advanced countries and in which companies, although they are active multinationally, remain committed to national bases and conduct the bulk of their business within their home region. Such a system is quite different from a *global* economy in which national economies have been subsumed, in which markets have autonomized themselves on a world scale, and in which stateless transnational corporations predominate.

It may be that after a decade of making the running in the media, globalist rhetoric is running up against inconvenient facts. Some mainstream commentators are now denying that the state is as powerless before global pressures as we have been led to believe. Martin Woolf (*Financial Times,* 18 September 1995) points out that the current degree of international openness of the major economies is no greater than it was before 1914 and few people thought the state was powerless then. An editorial in the *Economist* (7 October 1995) argues that global economic forces are not causing states to converge in their policies, citing the wide variation in the proportion of public spending to GDP (from 20 per cent in Singapore to 68 per cent in Sweden).

Needless to say, globalizers reject such claims. Andrew Marr (*Independent,* 19 October 1995) contends that such high proportions of public spending to national income are an index of economic failure and high unemployment. For the moment, the state has the capacity to meddle, it can tax and spend, but long term it will have to conform to global economic realities or take the punishment inflicted by internationally mobile capital.

Against this, the level of public spending is not in itself an index of economic failure. Societies have different characteristics and public spending ratios reflect distinct political choices. Thus Sweden has had a high level of public spending to GDP for a long time, including the period when it was seen as a model of high-tech competitiveness and had very low unemployment. Swedes have accepted public social provision as both economical and efficient, spending very little on private health insurance, schools or pensions. Such things have to be paid for in a mature economy, whether in the public or private sectors. Singapore's low level of public spending is an artefact of its very rapid recent growth; it has been an industrializing rather than a mature economy. It will not be able to get away with 20 per cent for ever: spending on items such as pensions will rise considerably in due course as the population ages. What is crucial is not the level of public spending *per se* but that the internationally tradable sectors of a country remain competitive.

It is time to turn to the relevant facts about the international economy that tell against the credibility of the globalization thesis. The first point to be made about globalization is that Martin Woolf is right: the protagonists of a rapid and recent process of globalization have short memories. They tend to talk as if until the 1970s national economies were almost closed systems. Yet the international economy has changed frequently and radically since a modern industrial trading system was first developed in the 1870s. One does not want to be bogged down in history and statistics but the evidence is striking and surprising. In many ways the international economy was more open in the period leading up to 1914 than it is today. Indeed, if globalization ever existed it was during the *Belle Epoque*. Several major states had high trade to GDP ratios, and these were not exceeded in the period of rapid growth after 1945 – France's ratio in 1913 was 35.4 per cent and in 1973 29 per cent; Germany's 35.1 per cent in 1913 and 35.2 per cent in 1973. Capital was highly mobile, levels of foreign direct investment high, and the ratio of total capital flows to GDP higher for major international *rentier* states like Britain and France than in any subsequent period. The nineteenth century was the age of mass migration – European labour flowing freely to new growing economies abroad – whereas today economic migrants are feared and discriminated against. Finally, of course, the Gold Standard ensured that the international monetary system was beyond the control of any state, even the UK. States had to adapt to monetary movements but they could not directly control exchange rates.

The point can also be made that the supposed golden era of national economic management from 1945–73 was in fact dependent on an *international* trading system controlled by *international* institutions that promoted growth and made the macroeconomic or industrial policies of the nation states possible. The liberal-managed multilateralism of the post-1945 world was largely an Anglo-American creation. It was sustained by US hegemony and by its willingness to bear the costs of underwriting the system. The Bretton Woods system of fixed exchange rates, Marshall Aid, GATT, large-scale American corporate investment abroad, and massive US military aid all helped to promote domestic growth in allied states and boost world trade. Indeed, international trade grew faster than did domestic output in the period 1950–73, and at a faster rate relative to domestic output in that period than in the supposed era of globalization after 1973. The point to emphasize here is that national controls over exchange rates, foreign exchange transactions and capital movements were made possible by a system of international institutions underwritten by a hegemonic state. The dismantling of this system was driven largely by national, and often short-term, policy considerations: states deregulated and abandoned exchange controls from the late 1970s, mainly because of internal political agendas rather than as a result of the pressure of international markets.

Secondly, the ungovernability of major financial and other markets is consistently overemphasized by the globalizers. The greatest economic turbulence in modern times was caused by deliberate acts of price-fixing by nation states – the oil price-hikes of OPEC in 1973 and 1979. It is certainly true that the 1970s and early 1980s were a period of intense volatility in currency markets and free-floating exchange rates. Given the intensity of the inflationary crisis of the 1970s, it is difficult to see how any international monetary regime could have survived. Yet efforts were being made to reregulate the major financial institutions at the micro-level in the 1980s, especially through the co-operation of the central banks of the major industrial states. Equally, the Plaza Accord of 1985 and the Louvre Accord of 1987 did effect some stabilization in exchange rates between the G-3 – Europe, Japan and the USA. Similarly, the EMS served to stabilize exchange rates in Europe from 1979–92. At present the battles between public policy and the major currency markets are far from settled – one reason being that no one state is willing to underwrite the system and the major players have divergent interests. Thus current currency problems, especially the over-valuation of the DM and the Yen, are exacerbated by a difference of interest between the US and the Japanese governments.

It is true that the volume of international financial trading is so great as to limit market-making by central banks and that it dwarfs the real economy of international trade. Yet these volumes represent short-term and repeated market transactions by financial institutions, and these casino-like trading patterns could be rapidly "cooled" by a modest turnover tax on short-term transactions like that proposed by James Tobin.[1] The problem here is not merely to get governments to agree, to plug loopholes and the like, but to change perceptions in the international financial community that insti-tutions use these transactions to *avoid* risk and that there is no shortage of capital to finance trade or fixed investment. Thus unless volatility becomes a real concern to financial institutions and major companies it is unlikely that the major states could be persuaded to act in concert to limit short-term international financial trading and to plug loopholes. Speculators apart, business has no direct interest in high levels of market volatility or states of uncertainty about major financial movements. They make both trade and meeting commitments arising from financial assets like pensions or insurance policies more difficult. Incalculable risks created by volatile markets are an investment and trade and, therefore, growth killer.

The present international currency and other financial markets are thus relatively lightly governed, but they are not beyond control in principle. What prevents greater governance is not market forces *per se* but the divergent interests of the major nation states and the belief in business circles that current risks do not justify the inconvenience of greater regulation. The notion that the major states are powerless in the face of global markets is thus highly exaggerated. The difficulties of the EMS in 1992–93 do not gainsay this judgement. The policies of several nation states, but especially the UK, provoked the markets by being stubbornly committed to unrealistic and unsustainable rates against the DM. Stupidity in public policy is no reason to believe that all governance is ineffective, simply that it should not grossly violate the interests and expectations of economic actors.

Thirdly, true transnational companies are relatively rare. Most multinational companies are based in a major industrial state, and conduct the majority of their business within their home region, such as North America, Asia-Pacific or Europe; typically the figure is around 60–70 per cent of sales and about the same for assets.[2] This does not mean that companies are not internationally oriented, but that they have a recognizable national/regional "base" from which they operate, and in which they keep the key value-adding parts of their activities such as R&D and core manufacturing. Companies use foreign direct investment in subsidiaries and branch plants in other countries to facilitate trade, but they remain distinctly "national": Ford is unmistakably an American company despite its global reach, and Sony distinctly Japanese despite its large acquisitions in the USA. Firms continue to derive substantial benefits from being nationally based, even if the days of interventionist state industrial policy and "national champions" are over. Companies benefit from the complex of institutions that form a national business system, particularly with nationally rooted financial institutions that provide the bulk of their capital. They also benefit from the cultural intangibles that generate common attitudes and expectations, something a supranational company will lack. There is little sign that companies are shifting from such nationally based patterns of multinational trading to a truly transnational scale of activity; the current national/regional concentration is not just a historic artefact. The point of this is that national companies show that distinct national economic systems remain, and therefore the relevance of national policy in promoting corporate performance and in ensuring regulations of companies through their national home bases. Will Hutton's influential book, *The State We're In* (1995) shows what happens when the complex of national institutions fails to sustain the manufacturing sector; national policy is not an irrelevancy, but in no country has the myth of globalization and the impotence of the state taken stronger root than in the UK.

Fourthly, further supposed evidence of globalization is to be found in the twin processes of foreign direct investment in less developed countries and the rapid growth of a large part of the third world, countries like China and India, that will alter western dominance and create a truly global economy in the early twenty-first century. At present trade and investment remain distinctly lumpy; the rich world of North America, Japan and Europe accounted for 14 per cent of the world's population, but 75 per cent of investment flows in the period 1980–91; in 1992 the same countries accounted for approximately 70 per cent of export trade.[3] Capital is not fleeing the developed world to low-wage countries. Foreign direct investment is flowing to a select minority of developing countries – Singapore, Malaysia, Mexico and the coastal provinces of China taking the lion's share. At face value the volumes of FDI flowing to less developed countries seem huge, for example, they surged from $31 billion in 1990 to $80 billion in 1993. This increase is closely correlated with a severe recession in the developed world and a downturn in investment opportunities there. Moreover, even large numbers can be misleading out of context – $80 billion appears an enormous sum until one considers that in 1992 the total population of India and China alone amounted to some 2 billion, and that if the whole of FDI to the third world in 1993 were invested in these two countries it would amount to $40 per capita. Paul Krugman has calculated that the entire net outflow of investment between 1990 and 1994 has reduced the total capital stock of the advanced world by a mere 0.5 per cent.[4]

It is possible that China and India will grow rapidly into the twenty-first century, but by no means certain. They will need to, since it is estimated that both will have populations of 1.5 billion by 2025. At that point China may well have to support 300 million people over 60 and perhaps up to 250 million unemployed. The truth is that prospects for growth in the third world are uncertain. Latin American growth rates are notoriously volatile – Mexico has gone from success story to basket case in a few months. East Asian growth rates have been spectacular in countries like Singapore and South Korea, but they are unlikely to continue to grow at rates of 9 per cent per annum indefinitely. In part these rates are once and for all investment driven, part of the process of conversion to a modern market society. Singapore, for example, doubled its labour participation ratio from 27 per cent to 51 per cent in just over two decades, and invested something like 40 per cent of output.[5] Moreover, countries like Singapore have staggeringly high export to GDP ratios – 185 per cent in 1991 – proving its role as an *entrepôt* and confirming that the growth of such Tigers depends directly on first-world prosperity. The odds are, therefore, that the three most wealthy regions in the world will retain their dominance of output, investment and trade.

That means they will continue to dominate the world economy and to have the capacity to regulate it effectively if they choose to do so and can agree. The EU and NAFTA (USA, Canada and Mexico) remain, moreover, quasi-autarchic – they still exported only about 10 per cent of their GDP in 1990, and even Japan exported only 11 per cent. If they wished, the major regional trade blocs of the EU and NAFTA could go it alone, imposing distinct regional policies and maintaining distinct regimes of welfare and labour rights. This would involve a measure of protectionism, and apart from its likely effects in constraining the growth of world trade, a world divided into regional economic blocs is likely to be more politically uncertain and unstable than one in which the major powers act to sustain an open world economy and to help its weaker members.

These examples should indicate that the scope of national policy in the advanced world has not been diminished to the degree the globalizers believe. However, if we are not at the mercy of uncontrolled market forces, the managed multilateralism and the activist macroeconomic steering at national level that characterized the period between 1947–73 are unlikely to return. The world economy is governable to a degree: curbing the volatility of world financial markets, promoting free trade through the WTO, attempting to impose social and environmental conditions on investment in poorer countries through home regulation in the advanced world, and so on. States need to co-ordinate national policies and to act in concert to support international forms of regulation. States will increasingly be effective if they act to promote international regulation, co-operating to pursue common goals and to pool their powers. Thus the national policies of economic management will be increasingly concerned with international issues; states will be effective as representatives of their populations at the supranational level. This will require a new outward-looking orientation on the part of national politicians and informed publics. The problem with the notion of globalization is that it denies this international orientation of national policy by insisting that the world market system is beyond all control. Globalization is a myth, unsustained by the evidence. It is a myth that serves the interests of neither business nor labour. Companies need a calculable degree of risk if they are to invest and promote growth, and uncertainty can only be contained by governance of markets and by an effective framework of regulation at national and international levels. In such a context labour can defend its welfare and its rights. A regulated international environment, in which the advanced states feel secure, is more likely to benefit the bulk of less developed economies than a volatile free for all. Globalization is a myth that the left and those conservatives concerned to maintain social stability and solidarity should never have fallen for in the first place. Never have ill-founded and ill-substantiated ideas been so pernicious. It is time they were abandoned and we returned to exploring the practical possibilities of active economic governance at national and international levels.

Notes

1. See Tobin (1994).
2. See Hirst and Thompson (1996), Ch. 4.
3. See Hirst and Thompson (1994).
4. See Krugman (1994a).
5. See Krugman (1994b).

14

The international origins of national sovereignty

Political theorists and sociologists commonly assert, following Max Weber, that a distinctive and definitive feature of the modern state is the effective control of the means of violence in a specific territory. Weber says: "The claim of the modern state to monopolise the use of force is as essential to it as its character of compulsory jurisdiction and continuous operation" (1968, Vol 1: 56). Yet in the sixteenth and seventeenth centuries – supposedly the key period in the rise of the modern state – this claim was frequently unsustainable. Many political entities could not consistently make this claim for the whole of their territories, and other rulers could not make such a claim. Thus, the French monarchy after the Edict of Nantes (1598) had explicitly ceded the control of certain fortresses to the Huguenots. Likewise, the Holy Roman Emperor's ability to regulate the use of force by lesser rulers within the territory of the Empire or to call on rulers to provide him with military forces was distinctly circumscribed. Some states were no more able to sustain this claim than the Lebanese state could control the armed militias in its territory in the early 1980s. France, at certain points during the religious civil wars, was close to the anarchy we have become familiar with in Beirut, Bosnia or Liberia today.

In what is supposed to be the period in which the larger territorial monarchies prevailed over other political entities, over feudal nobilities, universal institutions like the Papacy or the Empire, city states, and leagues of free cities (like the Hanseatic League), many major states actually had for long periods of time few means to control the loyalties of or the use of force by their citizens.[1] The supposed subjects of the monarch or ruler were committed to rival forms of social organization, to churches and religious sects, that had most of the attributes of states: that demanded a supra-political loyalty, that taxed their members' incomes, that imposed religious justice, and that controlled confessional armed forces. Given that religion was the main issue promoting dissent and conflict in the sixteenth and seventeenth centuries, dividing the populations of political bodies on primarily confessional lines, it inevitably became the main focus for political loyalty.

As Carl Schmitt (1976) argued, the issues that define the political are openended; ultimately they concern whatever drives people to group themselves into conflicting camps and compels them to create forms of political order – foci of loyalty and means of common decision-making – that enable them to contest with their enemies. Schmitt's views remain controversial and certainly only capture one aspect of politics, but his was a position shaped in part by reflection on the religious civil wars, and it is sharpened in its contemporary relevance by the experience of Bosnia. The aspect of politics that Schmitt emphasizes, friend–enemy relations, remains central, and Schmitt stresses the uncomforting truth that what order there is in politics arises either from the stabilization of conflict or by the defeat of one of the contending parties within a given territory.

Religious conflict thus had the capacity to disrupt the processes of state-building. The Reformation was central in this respect because it allied religious dissent to political power, and enabled lesser rulers to escape the hegemonic claims of the Emperor. Protestantism survived, unlike many previous movements for reform like the Lollards and Waldesians, because Luther was shrewd enough to ask for the support of disaffected elites and thus ensure that the new reformed religion did not become a "heresy", wholly outside the orbit of established power.[2] But even though Protestantism attracted certain established elites and rulers, it also created dissent within and between states, in France and the Empire in particular. The Reformation also gave rise to radical sects, Müntzer and his followers, the Anabaptists and the like, who rejected any form of covenant with the powers that be.[3] In large areas of Europe rulers could not rely on the religious, and therefore the political, loyalty of their subjects whether mean or mighty. Noblemen and peasants, journeymen and members of the urban patriarchate could turn revolutionary under the influence of religion. Huguenot nobles and bourgeois Calvinist elders in Scotland show that radical religious dissent was not merely a product of revolt by the poor and excluded. Moreover, religious dissent was not merely a threat that came from the Reformed religion. The Catholic League was a revolutionary organization that was willing to browbeat and even to cast aside the French monarchy in the pursuit of its goals. In such circumstances state-building could not follow a steady course, prevailing over feudal lords and lesser political entities, steadily acquiring control and constructing uniform systems of administration within their own borders.

Large states did not enjoy the inherent advantages over lesser powers in military and taxation terms if in fact they were subject to extensive disruption by religious dissent – entire regions or social strata rejecting the rule of the centre. Indeed, given a certain tax base and a loyal local population, the new military means that developed rapidly in the sixteenth century did not necessarily favour central power.[4] The new artillery fortifications could enable dissident regions to survive, as the alliance of rebel provinces in the Netherlands defied Spain, the greatest military power in the period, in an 80-year war of independence demonstrates. This was a protracted war of sieges behind new fortifications and water lines. The Protestant minority in France, led by local noble and urban elites, although outnumbered and geographically scattered, held out in a network of local fortresses until Huguenot power was finally crushed at La Rochelle in 1628.[5] In Holland's case Protestant foreign aid and access to the sea enabled survival at certain crucial moments in the war. La Rochelle fell because the English navy failed to break through and bring relief. Without that contingency, the course of absolutist state building in France might have been rather different.

Whether in Germany or Holland, France or England, religious dissidents could expect help from co-religionists abroad. In a genuine sense the Protestant and Catholic religions created true "internationals" in the sixteenth and seventeenth centuries. Princes and apprentices alike were willing to make efforts and sacrifices for the cause. States aided foreign rebels and also made war to help other states. They promoted civil war and encouraged ideological rebellion. Catholic Recusants in England, Huguenots in France, could expect foreign help, whether it be secret Papal agents or subsidies, or bibles smuggled through concealed in herring barrels by Dutch traders. Elizabeth I or Gustavus Adolphus were of course pursuing the political interests of their states, but that *realpolitik* was conducted within an international system in which the religious affiliations of states mattered. Thus to see the Thirty Years War as exclusively a matter of conflicting *state* interests – as a Hapsburg bid for hegemony that was resisted by other powers and as a series of local conflicts caught up in the bigger struggle – is as mistaken as it would be to view it as a *purely* religious war.[6]

States thus frequently could not begin to substantiate claims to "sovereignty" in a given territory, nor were they under effective international pressure to abide by a rule of non-intervention in their neighbours' internal affairs. On the contrary, non-intervention could only come to be seen as an issue when the religious conflicts had escalated beyond all bounds. Religion promoted ideological internationalism and civil war driven by political ideas. In that sense religious conflicts were comparable to the ideological conflicts of the twentieth century between left and right, between communists and fascists. Indeed, religious belief was if anything more international, since confessional allegiances could make existing frontiers irrelevant. Class conflicts remained stubbornly national by contrast, social interests struggling to seize power and sovereignty in nation states. Genuine popular acts of internationalism were rare among socialists, and the example of 1914 remains notorious. Confessional groups gave more than lip-service to international solidarity.[7] State-building could not have been effectively continued in several key European regions until the supra-national appeal of religious belief could be curtailed. The claims of loyalty to sovereign had to prevail over confessional loyalty, and the only way to do that was to make confessional loyalty and political loyalty coincident, to territorialize religion.

It is in this context that we should look, once again, at the Treaty of Westphalia. It has become fashionable to argue that the Westphalian states system is coming to an end and that the political universe will continue to diversify, to become more complex and pluralistic in the type of entities it contains, leading to the demise of the nation state as the predominant political entity.[8] On the other hand, Stephen Krasner (1993) argues that Westphalia *was* actually not the founding moment of the modern system of states, and that it did not usher in an international arena made up exclus-ively of sovereign nation states interacting externally one with another. Both of these arguments may be true to a degree, but I want to try and make a case for a rather different proposition. My claim is that Westphalia was a decisive moment in the formation of the modern system of states, but not because an already internally created and domestically secured state "sov-ereignty" was recognized there; rather the point is that by successfully reducing international religious conflict below a crucial threshold, states were able to gain control of their societies.

The negotiations of 1648 brought the Thirty Years' War to an end.[9] In that sense the Treaty marked the end of a long century of religious civil wars and of interstate conflicts with a strong religious dimension that had begun with the Hussites and had accelerated after Luther was able to win over some of the German princes. By 1648 religious conflict had begun to be seen as self-defeating; the miseries of the wars were perceived as bringing general discredit on religion. Much of Germany was devastated, or so contemporaries believed. Even the victors of the peace, France and Sweden, were close to exhaustion.

What the Treaty did was to attempt to stabilize religion and territory in Germany, and to make the main external powers who had intervened parties to and guarantors of that peace. The ruinous effects of the war led key political elites in Germany to put social peace before supraterritorial confessional ambitions and obligations. Westphalia worked in that it did strengthen the principle that the confessional status of a territory should be unambiguously clear, and that internal and external actors should not attempt to alter it. In this it follows previous efforts to end the religious conflicts but with more success. Thus the Peace of Augsburg of 1555 had attempted to stabilize religion and territory on the principle of *cujus regio ejus religio* – that the religion of the state is that of the prince. But it had failed to institutionalize it: dissident subjects and rulers who changed religion when the mass of their people did not were beyond control.

Moreover, the peace of 1555 was an agreement within the Empire, it was not underwritten by the major non-German rulers, who were thus at liberty to aid their allies in Germany.

Subject to certain guarantees and concessions to particular interests, Westphalia attempted to legitimate and to reconstruct a religious *status quo*, to freeze the relationship between religion and territory as Augsburg had, but to generalize it so that non-German states accepted that a religious division of power could be made to prevail within the Empire. States and the political entities in Germany had to accept that the confessional status of neighbouring powers was fixed and not subject to change by military force or by the support of sedition. Religious change thus ceased to be an object of interstate policy. States became Catholic, Calvinist or Lutheran according to the will of their rulers or to local agreements as to consent by subjects, both principles being present in the Treaty.

Thus over the remainder of the century that followed 1648, religion became "depoliticized" in Carl Schmitt's terms (Schmitt 1976). That is, it ceased to be a matter that led different groups to organized conflict. Subjects could no longer effectively dispute the claims of their sovereign to rule on the basis that they wanted to pursue a form of religious belief different to that of their lord, and increasingly this was because they could not rely on other states intervening to help their cause or allowing co-religionists among their subjects to do so. If religion began to cease to be a source of conflict, at the same time economic affairs had yet to become "political".[10] Social conflicts were limited in scope and preideological in nature – class war had yet to replace religious war. Hence as a consequence of the depoliticization of religion, the state could begin to assert more power over society than it had been able to do heretofore. The scope for "political" conflict *within* states was considerably lessened and the main forms of conflict came to be those that took place *between* states. This change increased the claims that states could credibly and legitimately make on their subjects. As *enemies* became increasingly external, states were able to call forth new forms of loyalty on the part of their members, and the ruling elites could begin the project of identifying the subjects with a territory and with the state. The regimes that were most successful in this process could draw more deeply on the lives and property of their subjects to fight foreign wars. In this context of de-politicization and the externalization of military conflict, it becomes possible for states to construct or resume the construction of systems of relatively uniform administration in their territory, to subject their subjects more effectively to their hierarchical control and organizational hegemony. Given such administration, the means of violence could then be controlled, appropriated and monopolized. The development of a monopoly of the means of violence is thus closely associated with the limitations on the scope of political conflict that were at least in part

brought about by agreements between states. The monopoly thus established is then used more effectively to direct violence outwards in a long
struggle for territory and hegemony in the shifting balance of power
between European states – from the 1680s onwards.

Westphalia established the principle that states agreed not to intervene in
other states' affairs in matters of religion, to accept a world of religiously
diverse territories. Catholics and Protestants abandoned claims to universalism. States accepted the legitimate existence of other religions in
other territories. This was the case whatever their internal religious policy,
whether they practised a policy of religious toleration, subject to minorities
accepting conditions, as in Holland, or sought to impose religious homogeneity by force, as did Louis XIV when his regime revoked the remaining
provisions of the Edict of Nantes in 1685, and began the dual process of the
expulsion of the Huguenots and the "Catholicization" of France. Either
policy made possible the consolidation of political authority by making state
power legitimate in religious terms.

Thus it is misleading to present the state as if it acquired its effective
monopoly over the means of violence by its own internal efforts, slowly
eliminating feudal military powers and the privileges of free cities. This is
the case even if it is accepted that this growth of military monopoly was
stimulated by external conflicts and the need to further them. States could
not consolidate by state-building alone – constructing administrative systems
for their territories and steadily adding to their powers to tax, to make laws,
and to regulate the raising of troops.

Even in England, where monarchical legal and administrative centralization had proceeded considerably by the later Middle Ages, the decisive
periods of Renaissance state-building were closely connected with religious
conflict. In Henry VIII's case religious dissent legitimated the acquisition of
further powers and resources with the dissolution of the Monasteries and the
assertion by the Crown of the right to determine the form of religious belief.
Later the struggle against Spain legitimated royal power and provided a basis
for growing internal political supervision of belief. It is only in retrospect that
England can be presented as a steadily growing monarchical-territorial state.
In the mid-fifteenth century it was in crisis. Its project of domination in
France had been destroyed – but for that it would have been a supranational
imperium. Equally, the Wars of the Roses reduced England to anarchy in the
aftermath of defeat in France. Thus to present England as an early example of
a territorial sovereign state as Krasner (1993) does is hardly accurate. It is so
only if one constructs a teleology of the "true course" of English state-
formation, one that ignores or sidelines the crises, uprisings, the Civil War,
and the Crown's dream of recovering its dominions in France that continued
well into the sixteenth century. England remained a relatively backward and
fragile Renaissance state. To ignore this is to indulge contemporary projects

of presenting the stability and continuity of the English state, those of the late Elizabethan era, and those of the Whigs. The religious conflicts at times helped to promote state power, in that they provided the Tudor monarchy with the means to construct and enforce a "national" confessional homogeneity, and at other times, most notably the Civil War, they undermined central royal authority.

Until religious conflicts could be contained from spreading across borders, no state subject to religious dissent could hope to develop uninterruptedly those attributes of sovereignty claimed as definitive of modern statehood by Weber. Those states that were able to avoid such disruption had managed to preserve or construct forms of religious homogeneity – Spain did so by an early practice of religious "police" directed against Jews and Moorish converts. Religion was *the* central political issue, and the capacity to prevent, eliminate or contain religious conflict was vital to building an effective *political* foundation for state power.[11] Thus by exploiting the freedom from external interference underwritten by international treaty and gradually extended throughout western Europe as the core principle of the emerging international law, states were better able to enforce "sovereignty" on their societies. The agreement of most of Europe's most affected states to avoid interference in the religious peace of other states changed the terms of conflict between territorial authority and confessional groups in the former's favour. To a significant degree the capacity of state elites to assert "sovereign" control over territory came from *without*, from agreements between states in the developing society of states. To a considerable degree therefore, the capacities of the state grew inward from the *international* recognition of its rights to certain key powers by other states.

This process was complex and by no means complete in 1648. But Krasner is wrong to talk down Westphalia as a watershed. States did not create fully uniform and effective administrations in most cases until the nineteenth century. France in 1789 was far from "absolutist"; it remained a patchwork of internal jurisdictions, status privileges and particular liberties. The process of state-building from above, imposing royal or state power, was subject to many limitations even in the supposedly "absolute" monarchies. But at least that project could be essayed once peace was assured in confessional matters, whereas it was radically delayed and undermined by the religious civil wars.

Krasner is right to point out that 1648 did not immediately result in a monoculture of sovereign states, displacing all other political entities both supra- and sub-territorial. But his interpretation of Westphalia in the matter of religious conflict seems somewhat forced. He is right to say that:

> Even the exercise of authority over activities exclusively within given territory, generally regarded as a core attribute of sovereign states, has

been problematic in practice and contested in theory. The most dramatic challenge has involved efforts by external actors to control the way a state treats its own citizens or subjects. (1993: 237)

This is certainly the case; the content and scope of sovereignty have been subject to constant conflict and redefinition. But he treats Westphalia in matters of religion as if it were a limitation of sovereignty, rather than an attempt to reinforce it. He says: "In the sixteenth and seventeenth centuries, states concluded international agreements containing provisions in respect to the treatment of religious dissenters" (*ibid.*). This is true, but Westphalia was an attempt to *limit* the grounds on which states could intervene by cementing a religious peace and delimiting confessional territories.

Curiously, Krasner recognizes this, without drawing the conclusion that Westphalia was a turning point. He says that "the more general problem therefore . . ." at issue in 1648 ". . . was to find some way of dealing with the religious disorders that had torn Europe apart for a century" (*ibid.*: 240), and "Westphalia attempted to insulate religion from politics" (*ibid.*: 242). The latter terms might well be reversed to sum up the impact of the Treaties. Certainly the peace tried to freeze the religious *status quo* as it had existed, and thus to a degree limited the absolutism in religious matters of rulers within Germany. But to say that Westphalia "was less consistent with modern notions of sovereignty than Augsburg" in 1555 is surely to miss the point of these provisions. The aim of the 1648 Treaties is to cement the provisions of the previous peace in the new context. Treaties are almost always complex amalgams of items agreed by difficult negotiations, and the agreements at Münster and Osnabrück were no exception. Nevertheless, key articles of the Treaty make clear that the aim was to reinforce Augsburg, not to set it aside. For example, the Treaty of Osnabrüch between Sweden, the Emperor and the German princes reads:

> . . . The Religious Peace of 1555 . . . shall, in all its articles entered into and concluded by the unanimous consent of the emperor, electors, princes and states of both religions, be confirmed and observed fully and without infringement. (Article 5, para. 1)

Whereas all immediate states enjoy, together with their territorial rights and sovereignty as hitherto used throughout the empire, also the right of reforming the practice of religion; and whereas in the Religious Peace the privilege of emigration was conceded to subjects of such states if they dissented from their territorial lord; and whereas later, for the better preserving of greater concord among the states, it was agreed that no one should seduce another's subjects to his religion, or for that reason make any understanding for defense or protection, or come to their aid for any reason; it is now agreed that all these be fully observed by the states of either religion, and that no state shall be hindered in the rights in matters of religion which belong to it by reason of its territorial independence and sovereignty. (Article 5, para. 30) [12]

In these provisions it is clear that Augsburg *limited* the powers of sovereigns radically: they could not enforce conversion and compel subjects to stay, subjects had a right to belief even if this meant exile. States thus had limited controls over their populations; they could not by right prevent emigration in the way that many states, especially the communist regimes of the twentieth century, have done. This limitation was in the interests of religious liberty – perhaps the first internationally recognized civil right. At the same time rulers had rights too, under the principle of *cujus regio ejus religio.* Moreover, the principle of non-intervention is defined in the 1648 Treaty as reinforcing an attribute of sovereignty, the right of states to order their own affairs. The upshot of this parcel of rights – for subjects, rulers and sovereign states – is to cement the ties of confession and territory, to prevent arbitrary acts against this state of affairs by subjects (they may leave but not rebel in the name of religion), by rulers (they may not subsequently and arbitrarily alter an established religious constitution agreed by prince and people), and other states (they may not legitimately intervene to aid co-religionists). Therefore, the internationally recognized rights of these diverse subjects reinforce state sovereignty rather than undermine it. The architects of Westphalia were not explicitly intending to create a new international order or to define sovereignty in a new way. But the effect of Westphalia was to cool the centre of religious conflict and make possible a form of connection between cultural homogeneity and political power, that is, confessional conformity and the exclusive control of a territory by one principal political body. That model of a coherent culture and a coherent territory being ruled by a single political entity could then subsequently generate "nationalism", that is, the requirement that cultural homogeneity extend to far more than religion, to whatever defines the "nation" as a specific socio-political construct. The notion of a confessionally coherent territory is thus the foundation for the idea that states and their subjects should have common and distinctive attributes. Before this notion of confessional conformity, peoples and rulers could have very diverse attributes, conflicting and overlapping loyalties and obligations, identities and beliefs.

Of course as Krasner argues, the Holy Roman Empire survived until 1806, but few contemporaries doubted that the Imperial Party were the main losers in the wars that followed the Edict of Restitution in 1629. The Edict was a bid by the Emperor to alter the religious balance between Protestants and Catholics in Germany in the latter's favour. It was backed by the threat of Wallenstein's army of 134,000 men. The Edict threatened not merely the

Protestants, but the autonomy of the Princes of the Empire, and it also provoked the intervention of the Swedes in 1630. The main beneficiaries of Westphalia *within* the Empire were its principal territorial states, who gained both more autonomy and a greater say in the conduct of Imperial affairs. The Papacy was very clear that the Catholic cause was the main loser in the peace and in the changes in Imperial government. The Pope was not a party to the negotiations and he fired off an angry Bull, "Zelo Domus Dei", repudiating the terms of the Treaty. Innocent X clearly did not believe nothing had happened – rather the "heretics" as he called them were accepted as a stable part of the political system of Germany both by Ferdinand III and the French.[13]

Krasner's scepticism is not unwelcome, since the conventional account of the rise of the modern state too readily assumes a sharp break between medieval and modern political forms. My difference with him is over the role of the Treaty of Westphalia in creating certain of the conditions for the territorialization of political-religious authority, and thus the building of the modern state. In the last few years international relations theorists like John Ruggie (1986), Brian M. Downing (1992), Hendrik Spruyt (1994), and Janice E. Thomson (1994) have begun to ask new questions about the formation of the modern sovereign state and to take the discussion of the development of a monopoly of the means of violence beyond Max Weber. They recognize that both the units of political power and the relationship between them, the system of states, changed in early-modern Europe.

Brian Downing's *The Military Revolution and Political Change* (1992) emphasizes the impact of the military revolution of the sixteenth and early seventeenth centuries on state formation and as a determinant of the type of political authority that emerged. He argues that the fiscal exigences of the military revolution in conditions of intense conflict fostered the development of military bureaucratic absolutism. Where rulers were forced to tax the agrarian sector heavily in order to survive, they were compelled to abrogate the local powers and the representative institutions of medieval constitutionalism. Brandenburg-Prussia and France moved in the direction of absolutism, whilst England and Holland were able to use the advantages of an advanced economy, alliances and geographic position to finance war on a basis that did not threaten the limits to taxation that their representative institutions were willing to grant. Sweden escaped the worst effects of absolutism because to a considerable degree it could make foreigners pay for its wars.

The argument is well marshalled, but it ignores how chaotic were the political and military institutional arrangements in much of Europe during the religious civil wars and the Thirty Years' War. Funds for armies were often raised by mere extortion and pillage – forms of "taxation" beyond the control of either medieval assemblies or "modern" absolutisms. Again

225

religious fervour could call forth resources that normal political purposes could not, changing the terms on which representative institutions were willing to act. Armies were far more makeshift than the term "military revolution" implies, composed of mixtures of volunteers, local levies and mercenaries armed with whatever came to hand. Often in the French civil wars or the Thirty Years' War, armed bands degenerated into an anarchy close to generalized banditry. A casual reading of Grimmelshausen's *Simplicius Simplicissimus* (1669) will reveal what was typical not only of the Thirty Years' War in its later stages but of many other conflicts: a broken-backed form of war conducted by armed bands directly feeding off the people and beyond any form of central or bureaucratic control. Religious zealots, mutinous unpaid mercenaries, impressed ploughboys, and rebellious peasants made up much of the "armies" of this period – forces far removed from the orderly schemes of Maurice of Nassau or Gustavus Adolphus, and principally armed with the cheap and cheerful pike and that low-tech, low-skill substitute for the crossbow, the arquebus.[14]

Hendrik Spruyt's *The Sovereign State and its Competitors* (1994) asks the entirely reasonable but very original question: if feudal authority was in decline and a new form of political order was necessary in a more commercial and urban society, why did it take the form of the modern territorial sovereign state? Spruyt examines the possible competitors, city states and city leagues, and attempts to explain why the territorial state emerged as the dominant form. Central to Spruyt's explanation is that the sovereign state was a more effective institutional arrangement than its competitors. He claims that:

> Organisational types that were fraught with free-riding and factionalism, that had problems rationalising their economies and reducing transaction costs – in short, those that could not make the transition to consolidated national economies – were less effective and less efficient in mobilising resources than sovereign states. (1994: 178)

The emergence of the sovereign state and the system of states went together: "The system selected out those types of units that were competitively speaking less efficient" (*ibid.*: 180). Thus the Hanseatic League was excluded as a distinct party at the peace negotiations of Westphalia, Spruyt argues, because it was not a territorial state. Rather the issue seems to turn on the delicate issue of religious power in Germany. The League was not a party to the Religious Peace of 1555 and its *German* cities were either directly or indirectly represented in the negotiations of 1648. The delicate balance between Protestants and Catholics could well have been undermined by such double counting, if the League was represented as a power and some of its member cities like Lübeck were also there because of their status in the Imperial constitution. The League's nature as a non-territorial form of organization seems less the point in and of itself, than the danger that it would alter the balance of forces further against the Catholic party.

Many of the "territorial" states at Westphalia were hardly in the position where they could cope with "factionalism". The weaknesses Spruyt sees in city states and city leagues were real, confronted with a territorial state in which sovereignty was effectively asserted. But many states at different points in the sixteenth and seventeenth centuries were in a state of religious civil war, or of aristocratic or local revolt; they were thus not inherently superior to other forms. Authority remained fragile and provisional in this period to a degree that makes theoretical analyses of the competitive advantage of forms of state hypothetical to say the least.

Janice E. Thomson's *Mercenaries, Pirates and Sovereigns* (1994) concentrates on the issue of sovereignty as the state's control of non-state violence beyond its borders. She argues that the monopolization of the means of internal violence by the state is only one aspect of sovereignty; what she calls its "constitutive dimension" defines "the state as *the actor* in international politics by designating the state, rather than a religious or economic organisation, as the repository of ultimate authority within a political space that is defined territorially" (1994: 16). This decisive element of sovereign statehood is in no way accomplished by the end of the seventeenth century: "The state's monopoly on external violence came very late and through a process spanning several centuries. For three hundred years non-state violence was a legitimate practice in the European state system" (*ibid.*: 143). She recognizes the extent to which this responsibility for external action and sovereignty over such action was internationally established and enforced. States gradually asserted control or were required to assert control over all actions emanating from their territory: "Interstate relations and not domestic politics were the crucial determinants in this trans-formative process" (*ibid.*: 19).

Her work draws on numerous sources, but in particular owes its key insights on the international aspect of national sovereignty to Charles Tilly. Tilly (1975, 1990) sees state-building, the growth of territorial sovereignty and its legitimacy, in stark and brutal terms. He argues that states were built by power-hungry elites, who used the force available to them to amass wealth and the instruments of hierarchical control. Central to the legitimacy of such power-grabbers were not the opinions of the mass of the ruled; given a certain capacity for coercion they could be ignored and compelled to obey. Power in early-modern Europe was seldom beneficial to the common people. Instead, states depended on the acceptance of their existence and their capacity to control territory by others: "Legitimacy is the probability that other authorities will act to confirm the decisions of a given authority" (Tilly 1985: 171). Anthony Giddens (1985) argues that the *nation* state, recognized within a definite territory and accepted as the legitimate agency for determining the scope and scale of governance within these borders, is a distinctively modern form. He argues that this extended sense of sovereignty depends upon mutual recognition by states, "upon a reflexively monitored set of relations between states" (1985: 263–4).

These various arguments confirm the role of interstate agreements and international processes in generating and cementing aspects of state sovereignty. The forms of non-state and state-sanctioned "private" violence that Thomson analyses clearly limited the capacity of the state to assert sovereignty in the sense of an *internal* monopoly of the means of violence in the seventeenth century. Private armies, mercenary forces for hire, privateers and pirates at sea, all contributed means of intervention in *other states'* territories and affairs, they limited the affected states' capacities to protect and monopolize control over their own citizens and commerce. The possibility of hiring mercenary armies and foreign troops (often on credit) strengthened some rulers against their peoples, but this could also provide rebel strata and provinces with the means to resist central power and royal authority.

Westphalia clearly did not end such practices as mercenarism and piracy, and they persisted until major liberal states made determined efforts to limit them or stamp them out in the nineteenth century. As we have seen, however, Westphalia did attempt to limit aspects of external intervention by controlling and curtailing the right of states to interfere in others' religious affairs, irrespective of whether they were Reformed or Catholic. In one sense Westphalia could be called the international triumph of the *Politiques* – the liberal Catholic faction in the French religious wars who argued for the primacy of social peace and a stable political order over the claims of purity of religious doctrine and the right to propagate one's religious practices at whatever cost.[15] As Reinhart Koselleck (1988) argues, there is at this period a fundamental shift in political theory towards seeing the state as a neutral public power, above society, that can impose order on the warring factions of citizens. Civil society is seen as problematic and incapable of sustaining itself without political control over religious disputes.

Bodin (1576) and Hobbes (1651) both argue for the primacy of sovereign *political* authority within the state, determining what religious practices and beliefs are legitimate, and imposing its will as an uncommanded commander. Given this concept of the state as a neutral power internally, it is evident why international relations should be viewed as a realm of deideologized power-technique too. Hobbes saw interstate relations as an anarchy in which all powers are morally equivalent; states have interests and capacities but they are not part of a civil order. Thus the norms of interstate relations are prudential and based on things as they are, not as they ought to be. This concept of the state as a supreme public power can easily be accepted by other states, it imposes no ideological condition for conformity or moral test of conduct. One can deal equally pragmatically with Turk or Christian, and treat Reformed and Catholic regimes as entities of the same kind, as potential allies or foes. The new concept of state raises guilty *realpolitik* to the status of legitimate behaviour, sanctioned by high theory. The way is then clear for the kind of international law based on sovereignty and non-intervention fully developed in the eighteenth century by such theorists as Vattel.

Koselleck's argument is a powerful one, linking political theory and practice; it explains why, in the context of the mutual exhaustion of the religious wars, the notion of the state as a power above society could acquire a definite legitimacy and an attraction to a wide variety of social actors. Kings, counsellors and peasants could all agree that Paris, and peace, is worth a mass. Thus although Tilly is right that most ruling elites were driven by a ruthless will-to-power, one has to explain why rulers and peoples were willing to forgo their strongly held beliefs to the primacy of their own religion, and accept beyond their borders other states legitimately practising alien beliefs. One has to explain why non-elite social actors also wished to stabilize political authority, to have order, and to reinforce domestic peace by international recognition in a treaty. Legitimacy did not just come from without, it was sanctioned by tired and frightened people within. Most citizens or subjects had few illusions about the state, but they had even fewer about the capacity of "civil society" to live at peace unaided. Rulers who could offer order within had something to offer peoples, even at the price of foreign wars and taxes, if they put an end to the religious sects and zealots who tore the body politic apart in the reckless pursuit of their own beliefs. Westphalia marks a watershed because the ruler-sanctioned, confessionally stable state, recognized by other states, was part of the answer to the social crisis and crisis of authority brought about by the religious schisms.

The reason the analysis of the religious conflicts is not well-integrated into accounts of state-building in the sixteenth and seventeenth centuries based on international relations theory and political science, is that religious struggles tend to be fully considered in social and cultural history rather than political history. We forget how real and important religious belief was as a source of motivation for actors in this period, both princes and people.[16]

The burden of this chapter has been to argue that the territorial sovereign state was able to develop its distinctive attributes at least in part because of international agreement between states to limit intervention in each other's affairs in matters of religion.[17] Modern nation states have been built on these seventeenth-century foundations. Sovereign power did not originate at the national level alone. It is now widely claimed that the modern state is threatened with obsolescence as the processes of globalization and the trends towards localism that accompany them strip out its powers above and below the national level. In consequence some people look back to the Middle Ages – before the formation of the modern sovereign territorial state – for models of the type of patterns of power that may prevail.

Perhaps there are still some lessons to be learnt from the period of the formation of the modern state and the modern states system. If the international and the national interacted so closely as they did in the seventeenth century, then it may be that they will interact in equally complex and surprising ways today. It is indeed the case that certain vital dimensions of governance are beyond the competence of even the largest states today, for example, creating a set of rules and an agency to regulate world trade, or controlling global environmental change. International governance is now a necessary part of the division of labour in government. It does not follow, however, that national states are therefore powerless and that all they do is cede sovereignty and competencies to international agencies and thereafter cease to have any role. On the contrary, international governance, no matter how indispensable, cannot exist without the continued consent and co-operation of at least a crucial sub-set of powerful national states. Without such nationally derived consent, such international agencies will lack legitimacy. States can provide such legitimacy most effectively, because it is they alone who can speak for territorially bounded populations. They can ensure compliance within their own territories and can also support supranational bodies in dealing with other more refractory states. States with definite boundaries and at least minimally democratic governments can credibly speak for their people and commit their part of the globe to a common supranational policy with authority. Without such territorially derived democratic legitimacy, international arrangements and agencies will be ineffective.[18]

It is also the case that if effective economic and social governance increasingly depends on the actions of regional and local authorities, the nation state retains a crucial role in providing the constitutional ordering for such governments. The nation state distributes powers and competencies within, ensuring lesser authorities have the right scope, powers and access to resources. It provides local and regional governments with political stability and physical security. Nation states are thus not losing "sovereignty" upwards and downwards – to the international system and to regional authorities. That would be so only if sovereignty could only be conceived of in narrowly Bodinian terms – as an exclusive possession that can be neither divided nor delegated. That view may have made sense confronted with the religious strife of the sixteenth century, but in relation to the complex division of labour that is necessary to modern governance it is outdated. The new national sovereignty is above all the power to confer legitimacy and governmental competence to other agencies, international and local, but then to continue to support and sustain those agencies as a co-operative partner in a new scheme of authority. The nation state does not thereby become functionless, rather it becomes the key node (the main source of legitimacy that ties the whole together) in a complex web of governing powers. If that is so, then the new and emerging patterns of supranational governance will not simply supplant the nation state but will continue to depend upon it. This relationship is quite different, indeed the reverse, of that postulated as an effect of the Treaty of Westphalia, when international agreements empowered the territorial state, but it is a reminder that the national and the international levels have been closely and reciprocally interlinked since the beginning of the modern states system.

Notes

1. On this process of competition between different forms of political organization in early modern Europe, of which the sovereign territorial state has only one of a number of contenders to replace the feudal system in advanced decay, see Spruyt (1994).
2. On the history of heretical movements before Luther, Lambert (1977) remains a comprehensive survey. On the failure of an influential "reform" movement and its decline into heresy and its defeat, see McFarlane (1972).
3. See Cohn (1970), Ozment (1973) and Williams (1962) for the radical ideas, sects and movements spawned by the Reformation.
4. It is a commonplace of the literature on early-modern state-building in Europe to refer to a "military revolution" that is supposed to have taken place between the early sixteenth and the mid-seventeenth century and to argue that the new military technologies and structures favoured large-scale authority and thus shifted the balance of power in favour of the central state and against aristocratic and municipal localism. The concept of a "military revolution" between 1550 and 1660 derives from the classic paper of Michael Roberts (1956); for a sympathetic discussion see Parker (1979) (1988: Ch. 1). In the 2nd edition of *The Military Revolution* Parker tries to defend his own version of the concept against criticisms, but in my view not wholly convincingly. The idea of a distinctive revolution in the art of war in this period is actually rather difficult to defend. Of course there was a great deal of change, but over a longer temporality of 1500 to 1800 and certainly not in one definite direction. What undermines the notion of a "revolution" is that the conditions underlying military organization and military operations remained remarkably stable, a *longue dureé* in the underlying structures of conflict. These underlying constraints on warfare meant that innovations were rapidly absorbed into a set of circumstances that tended to impose continuity in the actualities of conducting operations. Given the fundamental limitations imposed on mobility by bad roads, on logistics by low agricultural productivity and therefore limited surpluses in even the most advanced regions, and the inability to keep armies in the field in winter, warfare tended to degenerate into ineffectual sieges and into raiding the most accessible enemy province. Armies remained fiscally and

logistically fragile, as the work of Parker on the most organized and competent army of the time (Spain's) demonstrates; Parker (1972).

It is certainly the case that the size of armies increased dramatically from 1500 to 1700, but until remarkably late they were organizationally ramshackle. Most units were raised by military contractors for the duration of a campaign. The hosts assembled at the start of a war or campaign tended to melt away with astonishing rapidity. Most armies seldom stayed coherent or efficient for long: disease, desertion, the corruption of military contractors, mutiny for arrears of pay, and the general tendency of armies to scatter into bands to loot and forage for supplies meant that the numbers on payrolls meant little in terms of effectives who could be assembled to any strategic purpose. Black (1991, 1994) is sharply and tellingly critical of the notion of a military revolution. Anderson (1988) and Tallett (1992) are particularly informative on the composition of armies, military contracting and logistics, and the impact of war on society.

The problem with the notion of a "revolution" is not that there are no changes, but that the effects of these changes are ambiguous. If there was no distinct "military revolution" with a definite set of outcomes, then there are unlikely to have been effects on the process of state formation stemming from military organization that worked unambiguously in favour of the central state apparatus in this period. To take a key example; the new Italian-inspired artillery fortifications of the late 1520s/1530s. These are often presented as an inevitable effect of the French invasion of Italy in 1494, which finally demonstrated that medieval walls were obsolete. The new fortifications were expensive, as were the new siege cannons, and thus are supposed to have worked in favour of central authority.

Actually, what it meant was that effective sieges were difficult to conduct because cannons were scarce until the early seventeenth century; they were expensive because they were cast in bronze. Once the lessons of 1494 had been absorbed, military engineers and soldiers could devise cheap and cheerful ways of defending medieval town walls and castles: first, by building bastions only at the most threatened points; secondly, erecting temporary earthworks in front of or behind breaches in old walls. As Pepper and Adams (1986) show, in the most detailed study of Italian siege warfare, weak places could offer an effective and prolonged defence, costly to the besiegers. Montalcino made an effective resistance, despite being a very weak place. Siena held out in the prolonged siege of 1554–55, the old walls being reinforced by bastions on the most likely avenue of attack and bolstered by temporary earthworks. A spirited defence could thus challenge and even repel central power at a modest cost. Fortifications limited mobility, and thus worked against larger armies, dissipating their advantages. Warfare is usually more subject to contingency than historians allow; in this period it was frequently chaotic and thus quite unsuitable for the neat generalizations of political scientists.

5. Historians have a distinct tendency to write victor's history in the case of French absolutism, which doubtless would have been comforting to Richelieu, confronted with liquidating the Huguenot state within a state, and Mazarin, faced with the multifaceted revolts of the Fronde, had they been privy to the outcome. Lublinskaya (1968), esp. Ch. 5, although stalwartly an orthodox Marxist, explains the political situation of the suppression of the Huguenots exceptionally well and also indicates that it was more of a "close run thing" than

many accounts of French state-building allow. On the siege of La Rochelle see Duffy (1979).

6. Reinhart Koselleck remarks on the status of the Thirty Years' War that it was a *civil* conflict that subsequently became perceived as primarily an inter-state conflict;

> And if in Germany we do not refer to the Thirty Years War as a civil war – as corresponding events in neighbouring countries are called – it is because the Imperial constitutional character of this war has been altered with the termination of thirty years of struggle. What had begun as a civil war between the Protestant Imperial orders and the Imperial party ended in a peace treaty between almost sovereign territorial states. Our religious civil war could thus be interpreted *ex post* as a war between states. (1985: 44).

7. Michael Mann (1986) takes a contrary view:

> Up to the seventeenth century grievances expressed in religious terms were paramount in social struggles; yet they took on an increasingly state-bound form ... Religious wars came to be fought either by rival states or by factions who struggled over the constitution of the singly, monopolistic state in which they were localised. (1986: 435)

This is not wholly convincing: co-religionists *did* aid others, religious mercenaries and volunteers were commonplace, and subjects struggled against their rulers for religious goals and against central state power. Luther's "nationalism", for example, was *cultural* – addressed to "Germans", not to the members of a definite state – see Dickens (1974).

8. For examples of such arguments within international relations and social theory respectively see Zacher (1992) and Held (1995) esp. Part II. The "Westphalian model" it is argued is threatened by economic, environmental and cultural changes on a world scale that are undermining the governance capacities of the nation state and the system of international relations based upon it. For an attempt to argue that the nation state remains crucial and especially as a foundation for international governance, see Hirst and Thompson (1996).

9. For an exhaustive military, socio-economic and political assessment of the war, see Parker (1987) and for a modern historiographic survey see Limm (1984). For the text of the Treaty of Munster see Symcox (1973).

10. This should emphatically *not* be taken to mean that there were no conflicts over economic resources. For example, trade, piracy and warfare in the Mediterranean were inextricably intermingled in the sixteenth and seventeenth centuries, see Guilmartin (1974). Rather the point is that in such conflicts the protagonists did not tend *systematically* to group themselves as friend and enemy, they were episodic and shifting as specific crises or trade conjunctures developed and changed. Marxist historians attempted to portray the conflicts of this period as based on class struggles and as part of the general process of transition from feudalism to capitalism. Strong versions of such arguments, such as Porshnev's (1963) interpretation of popular uprisings in France before the Fronde, or Hobsbawm's version of a "general crisis of the seventeenth century" (1954), have not worn well in subsequent critical debate. Zagorin (1982) is an authoritative review of the modern historiographical literature and an

examination of the major examples of localist, social and religious revolts and civil wars.

11. Without a stable relationship between confessional organization and political power it was difficult to impose religious discipline and to begin the process of "Christianization" in terms of subordinating popular piety to elite beliefs and practices that began with the Reformation but in many Catholic countries was hardly accomplished in the Counter Reformation and only got under way in the late seventeenth century. See Delumeau (1977, 1988) and Muchembled (1978). Larner (1981) and Muchembled (1979) argue that the witch trials of the sixteenth and seventeenth centuries were part of this process of acculturation of the people and, in conditions of weak religious and secular authority, an attempt to assert social control. Catholic regimes in Italy and Spain were relatively efficiently able to control religious dissent. For example, in the Basque country in the early seventeenth century the Inquisition paid little attention to witchcraft as heresy, regarding self-confessed witches as self-deluding and mentally ill, see Henningsen (1980). Even in Spain, however, religious dissent could weaken the state at crucial junctures, as for example the Morisco Revolt of 1568–70.

12. Cited in Elton (1968), pp. 240–41.

13. Cited in Limm (1984), pp. 106–7. I am grateful to Dr Anthony Pagden for emphasizing this point to me during the discussion of my paper at the conference on which this essay is based.

14. This point about the low skill involved in the key weapons of the "military revolution" is made effectively by Guilmartin (1984), pp. 150–5. He does so in the context of explaining why Lepanto 1571 was such a blow to the Ottomans. This was because so many highly skilled archers holding land by military tenure were lost and they could not be quickly replaced – unlike galleys and their rowers. In effect the pike and the arquebus "de-skilled" war – they made it easy rapidly to train urban militias, impressed men and mercenaries. The effects of this were various: rebel armies could be improvised – as with the forces of the French or English civil wars; armies could become larger – as such low-skill soldiers were relatively cheap; and battles were thoroughly ineffective in settling wars, however "decisive" the victory, since new armies could be raised relatively quickly. To illustrate this latter point, the Swedish victories at Breitenfeld (1631) and Lützen (1632) failed to end the Imperialist capacity to wage war, nor did the shattering French victory over the Spanish at Rocroi (1643) quickly alter the outcome of the war, as Spain held out in its dense network of fortified positions in Flanders.

15. For the religious beliefs and practices of the Huguenots and the relationship to their political and constitutional doctrines see Kelley (1981); this linking of ideas and political practice he argues represents the "beginning of ideology". In that sense the *Politiques* represent an early and rapid disenchantment with ideology and political fanaticism – see Skinner (1978) Vol. II and Zagorin (1982) Vol. II for the political ideas of the French religious wars.

16. Ruggie (1993) presents an example of this. Having extensively reviewed the literature and prospectus on the transition to territorial states in early-modern Europe, he notes the role of the religious civil wars and remarks: "Still an international politics morally autonomous from the realm of religion did not become fully established until the Peace of Westphalia (1648), ending the Thirty

Years War" (1993: 163). The event is registered, but not its full consequences for state-building.

17. Gourevitch (1978) is a useful review and analysis of the relationship between international and domestic policy and structures, but it does not explicitly examine the issue of the foundations of sovereignty in its international dimension.

18. For a fuller version of this argument see Hirst and Thompson (1996), Chs. 6 and 8.

15

Why the national still matters

It has become a commonplace of political debate in the 1990s to assert that the role of national political institutions and the scope for ideologically based party politics are both rapidly diminishing. It would be difficult to deny that the arenas and the objectives of political action are changing, or that such changes require a radical rethinking of political ideas. These changes have been seen to affect the left above all, and to render its old certainties and solutions obsolete.

This new perception became firmly established in the 1980s with two very different but influential bodies of ideas that were directed more or less explicitly against the left. The first, that of the new right, was directed against western social democracy and liberal collectivism. The new right reacted against these forms of pragmatic politics with an ideological vehemence hitherto reserved for the critique of Soviet communism. It was argued that Keynesian national economic management and comprehensive social welfare had produced the crisis of the 1970s. Attempts to civilize capitalism, to maintain full employment and to sustain growth had led to evils analogous to full-blooded socialism: accelerating inflation, excessive public borrowing and spending, the crowding-out of private capital, and the growth of inefficient big government. The solutions lay in rolling back the state, increasing the scope of market forces, and opening nationally regulated economies to international competitive pressures. The failure of new right policies has not, however, led to a revival of social democracy. On the contrary, as a specific accommodation between labour and capital, it is seen as ineffective in a world where national-level solutions to economic problems are no longer possible.

The second argument, that of postmodernist philosophers and social theorists, occupied a more rarefied intellectual niche, but it was significant in undermining the intellectual foundations of the radical left. The post-modernists sought to replace a rhetoric of progress derived from the Enlightenment, central to Marxist beliefs, with a sceptical stance that emphasized the uncertainty of the future and the ambiguity of all meaning, and therefore, the problematic nature of political ideologies. The grand "meta-narratives", the necessary futures, that had governed political imagination were exhausted and irrelevant. Chief among these was the socialist belief that it could replace capitalism with a new social system. Such totalizing projects inevitably led to new oppressions and made a mockery of the claim that socialism would realize human emancipation.

The collapse of the Soviet Union and its satellites seemed to confirm these very different arguments. Communism was dead and with it the political credibility of any form of socialism. The revolutions of 1989 and after led to a brief mood of liberal capitalist euphoria. The hope of a "New World Order" based on democracy and the market was rapidly dispelled by stubborn political realities, but this did nothing to restore the credibility of the left. The conflicts in the former Yugoslavia and the failure of the states of the former Soviet Union to make an effective transition to market economies simply confirmed to many how deep were the deformations of institutions and attitudes produced by socialism. If the old nationalist identities and antagonisms were tenacious, they were a politics for losers. Multinational states might break up, but nationalist politics were no real alternative to the need to adapt to the world market.

To these various perceptions of the limitation of national and socialist solutions must be added the newest rhetoric; that of "globalization". From management gurus to the ideologues of the radical left, it has become fashionable to assert that our era is witnessing the growth of a truly global economy dominated by internationalized financial markets and transnational companies. National economies are being subsumed within the global and as a result national-level solutions of any kind are ineffective in the face of the dominant world markets and international competitive pressures. States will be forced to trade down their labour market policies and social spending to a level consistent with matching the competition from the newly industrializing countries of the Pacific Rim, and will have to adapt their monetary and fiscal policies in order to avoid the defection of internationally mobile capital that is concerned only with getting the highest possible returns on a world scale. For the right the rhetoric of "globalization" offers a whole new lease of life against the claims of nationally based labour at a time when the new right claims of the 1980s have worn thin. For the radical left, this is proof at last of the reality of the world capitalist system and the futility of national reform strategies, even if it is bought at the price of political impotence.

Globalization threatens national strategies based on the collaboration of locally organized capital and organized labour. Modern capitalism is dissolving the old allegiances of national capitalist industrialism. With occupational differentiation, the decline of mass manual employment in traditional manufacturing industry in the advanced countries, and the rise of new internationalized knowledge-based industries and mass media, class

237

in its traditional sense is seen to be less and less relevant. The social basis of traditional party affiliations is disappearing. The role of the party is less and less significant as ideology declines and the media replaces party workers as a means of reaching the electorate. Traditional politics matters less because states can do less and can therefore offer fewer satisfactions in return for citizens' identification with them.

Sections of the reforming left have accepted these arguments as the basis for rethinking a radical politics. They have followed the logic of Robert Reich's *The Work of Nations* (1992) in claiming that the role of national governments is to ensure that their societies are internationally competitive, that they can offer to international capital attractive locations based on efficient infrastructure at low cost and a highly trained labour force. National governments are the municipalities of the global system, they offer locally the public goods that business needs. This is in essence what much of the argument for "supply-side socialism" amounts to: public provision to ensure a thriving market economy.

Sections of the left have also recognized the need to adopt a politics of democratic renewal that accepts the decline of traditional party politics and the weaknesses of centralized representative democracy. They embrace a politics in which it is claimed that the media are dominant, in which single-issue campaigns and social movements capture much of the traditional energy and idealism that once went into party politics, and in which new forms of democracy through referenda, consultation of citizens through new information technologies, and local direct democratic control become possible.

15.1 Globalization: a new grand narrative

The problem with such attempts to redefine the left is not that new thinking and a new radicalism are not necessary – they are – but that they over-emphasize the extent to which national states and the institutions of national democracy are obsolete and ineffective. The rhetoric of "globaliz-ation" creates the belief that the world economy is beyond control and that national-level processes are increasingly being superseded by global ones. Ironically, like classical Marxists, the globalists believe that economic logics are driving us toward a necessary future, in this case one in which an unaccountable world capitalism is dominant. At its worst this is a meta-narrative of pessimism rather than progress.

"Globalization", however, remains more myth than reality.[1] This is because the world economy is still predominantly determined by competitive pressures and products generated at the national level and dependent on national social and political institutions. Truly transnational companies are in fact few; most major companies are still nationally based even if they trade and produce internationally. These national bases contribute to the productive efficiency of these firms. This is particularly true of Germany and Japan, but it also applies to the USA. Truly transnational companies would have to reproduce within the firm the advantages they obtain from national institutions, creating, for example, their own multi-national, but cohesive managerial elite. As yet the institutional means to build non-national companies as the normal form of economic organization are far from clear.

Companies actually *benefit* from distinct national managerial styles. They also benefit from being embedded in a complex network of national relationships with central and local governments, with industry associations, with local capital suppliers, with regulatory and standard-setting institutions that help to protect their rights and interests against unfair competition, and with national systems of skill formation and labour motivation. This is as much the case for large, internationally oriented firms as it is for small and medium-scale enterprises in regional economies and industrial districts.

Unregulated global markets in national currencies and equities pose almost as great a threat to companies as they do to international trade. The international governance of major financial markets promises a stability that companies desire as much as anyone else. Calculable trade rules, settled standards for property rights, and a measure of stability in exchange rates are conducive to corporate planning, and, therefore, to investment and growth. Volatility and uncertainty are not. In response to periods of extreme volatility the major nation states of the G7 have attempted regulation, as with the Louvre and Plaza Accords. The tendencies in the governance of the world economy are still unsettled in their direction, but measures towards the reregulation of currency markets and the stabilization of key sectors through international governance are as likely as not.

In such schemes of international governance nation states retain a crucial role. Nation states were effective managers of their own national economies in the post-1945 period mainly because they could rely on a measure of exchange rate stability and trade liberalization conferred by a multilateral regime of international regulation. If a new international regulatory regime is established it will be because the major nation states agree to create it and to confer legitimacy on it by pooling sovereignty. National claims to "sovereignty" have been more myth than fact: states have never been all-powerful or omnicompetent. If sovereignty means anything now, it is as a source of legitimacy in transferring power upwards and downwards, both through agreements between sovereign states to create international agencies and regulatory regimes and to abide by treaties, and through the constitutional ordering of power between central, regional and local government and publicly recognized bodies in civil society. Nation states are linchpins in the art of distributing power, ordering government by giving it legitimacy. They can only be effective in this if they are democratic and can credibly present such decisions as having popular support.

In a system of international regulation states become crucial agencies of representation. They are the "global electors" and the means of ensuring that in some mediated degree such international bodies are answerable to the world's people. Such representation is far from direct, but it will be more effective to the extent that states are answerable to their populations and that those populations are informed and roused by a world "civil society" of NGOs. States will continue to have a function; without them international regulation is inconceivable. And without international economic regulation, the majority of companies will lose rather than gain: a world of volatile markets is one in which success and failure are capriciously distributed, in which companies cannot plan (as they must if they are to develop new markets and products), and where investments and returns on capital are radically insecure. Such a world is sufficiently unsustainable that it will not persist, it will lead either to international regulation or to emerging forms of regional protectionism based on the major trading blocs.

15.2 Altered states

Paradoxically, therefore, the degree to which the world has internationalized reinforces the need for the traditional national democratic state, not as the sole or "sovereign" political agency, but as a crucial relay between international processes and the articulate publics of the developed world. Not all states will matter in this process, which will remain confined to the great powers and the most prosperous nations. Nor will all states be able to achieve a satisfactory internal settlement that enables them to benefit from such international stability as can be created and contained. States and their economies will benefit from existing institutional inheritances that contribute to the co-operation of the major social interests and industrial sectors. Those states like the UK, which have the least social solidarity, the least commitment to major interests, to "national" goals, the weakest institutions of informal economic co-ordination, and the least developed local and regional structures of economic governance, will tend to fail.

The odds are that relatively solidaristic countries like Germany and Japan will continue to be successful. Wealth and economic success will continue to be highly concentrated, even if new societies with strong national centres of economic co-operation like Korea and Singapore join the ranks of the successful. Macroeconomic policy continues to be crucial in promoting prosperity, at the international level by ensuring stability, and at the national and regional levels by balancing co-operation and competition. Governments are not just municipalities in a competitive global market-place. Supply-side socialism is at best one-sided. Unless the conditions for stability and growth are created, it amounts to little more than spending public money in an attempt to attract capital. But even the best-trained labour forces can be idle in a world of radical uncertainty and instability.

Politics and governance is becoming ever more polycentric. Nation states are merely one level in a complex system of overlapping and competing governing agencies. Some of those agencies are not public bodies at all; they are private governments or voluntary bodies in civil society. Citizens in advanced countries have multiple foci of association and identification, while societies are becoming more pluralistic and their members more indi-viduated. They are less willing to give unqualified allegiance to collectivities or subordinate their own interests to a single political entity, be it a party, trade union or state. All of this is true, but it does not gainsay the con-tinuing role of nation states. If the state retains a role because of its place in the securing of international regulation, it also retains a role *within* national societies because of this very polycentricity and complexity.

15.3 A weak argument?

It has become fashionable to downgrade the role of representative democ-racy and of central political institutions. Geoff Mulgan, for example, has been an important, and almost invariably very constructive voice pressing the left to rethink and adapt to new realities.[2] Yet he is strongly critical of traditional political institutions. He sees such institutions as forms of "strong power" that developed in an era when the nation state became the central political community. In his essay "Party-free politics", he expresses this view very clearly, that politics and nation states have prevailed for 200 years and now their time is passing. They depended on certain historical conditions: "our sense of politics as a formal system of activism, declarations of rights, manifestos, parliaments, constitutions and professional politicians . . . began . . . in the time of the spinning jenny, the musket and absolutist monarchy" (1994b: 15). "Politics" existed when power had clear boundaries: "the central institutions of politics, parties and parliament, remain stuck in a 19th-century form: centralised, pyramidal, national, with strictly defined rules of authority and sovereignty" (*ibid.*). These historically specific forms of "strong power" are being replaced by "new forms of soft or {weak power} that depend less on formally defined roles and strict rules of authority and cultivate instead greater flexibility, creativity and responsiveness" (*ibid.*).

The implication is that "formal politics" is weakening and with it the traditional institutions of state, constitutions, parliaments, and strictly defined legal rules about who has power. The problem with this view is first of all that the list of elements of the old "strong politics" – rights, manifestos, parliaments, constitutions and professional politicians – is not all of a piece. It can be broken down into at least two sub-sets. Thus parliaments, professional politicians and manifesto politics can all decline in significance without the codified rights of citizens or constitutional ordering suffering the same fate. The reason is that they relate to different aspects of governance. The former set is part of a substantive outcome-oriented politics concerned with win or lose contests within nation states, whereas the latter set is procedural and concerned with regulating social action in the widest sense.

In other words, even if nation states become less effective at deciding the affairs of their societies, national political institutions remain central in setting up the rules whereby various political bodies and social agencies play their games. This may not be "sovereignty" in the old sense, and the state may be highly pluralistic, but such a society requires a public power that ensures the rule of law.

Rights and constitutional ordering are central to the rule of law. Modern politics has only partly been about parties and ideologues. Modern western societies have been economically successful and relatively civilized in their treatment of their members, in large measure because they provided the security and certainty of the rule of law, limiting the actions that citizens and companies could do to each other and binding the government to obey the law in its dealings with citizens. The politics of parties, parliaments and ideologies has been capable of undermining and destroying the rule of law, so respect for it has depended crucially on the idea of constitutionally ordered authority. Potentially, the two sets in the list above are thus profoundly different in their consequences, and the decline of the former, far from implying the latter's decline, may actually help to sustain and enhance it.

If we do move into a more complex and pluralistic social and political system, then the rule of law will become more, not less important. Law here is meant in two senses: as a guide to action, giving citizens some certainty of expectation and a minimum of norms of conduct in an increasingly complex world; and as a means to regulate conflict between a large number of competing public and private bodies.

A society of diversifying political forces, issues and organizations makes it necessary for there to be a core public power regulating and guiding action, and safeguarding those irreducible elements of the common good that remain. The constitution is thus a *pouvoir neutre*, not part of "politics" in the old sense, but still essential to the emerging complexity of our national political systems.

Thus constitutional and civil law remain central, and the former protects the latter from undue political interference. Bills of Rights that protect individuals from the state and their fellows, and constitutional ordering of the public domain, preventing the state exceeding certain limits or other bodies appropriating powers that should remain public, are therefore inescapable and continuing elements of modernity.

Because politicians can make less of a claim to legitimacy or majority support, and because the power of common ideologies is waning, it becomes more and not less essential to define and regulate constitutionally the powers they do have. Mulgan's example of the motorway protestors may be the model of new political movements but they would have been aided by a constitution that limited the powers of the executive in pushing through the rape of Twyford Down.

15.4 Legal ruling

As the world economy internationalizes and modern states are at best one level of economic regulation, so the roles of international regimes based on international law and of an international "civil society", of organizations defending common human rights standards, become more necessary. The major national public powers and the private governments that are growing in significance must have internal constitutional limits and be capable of shaping, receiving and obeying international law. International law cannot be imposed on lawless states: it can be effective only if the members of the "society of states" are themselves law creators and are bound by the rule of law internally.

Without formal democratic legitimacy it is difficult to see how constitutional ordering and the law-making functions of states can be maintained. New forms of direct democracy could only shape a fraction of the laws. Representative democracy will thus remain central, and indeed, needs to be reinvigorated and enhanced in countries like the UK, where its institutions have become a mere appendage of the executive. Representative democracy requires parties and politicians, however little we may esteem them at the moment.

If the above arguments are true, then the scope for national politics is by no means over. Nation states will continue to have three key roles, whatever other functions they may gain or lose. The first is as a source of advocacy of, and of legitimation for, international economic regulation, and specifically the stabilization of financial markets. Such stability is essential for the long-term interest of the majority of companies and for the labour forces of the advanced nations. It is, at the international level, a commonality of interest between labour and capital of the same kind that has sustained social democracy in nation states. The second is as the orchestrator of social cohesion and economic co-operation between the major social interests at national level. Such co-operation (rather than technical macroeconomic policy) is the key to economic success. The UK under the Conservatives has suffered from a combination of reckless adventurism in macroeconomic policy and a refusal to build co-operation between the social interests, a function of the maldistribution of power within the state and the dominance of the central executive. The third is as guarantor of the rule of law and of enabling plural communities to co-exist without excessive conflict.

These roles may be slightly different from those of nation states in the past, but they give a place to national-level politics and its political parties. In an obvious sense, this offers a continued place for the reforming left, which has always been nationally based and has always sought an ongoing collaborative dialogue with business. Social democracy in this sense may have a future, but only if it sees the national as a political stage from which to operate upwards, promoting international regulation, and downwards, promoting social cohesion as well as appropriate forms of regional, local and private government. This is yet to happen. The left remains convinced that the global economy is unregulatable, and it has been too little interested in constitutional ordering and distributing power within the state, preferring to centralize power. Ideology may be unfashionable, but in an era in which the key role of the nation state is to practice the arts of government, orchestrating the power of others, ideas remain essential.

Notes

1. For a more extended and considered view of the issues see Hirst and Thompson (1992), (1994). For the clearest statement of the "globalization" position, see Ohmae (1990).
2. See Mulgan (1994a).

Bibliography

Albert, M. 1993. *Capitalism against capitalism*. London, Whurr.

Althusser, L. 1972. *Montesquieu – politics and history*. London, New Left Books.

Anderson, M.S. 1988. *War and society in the Europe of the Old Regime*. London, Fontana.

Andrews, G. (ed.) 1991. *Citizenship*. London, Lawrence & Wishart.

Bagnasco, A. & C. Sabel (eds) 1994. *Ce que petit peut faire: les petites et moyennes entreprises en Europe*. Poitiers, OCSEO.

Barnett, A. (ed.) 1994. *Power and the throne*. London: Vintage.

Barnett, A., C. Ellis, P. Hirst (eds) 1993. *Debating the constitution*. Cambridge, Polity Press.

Baude, R. & B. Lewis (eds) 1983. *Christians and Jews in the Ottoman empire*. New York, Holmes & Myrtle.

Bernstein, E. [1899] 1961. *Evolutionary socialism*. New York, Schocken Books.

Beccattini, G. 1990. The Marshallian industrial district as a socio-economic notion. In Pyke *et al.* op. cit.

Belloc, H. 1913. *The servile state*. London, T.N. Foulis. (reprinted 1977 Liberty Classics, Indianapolis IN.)

Black, A. 1984. *Guilds and civil society in European thought from the twelfth century to the present*. London, Methuen.

Black, J. 1991. *A military revolution? Military change and European society 1550–1800*. Basingstoke, Macmillan.

— 1994. *European warfare 1660–1815*. London, UCL Press.

Bobbio, N. 1987. *The future of democracy*. Cambridge, Polity Press.

—1988. *Which socialism?* Cambridge, Polity Press.

Bodin, J. [1576] 1992. *On sovereignty* (J.H. Franklin (ed.). Cambridge: Cambridge University Press.

Bourdieu, P. & J.S. Coleman (eds) 1991. *Social theory for a changing society*. Boulder CO, Westview Press.

Bowles, S. & H. Gintis 1986. *Democracy and capitalism*. London, Routledge.

Brusco, S. 1982. The Emilian model: productive decentralisation and social integration. *Cambridge Journal of Economics* **6**(2), 167–86.

Brusco, S. 1992. Small firms and the provision of real services. In Pyke & W. Sengenberger op. cit.

Carpenter, N. 1922. *Guild socialism: an historical and critical analysis*. New York, D. Appleton.

Cawson, A. 1986. *Corporatism and political theory*. Oxford, Basil Blackwell.

Cohen, J. and Arato, A. 1992. *Civil society and political theory*. Cambridge MA, MIT Press.

Cohen, J. and Rogers, J. 1983. *On democracy*. New York, Penguin.

— 1992. Secondary associations and democratic governance. *Politics and society.* **20**(4), 393–472. (Revised version reprinted in E. Olin Wright (ed.) *Associations and Democracy.* London, Verso).

Cohn, N. 1970. *The pursuit of the millennium.* London, Paladin.

Cole, G.D.H. 1920. *Guild socialism re-stated.* London, Leonard Parsons.

Commission on Social Justice 1993. *The justice gap.* London, Institute of Public Policy Research.

Cornford, J. A. 1990. *A stake in the company.* Economic Study No. 3, London, IPPR.

Cutler, A.J., K. Williams & J. Williams 1986. *Keynes, Beveridge and Beyond.* London, Routledge & Kegan Paul.

Dahl, R.A. 1948. Marxism and free parties. *Journal of Politics* **10**, 787–813.

— 1956. *A preface to democratic theory.* New Haven CT, Yale University Press.

— 1982. *Dilemma of liberal democracies.* New Haven CT, Yale University Press.

— 1985. *A preface to economic democracy.* Cambridge, Polity Press.

Davidson, R. 1983. The millets as agents of change in the seventeenth century Ottoman Empire. In Baude & Lewis (eds) op. cit.

Delumeau, J. 1977. *Catholicism between Luther and Voltaire: a new view of the counter-reformation.* London, Burns & Oates.

— 1988. Prescription and Reality. In Leites (ed.) op.cit.

Dickens, A.G. 1974. *The German nation and Martin Luther.* London, Fontana.

Downing, B.M. 1992. *The military revolution and political change: origins of democracy and autocracy in early modern Europe.* Princeton NJ, Princeton University Press.

Dore, R. 1986a. *Flexible rigidities: industrial policy and industrial adjustment in the Japanese economy 1970–1980.* London, Athlone Press.

— 1986b. *Taking Japan seriously: a Confucian perspective on leading economic issues.* London, Athlone Press.

Duffy, C. 1979. *Siege warfare – the fortress in the early modern world 1494–1660.* London, Routledge & Kegan Paul.

Durkheim, E. [1893] 1964. *The division of labour in society.* Trans. New York, The Free Press.

— 1957. *Professional ethics and civic morals.* London, Routledge & Kegan Paul.

Economist 1995. Editorial, The myth of the powerless state. *Economist* 7 October, 15–16.

Elton, G.R. (ed.) 1968. *Renaissance and reformation 1300–1648.* New York, Macmillan.

Etzioni, A. 1995. *The spirit of community.* London, Fontana.

Evans, P.B., D. Rueschemeyer & T. Skocpol (eds) 1985. *Bringing the state back in.* Cambridge, Cambridge University Press.

Figgis, J.N. 1913. *Churches in the modern state.* London, Longman, Green & Co.

Friedman, D. 1988. *The misunderstood miracle: industrial development and political change in Japan.* Ithaca NY, Cornell University Press.

Fukuyama, F. 1989. The end of history? *The National Interest* **19**, 3–18.

— 1992. *The end of history and the last man.* New York, The Free Press.

Galbraith, J.K. 1992. *A culture of contentment,* Boston, Houghton Mifflin.

Gamble, A. 1996. The limits of democracy. In Hirst & Khilnani (eds) op. cit.

Garton Ash, T. 1983. *The Polish revolution: solidarity.* London, Jonathan Cape.

— 1989. *The uses of adversity.* Cambridge, Granta Books in Association with Penguin Books.

Gerth, H. & C. Wright Mills (eds) 1948. *From Max Weber.* London, Routledge & Kegan Paul.

Giddens, A. 1985. *A contemporary critique of historical materalism – vol. 2 the nation state and violence.* Cambridge, Polity Press.

Glass, S.T. 1966. *The responsible society.* London, Longman.

Goldstein, J. & R.O. Keohane (eds) 1993. *Ideas and foreign policy: beliefs, institutions and political change.* Ithaca NY, Cornell University Press.

Gorbachev, M. 1987. *Perestroika.* London, Collins.

Gourevitch, P. 1978. The second image reversed: the international sources of domestic politics. *International Organisation* **32**(4), 881–912.

Green, D.G. 1993. *Reinventing civil society – the rediscovery of welfare without politics.* London, IEA, Health and Welfare Unit.

— 1996. *Community without politics – a market approach to welfare reform.* London, IEA, Health and Welfare Unit.

Grimmelshausen, H.J.C. von [1669] 1964. *Simplicius simplicissimus.* (Trans. H. Weissenborn and L. Macdonald). London, John Calder.

Grossman, V. 1986. *Forever flowing.* London, Collins/Harvil.

Guilmartin, J.F. 1964. *Gunpowder and galleys: changing technology and Mediterranean warfare at sea in the sixteenth century.* Cambridge, Cambridge University Press.

Gurney, P. 1988. George Jacob Holyoake: socialism, association, and cooperation in nineteenth century England. In Yeo (ed.) op. cit.

Habermas, J. 1984 and 1987. *The theory of communicative action, 2 vols.* Cambridge, Polity Press.

Hailsham, Lord 1978. *The dilemma of democracy.* London, Collins.

Hampden-Turner, C. & F. Trompenaars, 1993. *The seven cultures of capitalism.* New York, Doubleday.

Havel, V. 1987. The power of the powerless. In *Living in Truth.* London, Faber & Faber.

Hayek, F.A. von 1944. *The road to serfdom.* London, Routledge & Kegan Paul.

Hayward, J.E.S. 1960. *Solidarist syndicalism: Durkheim and Duguit. Sociological Review* NS **8**(1), 14–35 and (2), 185–202.

Hegel, G.W.F. [1843] 1956. *The philosophy of history.* (Trans. J. Sibree) New York, Dover.

— [1821] 1952. *Philosophy of right.* (Trans. T.M. Knox) Oxford, Clarenden Press.

Held, D. 1991. Democracy, the nation state and the global system. *Economy and Society.* **20**(2), 138–172.

— 1995. *Democracy and the global order: from the modern state to cosmopolitan governance.* Cambridge, Polity Press.

Henningsen, G. 1980. *The witches' advocate: Basque witchcraft and the Spanish Inquisition 1609–1614.* Reno, Nevada, University of Nevada Press.

Hindess, B. 1983. *Parliamentary democracy and socialist politics.* London, Routledge & Kegan Paul.

Hirschman, A.O. 1970. *Exit, voice and loyalty.* Cambridge MA, Harvard University Press.

Hirst, P. 1986. *Law, socialism and democracy.* London, George Allen & Unwin.

— 1987. Carl Schmitt's decisionism. *Telos* **72**, 15–16.

— 1988. Carl Schmitt: decisionism and political romanticism. *Economy and Society* **17**(2), 272–82.

— 1989a. The politics of industrial policy. In Hirst and Zeitlin (eds).

— 1989b. *The pluralist theory of the state: selected writings of G.D.H. Cole, J.N. Figgis and H.J. Laski.* London, Routledge.

— 1990a. *Representative democracy and its limits.* Cambridge, Polity Press.

— 1990b. An answer to relativism. *New Formations* **10**, 13–23.

— 1990c. Guilding the Factory. *Samizdat* **10**, 6–7.

— 1990d. From statism to pluralism. In Pimlott *et al.* (eds) op. cit.

— 1991. Labour and the constitutional crisis. In Andrews (ed.) op. cit

— 1994. *Associative democracy.* Cambridge, Polity Press.

— 1997. From the economic to the political. In Kelly, Kelly & Gamble (eds) op. cit.

Hirst, P. & S. Khilnani (eds) 1996. *Reinventing democracy.* Oxford, Basil Blackwell/ The Political Quarterly.

Hirst, P. & G. Thompson, 1992. The problem of globalisation: international economic relations, national economic management and the formation of trading blocs. *Economy and Society* **21**(4), 357–96.

— 1994. Globalisation, foreign direct investment and international economic governance. *Organisation* **1**(2), 271–303.

— 1996. *Globalisation in question.* Cambridge, Polity Press.

Hirst, P. & J. Zeitlin (eds) 1988. *Reversing industrial decline.* Oxford, Berg.

— 1988b. Crisis, what crisis? *New Statesman* 18 March, 10–12.

— 1989. Flexible specialisation and the competitive failure of UK manufacturing. *Political Quarterly* **60**(2),164–78.

— 1991. Flexible specialisation vs post-Fordism: theory, evidence and policy implications. *Economy and Society* **20**(1), 1–50.

Hobbes, T. [1651] 1960. *Leviathan.* (Ed. M. Oakeshott) Oxford, Basil Blackwell.

Hobsbawm, E.J. 1954. The crisis of the seventeenth century. *Past and Present* **5** & **6** (Reprinted in T. Aston (ed.) 1965. *Crisis in Europe 1560–1660.* London, Routledge & Kegan Paul.)

Holyoake, G.J. 1891. *The cooperative movement today.* London, Methuen.

Hunt, A. (ed.) 1980. *Marxism and democracy.* London, Lawrence & Wishart.

Hutton, W. 1995. *The state we're in.* London, Cape.

Jowell, R., S. Witherspoon & L. Brook 1988. *British social attitudes, the fifth report,* Aldershot, Gower.

Katzenstein, P.J. 1984. *Corporatism and change: Austria, Switzerland and the politics of industry.* Ithaca NY, Cornell University Press.

— 1985. *Small states in world markets: industrial policy in Europe.* Ithaca NY, Cornell University Press.

Kautsky, K. [1892] 1971. *The class struggle.* New York, W.W. Norton.

— 1909. *The road to power,* Chicago: Samuel A. Bloch.

— [1918] 1964. *The dictatorship of the proletariat.* Ann Arbor, University of Michigan Press.

Keane, J. (ed.) 1988. *Civil society and the state.* London, Verso.

— 1988. *Democracy and civil society.* London, Verso.

Kelley, D.R. 1981. *The beginning of ideology – consciousness and society in the French reformation.* Cambridge, Cambridge University Press.

Kelly, D., G. Kelly & A Gamble (eds) 1997. *Stakeholder capitalism.* Baskingstoke, Macmillan.

Keohane, R. (ed.) 1986. *Neorealism and its critics.* New York, Columbia University Press.

Kennedy, P. 1988. *The rise and fall of the great powers.* London, Unwin Hyman.

Kerblay, B. 1983. *Modern Soviet society.* London, Methuen.

Kingdom, E. 1991. *What's wrong with rights?* Edinburgh, Edinburgh University Press.

Knight, K. 1990. The myth of functional democracy, PhD thesis, University of London.

Kojéve, A. 1969. *Introduction to the reading of Hegel.* New York, Basic Books.

Koselleck, R. 1985. *Futures past.* Cambridge MA, MIT Press.

— 1988. Critique and crisis – *Enlightenment and the pathogenesis of modern society.* Oxford, Berg.

Krasner, S.D. 1993. Westphalia and All That. In Goldstein & Keohane (eds) op. cit.

Krugman, P. 1994a. Does third world growth hurt first world prosperity? *Harvard Business Review* July/August pp. 113–121.

— 1994b. The myth of Asia's miracle. *Foreign Affairs* **74**(6) 63–75.

Laclau, E. & C. Mouffe 1985. *Hegemony and socialist strategy.* London, Verso.

Lambert, M.D. 1977. *Medieval heresy: popular movements from Bogomil to Hus.* London, Edward Arnold.

Larner, C. 1981. *Enemies of God: the witch hunt in Scotland.* London, Chatto & Windus.

Laski, H.J. 1921. *The foundations of sovereignty and other essays.* London, Allen & Unwin.

Le Grand, J. 1990. Rethinking welfare: a case for quasi-markets. In Pimlott *et al.* (eds) op. cit.

Le Grand, J. & S. Estrin (eds) 1989. *Market Socialism.* Oxford, Oxford University Press.

Leites, E. (ed.) 1988. *Conscience and casuistry in early modern Europe*, Cambridge, Cambridge University Press.

Lembruch, G. 1997. From state of authority to neutral state: the German state in developmental perspective. In Muramatsu and Naschold (eds) op. cit.

Lenin, V.I. 1917. The state and revolution. *Collected works* Vol. 25. Moscow, Foreign Languages Publishing House.

Limm, P. 1984. *The Thirty Years War.* London, Longman.

Locke, R.M. 1995. *Remaking the Italian economy.* Ithaca NY, Cornell University Press.

Lorenz, N. 1989. The search for flexibility: subcontracting networks in French and British engineering. In Hirst and Zeitlin (eds) (1989) op. cit.

Lublinskaya, A.D. 1968. *French absolutism: the crucial phase 1620–1629.* Cambridge, Cambridge University Press.

MacFarlane, K.B. 1972. *Wycliffe and English non-conformity.* Harmondsworth, Penguin.

Macpherson, C.B. 1966. *The real world of democracy.* Oxford, Oxford University Press.

Mann, M. 1986. *The sources of social power Vol. 1.* Cambridge, Cambridge University Press.

Marcuse, H. 1964. *One dimensional man.* London, Routledge & Kegan Paul.

Marquand, D. 1988. *The unprincipled society.* London, Cape.

Marr, A. 1995. Stuck between the flab and a hard place. *The Independent,* 19 October.

Marshall, A. 1919. *Industry and trade.* London, Macmillan.

Marshall, T.H. 1963. Citizenship and social class. In *Sociology at the Crossroads* London: Heinemann pp. 67–127.

Marx, K. [1844] 1975. *Economic and political manuscripts. Collected Works Vol. 3.* London, Lawrence & Wishart.

— [1871] 1962. The civil war in France. In *Karl Marx and Friedrich Engels selected works Vol. 1.* Moscow, Foreign Languages Publishing House.

Matthews, J. 1989. *The age of democracy.* Melbourne, Oxford University Press.

Michnik, A. 1985. *Letters from prison.* Berkley CA, University of California Press.

Miller, P. 1996. Dilemmas of accountability: the limits of accounting. In Hirst & Khilnani (eds) op. cit.

Miłosz, C. [1953] 1985. *The captive mind*. London, Penguin.

Mouffe, C. 1988. *The civics lesson*. New Statesman and Society, 7 October, 28–31.

Mount, F. 1992. *The British constitution now*. London, Heinemann.

Muchembled, R. 1978. *Culture populaire et culture des elites dans La France moderne (XVé–XVillé siécles)*. Paris, Flammarion.

— 1979. The witches of Cambresis – the acculturation of the rural world in the sixteenth and seventeenth centuries. In Obelkevich (ed.) op. cit.

Mulgan, G. 1994a. *Politics in an antipolitical age*. Cambridge, Polity Press.

— 1994b. Party-free politics. *New Statesman and Society*, 15 April, 16–18.

Muramatsu, M. & F. Nasehold (eds) 1997. *State and administration in Japan and Germany*. Berlin, W. de Gruyter.

Nicholls, D. 1975. *The pluralist state*. London, Macmillan.

Obelkevich, J. (ed.) 1979. *Religion and the people 800–1700*. Chapel Hill NC, University of North Carolina Press.

Ohmae, K. 1990. *The borderless world*. London, Collins.

Olson, M. 1982. *The rise and decline of nations*. New Haven CT, Yale University Press.

Ozment, S.E. 1973. *Mysticism and dissent*, New Haven CT, Yale University Press.

Parker, G. 1972. *The army of Flanders and the Spanish Road 1567–1659*. Cambridge, Cambridge University Press.

— 1979. The "military revolution 1560–1660" – Myth? In *Spain and the Netherlands*. London, Fontana.

— (ed.) 1987. *The Thirty Years War*. London, Routledge & Kegan Paul.

— 1988. *The military revolution – military innovation and the rise of the west 1500–1800*. Cambridge, Cambridge University Press.

Pelezynski, Z.L. 1988. Solidarity and the rebirth of civil society. In Keane (ed.) op. cit.

Pepper, S. & N. Adams. 1986. *Firearms and Fortifications – Military Architecture and siege warfare in sixteenth century Siena*. Chicago, Chicago University Press.

Piore, M. & C. Sabel 1984. *The second industrial divide*. New York, Basic Books.

Pimlott, B. *et al.* (eds) (1990) *The alternative*. London, W.H. Allen.

Plant, R. 1988. *Citizenship, rights and socialism*. London, Fabian Tract No. 531.

Pocock, J.G.A. 1975. *The Machiavellian moment: Florentine political thought and the Atlantic republican tradition*. Princeton NJ, Princeton University Press.

Polan, A.J. 1984. *Lenin and the end of politics*. London, Methuen.

Polanyi, K. [1944] 1957. *The great transformation*. Boston MA, Beacon Press.

— 1971. *Primitive, archaic and modern economics*. (ed. G. Dalton) Boston MA, Beacon Press.

Porshnev, B. 1963. *Les soulévements populaires en France de 1623 á 1648*. Paris, S.V.E.P.E.N. (Excerpted in P.J. Coveney (ed.) 1977. *France in crisis 1620–1675*. London, Macmillan.)

Porter, B.D. 1994. *War and the rise of the state – the military foundations of modern politics*. New York, The Free Press.

Power, M. 1994. *The audit explosion*. London, Demos.

Prochaska, F. 1988. *The voluntary impulse*. London, Faber & Faber.

Proudhon, P.-J. [1863] 1963. *The principle of federation*. (Intro. R. Vernon) Toronto, University of Toronto Press.

Pyke, F., G. Beccattini & W. Sengenberger (eds) 1990. *Industrial districts and inter-firm cooperation in Italy*. Geneva, International Institute for Labour Studies.

Pyke, F. & W. Sengenberger (eds) 1992. *Industrial districts and local economic regeneration*. Geneva, International Institute for Labour Studies.

Reading, B. 1992. *Japan: the coming collapse*. London, Weidenfeld & Nicholson.

Reich, R. 1992. *The work of nations*. New York, Vintage.

Rendell, R. & C. Ward 1989. *Undermining the central line – giving government back to the people*. London, Chatto & Windus.

Roberts, M. 1956. The military revolution 1560–1660. Belfast, Queens University. (Reprinted in M. Roberts 1967. *Essays in Swedish history*. London, Weidenfeld & Nicholson.

Rosenau, J.N. & E.O. Czempiel (eds) 1992. *Governance without government: order and change in world politics*. Cambridge, Cambridge University Press.

Rossiter, C. 1948. *Constitutional dictatorship*. Princeton NJ, Princeton University Press.

Rousseau, J.-J. [1762] 1913. *The social contract*. In G.D.H. Cole (ed.) 1913 London: Dent (Everyman).

Ruggie, J.G. 1986. Continuity and transformation in the world polity. In Keohane (ed). op. cit.

— 1993. Territoriality and beyond: problematising modernity in international relations. *International Organisation* **47**(1), 134–72.

Rustin, M. 1985. *For a pluralist socialism*. London, Verso.

Sabel, C. 1989. *Flexible specialisation and the re-emergence of regional economies*. In Hirst & Zeitlin (eds) 1989 op. cit.

— 1990. Studied trust: building new forms of cooperation in a volatile economy. Paper No. 11, Conference on Industrial Districts and Local Economic Regeneration, ILO Geneva.

—1991. Moebius strip organisations and open labour markets: some consequences of the reintegration of conception and execution in a volatile economy. In Bourdieu & Coleman (eds) op. cit.

— 1994. Learning by monitoring: the institutions of economic development. In Smelser & Swedberg (eds) op. cit.

— 1995. Bootstrapping reform: rebuilding firms, the welfare state and unions. *Politics and Society* **23**(1), 5–48.

Sabel, C., G. Herrigel, R. Degg & R. Kazis 1989. Regional prosperities compared: Massachusetts and Baden-Württemberg in the 1980s. *Economy and Society* **18**(4), 374–404.

Sabel C. & J. Zeitlin 1985. Historical alternatives to mass production. *Past and Present* **108**, 133–76.

Sampson, A. 1962. *The anatomy of Britain*. London, Hodder & Stoughton.

Scharpf, F.W. 1991. *Crisis and choice in European social democracy*. Ithaca NY, Cornell University Press.

Schmitt, C. 1976. *The concept of the political*. New Brunswick NJ, Rutgers University Press.

— [1926] 1985. *The crisis of parliamentary democracy*. Cambridge MA, MIT Press.

— 1986. *Political romanticism*. (Trans. G. Oakes). Cambridge MA, MIT Press.

Schmitter, P. 1988. Corporatist democracy: oxymoronic? Just plain moronic? Or a promising way out of the present impasse? MSS Stanford University.

Schmitz, H. 1992. Industrial districts: model and reality in Baden-Württemberg. In Pyke & Sengenberger (eds) op. cit.

Schwab, G. 1970. The challenge of the exception. 1st edn. Berlin, Duncker & Humblot; 2nd edn. 1989. New York, Greenwood Press.

Skidelsky, R. 1995. *The world after communism*. London, Macmillan.

— 1996. Welfare without the state. *Prospect*, January, 38–43.

Skinner, Q. 1978. *The foundations of modern political thought. Vol. 2.* Cambridge, Cambridge University Press.

Smelser, N.J. & R. Swedberg (eds) (1994). *Handbook of economic sociology.* Princeton NJ, Princeton-Sage.

Soskice, D. 1996. The state we're in. *Prospect*, April, 31–42.

Spruyt, H. 1994. *The sovereign state and its competitors.* Princeton NJ, Princeton University Press.

Streeck, W. & P. Schmitter 1984. Community, market, state and associations. Florence, European University Institute Working Paper No. 94.

Stewart, J. 1992. The rebuilding of public accountability. London, European Policy Forum.

Symcox, G. (ed.) 1973. *War diplomacy and imperialism.* New York, Harper & Row.

Tallett, F. 1992. *War and society in early modern Europe 1495–1715.* London, Routledge.

Taylor, K. 1982. *The political ideas of the utopian socialists.* London, Frank Cass.

Thurow, L. 1980. *The zero sum society.* New York, Basic Books.

Tilly, C. (ed.) 1975. *The formation of nation states in western Europe.* Princeton NJ, Princeton University Press.

— 1985. War making and state making as organised crime. In Evans *et. al.* (eds) op. cit.

— 1990. *Coercion, capital and European states AD 990–1990.* Oxford, Basil Blackwell.

Thompson, G. 1990. *The political economy of the new right.* London, Frances Pinter.

Thomson, J.E. 1994. *Mercenaries, pirates and sovereigns: state-building and extraterritorial violence in early-modern Europe.* Princeton NJ, Princeton University Press.

Tobin, J. 1994. Speculator's Tax. *New Economy* pp. 104–9.

Trigilia, C. 1992. Italian industrial districts neither myth nor interlude. In Pyke & Sengenberger (eds) op. cit.

Turnbull, S. 1991. Reinventing corporations. *Human Systems Management* **10**, 169–186.

Van Wolferen, K. 1989. *The enigma of Japanese power.* London, Macmillan.

Venturi, F. 1971. *Utopia and reform in the Enlightenment.* Cambridge, Cambridge University Press.

Vernon, R. (1979) Introduction. In Proudhon [1863] op. cit.

Vibert, F. (ed.) 1991. *Britain's constitutional future.* London, IEA.

Vincent, S. 1984. *Pierre-Joseph Proudhon and the origins of French republican socialism.* New York, Oxford University Press.

Walzer, M. 1983. *Spheres of justice.* Oxford, Basil Blackwell.

Weber, M. [1919] 1948. Politics as a vocation. In Gerth & Wright Mills (eds) op. cit.

— 1968. *Economy and society Vol. 1.* New York, Bedminster Press.

Weir, S. 1996. From strong government and quasi-government to strong democracy. In Hirst & Khilnani (eds) op. cit.

Weir, S. & W. Hall 1994. *Ego trip: extra-governmental organisations in the UK and their accountability.* London, Charter 88 Trust.

Williams, G.H. 1962. *The radical reformation.* Philadelphia PA, Westminster Press.

Williams, K. & J. Williams (eds) 1987. *A Beveridge reader.* London, Allen & Unwin.

Wolf, M. 1995. Globalisation and the state. *Financial Times*, 18 September, 24.

Wright, A.W. 1979. *G.D.H. Cole and socialist democracy.* Oxford, Clarenden Press.

Yeo, S. (ed.) 1988. *New forms of cooperation.* London, Routledge.

Young, H. 1989. *One of us*. London, Macmillan.

Zacher, M.W. 1992. The decaying pillars of the Westphalian Temple: implications for international order and governance. In Rosenau & Czempiel (eds) op. cit.

Zagorin, P. 1982. *Rebels and rulers 1500–1660: Vol. I Society, states and early modern revolution, agrarian and urban rebellions; Vol. II Provincial rebellion revolutionary wars 1560–1660*. Cambridge, Cambridge University Press.

Zeitlin, J. 1992. Industrial districts and local economic regeneration. In Pyke & Sengenberger (eds) op. cit.

— 1994. Why are there no industrial districts in the UK? In Bagnasco & Sabel (eds) op. cit.

Index